Being Made Strange

SUNY series in Communication Studies
Dudley D. Cahn, editor

Being Made Strange

Rhetoric beyond Representation

Bradford Vivian

State University of New York Press

Published by
State University of New York Press, Albany

For information, address State University of New York Press,
90 State Street, Suite 700, Albany, NY 12207

Production by Kelli Williams
Marketing by Fran Keneston

Library of Congress Cataloging-in-Publication Data

Vivian, Bradford.
    Being made strange : rhetoric beyond representation / Bradford Vivian.
        p. cm. — (SUNY series in communication studies)
    Includes bibliographical references (p.) and index.
    ISBN 0-7914-6037-1 (alk. paper)
    1. Rhetoric—Philosophy. 1. Title. II. Series.

P301.V58 2004
808'.001—dc22   2003067295

10 9 8 7 6 5 4 3 2 1

for my parents

A speech ought to be a man:—the heart and soul of the speaker made manifest.

—Ralph Waldo Emerson, "Politics"

What matter who's speaking, someone said what matter who's speaking.

—Samuel Beckett, *Texts for Nothing*

Contents

Part III: Rhetoric and the Politics of Self and Other

Preface

The title of this book is meant to convey a double meaning. On the one hand, the word *being* may be taken as a noun. The nature of some*thing* familiar has been altered. According to the subject matter of this book, that thing is a kind of being: *human* being. Presently, we understand who we are in profoundly different ways than our culture once did. Nevertheless, we use a traditional and seemingly stable category (being) in order to do so. On the other hand, "being" may also be taken as a gerund, in which case what we normally consider a thing would in fact be an action, an occurrence. Our understanding of ourselves as kinds of beings is unsettled, subject to alteration, and we know it. Our ideas about the state of our being are informed by its gradual transformation, by its becoming other than what it once was. We do not merely recognize an objective difference between how individuals once defined human being and how we define it now; rather, the most influential conceptions of human being in the present era are characterized by a reticence at the prospect of naming its truth, of regarding it as a stable entity.

Such reticence characterizes the current social context as well as philosophical reflection. Technological or biomedical affiliations between humans and machines, the rapid reorganization of time and space achieved by modern information networks, and the questioning of Enlightenment ideologies centered on a universal political subject have prompted us to wonder if we truly can claim any essential human form or nature. Consequently, one is hard-pressed to name human being as *either* a noun *or* a gerund, as objective presence or pure process, as an unchanging state of matter or as the embodiment of changing states of affairs. At best, ours is an epoch in which one must approach the category of human being with an awareness of this double meaning: as *both* presence *and* process, as something we comprehend only in its transfiguration. This book investigates the ways in which such double meaning shapes what can be said about human being today.

What can be said, however, cannot be separated from *how* it is said. How, then, has the supposed truth of human being traditionally been said? Throughout the Western tradition, the alleged essence of human being has been expressed in the practice of rhetoric, in the refinement of reason applied to speech. Our supposedly innate capacity for eloquence has long been the organizing principle of what came to be known in our heritage as humanist ideals, including skill in political voluntarism, artistic, philosophical, or religious conduct, and the management of civic or professional affairs in general.

Speech so conceived is doubly representative. In its ideal form, speech allows human beings to represent, or lucidly communicate, transcendent phenomena—truths, laws, or values that would remain mute, mere intuitive impressions, if not for the expressive powers of human speech. As such, speech also represents the definitively human capacity of human beings, the activity in which humans personify the truth of their being.

By virtue of this representational logic, the discipline of rhetoric remained, for centuries, the primary pedagogical instrument in which the supposed truth of human being was said.[1] In 1837, Ralph Waldo Emerson reveled in this doubly representative nature of the orator when he proclaimed:

> Eloquence is the power which one man in an age possesses of piercing the superficial crusts of condition which discriminate man from man and addressing the common soul of them all. . . . By a few sharp and skillful statements he unites his various audience and whilst they stand mute and astonished, he touches their hearts as harpstrings until in the presence of the aroused Reason Good and Fair becomes practicable and the gravest material obstacles are swept away as the morning cloud. Under the dominion of a commanding sentiment Society becomes perfect, for individual interests, even personal identity melt into the swelling surges of the Universal Humanity. (1964b, 109–10)

Edwin Black, in his more recent encomium of rhetoric itself, likewise extolled the vibrant connection between rhetoric and a supposedly universal human condition when he declared, "The object of our study, then, is something that has been a vital, formative component of human experience for thousands of years. And it is likely to remain so for thousands more—for as long as creatures like us abide" (2001, 541). Ancient and modern rhetorical treatises alike are littered with such celebrations of the orator's innate skill and virtue, which ostensibly represent a universally noble human nature.

Throughout the twentieth century, philosophical, scientific, and political events called into question the authority of a universal humanist subject. Time and again, the belief in some fundamental truth of our being has led those with pernicious motives to claim privileged access to that truth. Time and again, authorities have exerted control over those who publicly affirm an ethic or ideology other than a patently Western version of humanism by compelling them to adhere to the allegedly universal and civilizing norms of liberal democratic discourse.[2] During the age of European expansion and imperialism, for example, explorers and colonists viewed the languages of native peoples around the globe as evidence of an inferior human nature. The arts of oratory offered a potent colonizing tool with which Christian missionaries and European settlers sought to assimilate so-called savages into Western forms of religious or civic life.[3] The historical practice of rhetoric proves that assuming an essential sameness among individuals, even in the spirit of Christian benevolence or democratic progress, can result in a denial of important cultural or ethnic differences. Nancy Fraser (1992) has demonstrated cogently that formal appeals to supposedly universal values and interests can informally, but nonetheless powerfully, exclude groups and individuals from social and political validation. Denying cultural or ethnic differences is often preliminary to, and in some cases indistinguishable from, excluding or even eradicating them.

Nevertheless, ideal conceptions of humanity and speech retain an impressive ethos in our culture. Even in its transformation, the heritage shaped by such humanist ideals continues to influence, in subtle but profound ways, how individuals conceive of the affinity between human nature and the powers of ordinary expression. Our traditional rhetoric of human being, which presupposes that humans are uniquely endowed with a capacity for eloquence guided by truth, reason, and virtue, operates throughout our culture in the guise of conventional wisdom even at this late date.

In this book, I investigate how the discipline of rhetoric, having for centuries sustained ideal conceptions of speech and human being, continues to promote humanist ideals (such as artistic and political autonomy or the inherent reason and eloquence of speech) whose ethical and political implications have rightly given pause to a host of modern scholars. Granted, virtually all humanistic or social scientific disciplines retain at least some commitment to these same principles; but rhetoric has long been the organ of Western education devoted exclusively to training individuals how to personify those principles in civic conduct. Indeed, Greco-Roman, Renaissance, and Enlightenment values have endured as crucial touchstones of contemporary Western culture largely because the discipline of rhetoric historically has functioned as their means of common expression and scholastic canonization.

Some modern rhetoricians would likely object to this claim and reply that rhetoric, throughout its many incarnations, has been defined as a counterpart to philosophy. By this reasoning, practitioners of rhetoric may be commended for professing the value of contingency rather than transcendence, of revisable standards instead of ideal values, and of *doxa* rather than *episteme*. This bifurcated arrangement indeed rendered philosophy and rhetoric separate, but not equal. To endorse such disciplinary boundaries is to endorse a definition of rhetoric originally conceived by, and beneficial to, philosophy (or, for that matter, any discipline organized by the ideals of essential truth or objective knowledge). Throughout the chapters to come, I demonstrate that rhetoric's apparent disciplinary autonomy paradoxically reflects its domestication by philosophy. In Aristotle's overwhelmingly influential system, skill in rhetoric was predicated upon one's skill in dialectic (*On Rhetoric*, 1.2.7). In Cicero's equally renowned balance of *sapientia et eloquentia*, eloquence acquired its value as an instrument of civic affairs only when one used it in accord with unassailable reason (*De Inventione*, 1.1.1). Both thinkers took for granted that rhetoric is domesticated by the imperatives of an unimpeachably moral and rational agent. One finds the tersest summary of such moral and intellectual assumptions, exhibited throughout the rhetorical tradition, in Quintilian's famous definition of a good orator as a "good man skilled in speaking" (*Institutio Oratoria*, 12.1.1). Rhetoricians that affirm ontological values opposed to those of traditional philosophy unwittingly affirm the dialectical logic and classical ideals by which rhetoric has been, at best, domesticated and, at worst, denounced.

One's affirmation of such values is compromised if one fails to question the broader logic that first gave them meaning. The purpose of this book is to question the logic of representation and, subsequently, to offer an account of rhetoric no longer sanctioned by the socially and intellectually prejudicial values of representational thought. In questioning that logic, however, my purpose is not to hastily abrogate the dominant ideals of the rhetorical tradition. Instead, my inquiry in what follows is conducted in a spirit of critical prudence modeled on Charles Scott's description of his own methodology: "What is questioned is not abandoned," he writes. "Questioning, as I use the word, is not a matter of indifference and ignorance, but a way of relating to something that holds its fascination or importance while it loses a measure of its authority. What is in question returns in the question, returns without elevation and without the power to produce heroes, returns without being a totality that is protected against the exposure of its limits and the fittingness of its mortality" (1990, 8). In this spirit, I question and thereby assign an unconventional sense and value to the universal conceptions of human being that have defined the art of rhetoric for centuries. I advocate, not the end of rhetoric in its traditional form, but the end of its "power to produce heroes" in the old style. Only by interrogating the frequently ignored "limits" and "fittingness" of categorical human ideals, I argue, can one conceive of rhetoric beyond the misleading lucidity of representation.

☙

Readers will note that I have retained, in quoted material, masculine pronouns prevalent throughout the literature of the rhetorical tradition. I leave such pronouns unaltered not to ignore them, but as a way of highlighting one of the many social prejudices historically characteristic of rhetorical theory and practice. I trust that the context of my argument in this study leaves no doubt as to my rejection of civic and scholarly exclusions, gendered or otherwise, based on partial and privileged notions of human being.

The authorial subject of this book is comprised of many different selves, perhaps too many to name. The present study (and much else in my scholarly development) would have been unthinkable without Denise Albanese, Bruce Manchester, and Sheryl Friedley. This book began as a dissertation at Pennsylvania State University. I thank the Department of Communication Arts and Sciences at that institution for their generous award of a Sparks Fellowship in 2000, which proved both timely and instrumental in the development of my project. Several of my doctoral cohorts meaningfully contributed to this book—either implicitly, as the result of both seminar discussions and informal conversations, or explicitly, by critiquing essays that eventually became chapters. More generally, I wish to acknowledge abundant departmental support throughout my time at Penn State; little more than a throw of the dice brought me to the program, and in it chance was affirmed.

The influences of the faculty with whom I worked at Penn State are consubstantial with this book, and will not soon fade from my future scholarship. Jeff Robinson and the late Richard Gregg courteously supported my research at awkward junctures. Rich Doyle's contributions to the present work prove that intellectual passions are often the result of unexpected infections, and I don't expect to encounter a more infectious intellect anytime soon. I have learned a tremendous amount from Charles Scott's sage commentary on earlier portions of this book; I continue to orient my thinking and writing according to his singular example of scholarly care and dedication. Thomas Benson provided, as he does for all of his students, a rare patience and attentiveness that signified, not simply sound pedagogy, but intellectual virtue. Above all, the length of this work would be dramatically enhanced were I to list the myriad ways in which I have benefited from Stephen Browne's unique and selfless tutelage. The entirety of my scholarship to date is devoted, in one way or another, to emulating his distinctive union of *sapientia et eloquentia*.

I thank Fran Keneston, Kelli Williams, Ronald Helfrich, and Priscilla Ross at SUNY Press for their indispensable assistance in developing my manuscript. Nor would I have realized this project without the knowing counsel and encouragement of my parents, who provided me with my earliest and most constant examples of dedicated scholars. Finally, Anne Demo's contributions to this book are unsurpassed; in countless ways, this text represents the inestimable outcome of all I have learned from her, and which I can, at best, only attempt to return—eternally, I hope.

Earlier versions of chapters 4 and 5 appeared, respectively, as "Style, Rhetoric, and Postmodern Culture" in *Philosophy and Rhetoric* 35 (2002):

223–43, and "Jefferson's Other" in *Quarterly Journal of Speech* 88 (2002): 284–302. I wish to thank those publications for permission to reproduce such material. The epigraphs are reprinted by permission of the publisher from *The Early Lectures of Ralph Waldo Emerson, Volume III, 1838–1842*, edited by Robert E. Spiller and Wallace E. Williams, p. 244, Cambridge, Mass.: The Belknap Press of Harvard University Press, Copyright © 1972 by the President and fellows of Harvard College. Copyright © renewed 1992 by Stephen Emerson Whicher, Robert Ernest Spiller, and Wallace Edward Williams; Grove/Atlantic, Inc. to quote from *Stories and Texts for Nothing*, by Samuel Beckett, copyright © 1967 by Samuel Beckett; and Penguin Press for permission to quote from *Twilight of the Idols/The Anti-Christ* by Friedrich Nietzsche, translated by R. J. Hollingdale, copyright © 1968 by R. J. Hollingdale.

Introduction

Prior to the twentieth century, the discipline of rhetoric could boast of Western culture's most complete and integrated system for understanding the manifold uses of language in human affairs. The following synopsis documents, in the most general terms, how rhetorical scholars historically have appealed to universal notions of human being to define and legitimate their discipline. The rhetorical tradition originated in Greece during the fifth and fourth centuries B.C.E., when skill in public address emerged as an essential requirement for one's success, most notably, in Athenian government and society. The demand for instruction in a style of speaking suited to the practice of civic affairs and professional advancement transformed rhetoric from a poetic and theatrical practice into a valued academic discipline.[1]

Isocrates (436–338 B.C.E.) helped to institutionalize rhetoric as a prominent feature of Greek education. Over time, his teachings influenced Roman education and, through this connection, Western education in general. In his *Antidosis,* he calls speech "that power which, of all the faculties which belong to the nature of man, is the source of most of our blessings" (253). Isocrates anticipates more than two millennia worth of conventional wisdom regarding the nature of speech and humanity:

> For in the other powers which we possess, as I have already said on a former occasion, we are in no respect superior to other living creatures; nay, we are inferior to many in swiftness and in strength and in other resources; but, because there has been implanted in us the power to persuade each other and to make clear to each other whatever we desire, not only have we escaped the life of wild beasts, but we have come together and founded cities and made laws and invented arts. . . . It is by this also that we confute the bad and extol the good. Through this we educate the ignorant and appraise the wise. (253–55)[2]

In Isocrates' account, humans transcend the life of "other living creatures" not simply by virtue of their capacity for reason, for founding cities, laws, and arts, but through the ability to cultivate and express their reasoning in speech. Without speech, our reason would make us no better than "wild beasts." According to Isocrates, "the power to speak well is taken as the surest index of a sound understanding, and discourse which is true and lawful and just is the outward image of a good and faithful soul" (255–56). Like so many in classical Greece, Isocrates maintained that reason, the very hallmark of human being, would lie dormant and useless without eloquence.[3]

Aside from Isocrates' considerable influence, contemporary rhetoricians frequently characterize the sophists, with whom he is often (and somewhat controversially) grouped, as Hellenistic counterculturalists or proto-postmodernists whose teachings provide a classical Greek template for civic education and discourse in the so-called postmodern era (Jarratt 1991; Vitanza 1997). Regardless of contemporary interpretations, the sophists generally affirmed conventional civic and intellectual ideals. Although the sophists' standards of truth and virtue were, indeed, often more flexible than Socrates or Plato's standards, most of them advocated moral education for the orator, celebrated the virtues of reason, and venerated both enlightened government and the gods (Kennedy 1999, 50). "[W]ho does not know," Isocrates opined, "that words carry greater conviction when spoken by men of good repute than when spoken by men who live under a cloud, and that the argument which is made by a man's life is of more weight that that which is furnished by words?" (*Antidosis,* 278). In this sense, Isocrates' influential espousal of the orator's contributions to Hellenistic culture strongly resembled widespread sophistic contributions to the establishment of reason, truth, morality, and eloquence as Western cultural ideals.[4]

Whereas Isocrates emphasized the virtuous capacities of the speaker, Plato (ca. 429–347 B.C.E.) emphasized the corrupt nature of rhetoric. In his *Sophist,* the interlocutors conclude that "skill in the region of discourse" enables one "to impose upon the young . . . images of all things in a shadow play of discourse, so as to make them believe that they are hearing the truth and that the speaker is in all matters the wisest of men" (234c). Nevertheless, Plato admitted that uniquely gifted individuals could use speech virtuously. For him, the only form of speech immune to the human penchant for deceit was spoken by the philosopher, by a lover of wisdom devoted to the reasoned science of dialectic and therefore able to intuit truth prior to the order of discourse and represent it transparently in speech.[5]

Plato's insistence on wisdom or truth as rhetorical standards may have indicated his distaste for the often combative and deceitful temper of public oratory in the Greek polis. The earliest recorded speeches in Greek literature, those in Homer's *Iliad,* demonstrate that lying was a common oratorical practice in Greek culture well before Plato's time (Kennedy 1999, 6–7). Plato rejected this practice and maintained that rhetoric was virtuous only if it was conducted by "a scientific practitioner of speech" who had attained a dialectical mastery of the subject at hand, a command of the different forms of speech, and (most important of all) a knowledge of the souls of one's listeners to which the discourse must be adapted (*Phaedrus,* 277b–c).

Plato's explication of wise and virtuous speech reflected his profound debt to Socrates' teachings. In W. K. C. Guthrie's summation, Socrates "reduced all the virtues to one and described that one as wisdom or knowledge—the knowledge of good and evil" (1975, 104–105). Hence, in Plato's *Meno,* Socrates reasons, "If then virtue is an attribute of the spirit, and one which cannot fail to be beneficial, it must be wisdom, for all spiritual qualities in and by themselves are neither advantageous nor harmful, but become advantageous or harmful by the presence with them of wisdom or folly. If we accept this argument, then virtue, to be something advantageous, must be a sort of wisdom" (88c-d). Actions performed without wisdom are harmful. Those performed with it are inherently beneficial. Wisdom, therefore, must be inherently virtuous. Plato's scrutiny of linguistic imperfections according to this ideal knowledge eventually became the standard according to which rhetoric often was evaluated and, not coincidentally, frequently excoriated.

Although Isocrates and Plato instituted differing schools of thought on the nature of rhetoric, both schools contributed to establishing the moral benchmarks of reason, truth, and transparency against which the use of rhetoric typically has been measured for two-and-a-half millennia. Isocrates did not dispute the moral criteria that Plato advocated in his conception of philosophical rhetoric so much as he insisted that one could not attain eloquence without wisdom, and thus a virtuous character. In his *Panegyricus,* Isocrates declares that "beautiful and artistic speech is never allotted to ordinary men, but is the work of an intelligent mind" (48). He, along with other sophists, shared responsibility with Plato for defining the very person of the orator in moral terms, which later influenced Cicero and Quintilian's own reverence for the orator and eventually became a pervasive feature of Greco-Roman rhetoric in general. For both Isocrates and Plato, the practice of rhetoric depended on an inborn moral aptitude for wisdom and eloquence. Despite their undeniable differences, Isocrates and Plato alike presumed that only a select class of students could best actualize the supposedly universal human potential for reason, truth, virtue, and eloquence—a belief that presaged the intellectual bias of such human ideals from the Greek classical period forward.

Aristotle (367–322 B.C.E.), Plato's student, institutionalized the value of speech as such by defining rhetoric as "an *antistrophos* [counterpart] to dialectic" (*On Rhetoric,* 1.1.1). Dialectic, he argued, is suited to the apprehension of truth, whereas rhetoric is suited to its responsible reproduction in discourse. In Aristotle's comparatively scholastic calculus of essence and appearance, one must use rhetoric like dialectic—as a means to distinguish between truth and falsehood (albeit in separate domains): "[I]t is a function of one and the same art to see the persuasive and [to see] the apparently persuasive, just as [it is] in dialectic [to recognize] a syllogism and [to recognize] an apparent syllogism" (1.1.14). This dialectical domestication of rhetoric was necessary, according to Aristotle, because "In the case of rhetoric . . . there is the difference that one person will be [called] *rhētōr* on the basis of his knowledge and another on the basis of his deliberate choice" (1.1.14), suggesting that wisdom and spurious intentions alike can motivate rhetorical practice. In his popular translation of Aristotle's *Rhetoric*, W. Rhys Roberts comments that "rhetorician" "can mean either a *trained speaker* or a *tricky speaker*" (1954, 24 n1). Understandably, then, training in rhetoric involved moral as well as practical instruction.

Aristotle's subordination of rhetoric to dialectic further codified instruction in the art throughout the Hellenistic world. It did so, moreover, by affirming the conventional belief that speech somehow typified the elevated nature of human beings—that, in Aristotle's terms, defending oneself with speech rather than with "the body" is "more characteristic of humans" (*On Rhetoric*, 1.1.12). His *Rhetoric*, after being overshadowed by newer handbooks in later antiquity and relegated to obscurity during the medieval period, once again became a leading influence on rhetorical education following its rediscovery and translation into Latin during the Renaissance. Contemporary rhetoricians view Aristotle's *Rhetoric* as an authoritative model of rhetorical theory and practice. Because of Isocrates, Plato, and Aristotle's profound influence in particular, instruction in rhetoric historically has been accompanied by at least some moral code guiding its use, personified in the ideal of a wise and virtuous rhetor.[6]

Classical Romans inherited this conception of speech as a defining feature of human civilization from the Greeks. Cicero's treatises on rhetoric proved uniquely influential "in forming the image of the orator as a culture-hero" (Vickers 1988, 10). In *De Inventione*, his first work on rhetoric, Cicero (106–43 B.C.E.) echoed Isocrates in celebrating the orator's exemplary status, not merely as a citizen, but as a human being. "I think that men," he wrote, "although lower and weaker than animals in many respects, excel them most by having the power of speech. Therefore that man appears to me to have won a splendid possession who excels men themselves in that ability by which men excel beasts" (1.4.5). Cicero's later texts, most notably *De Oratore*, continued to celebrate the ennobling and liberating capacities of eloquence guided by wisdom, such that "out of the innumerable company of mankind, a single being should arise" who "can make effective a faculty bestowed by nature on every man" (1.7.31). "In every free nation," he proclaimed, "and most of all in communities which have attained the enjoyment of peace and tranquility, this one art has always flourished above the rest and ever reigned supreme. . . . [T]he wise control of the complete orator is that which chiefly upholds not only his own dignity, but the safety of countless individuals and of the entire state" (*De Oratore,* 1.7.30–1.8.34). In addition to praising the civilizing qualities of rhetoric, Cicero credited them with maintaining nothing less than the peace and security of the state as a whole.

In turn, Quintilian (ca. 39–96 C.E.) echoed Cicero by calling oratory "the highest gift of providence to man" (*Institutio Oratoria,* 1.10.7) and insisted that a good orator must be a good person. Like his predecessor, Quintilian proposed that, by surpassing other individuals in the application of eloquence to reason, an orator personified the pinnacle of humanity (*Institutio Oratoria,* 2.16.17). His remarkably influential *Institutio Oratoria* treated rhetoric as an essential component in the instruction of social and political leaders as well as responsible citizens. For Quintilian especially, rhetorical education involved a lifelong training of the entire person and represented the centerpiece of one's education. The Roman presumption that rhetorical education refined one's social being has endured in modern justifications for the scholarly and civic value of rhetorical study. Edward Corbett's assertion that "rhetoric can be regarded as an enabling discipline not simply because it develops particular skills in those who study it but because it is also a discipline concerned with the development of the whole person" (1989, 207) could have appeared in any number of classical Roman handbooks on rhetoric. By virtue of this enduring connection, Cicero and Quintilian together exemplify the unsurpassed influence of Roman rhetoric on Western education and civic participation. "From Rome," Brian Vickers states, "rhetoric, in education, in public activity, and in all forms of writing, spread throughout the world, its influence waning only in the nineteenth century" (1988, 12).[7]

The Middle Ages produced few lasting innovations in rhetorical theory and practice. In an era of diminishing support for liberal education, even the influence of Plato and Aristotle waned considerably as pagan knowledge was transmuted into the basis for religious teachings. Not surprisingly, the widespread application of classical rhetorical principles to the art of preaching was the most significant innovation in rhetorical theory and practice at this time.[8] Augustine's (354–430) *De Doctrina Christiana* became the authoritative statement on Christian eloquence during the medieval period (1995).[9] For him, rhetoric was principally useful in allowing audiences to achieve a deeper understanding of the Scriptures and thereby incite good works on the basis of belief. Rhetoric thus became the instrument of the true believer, of a preacher committed to the indisputable truth and moral directives of Christian texts. Persuasion depended on prior belief in the Word of God rather than human eloquence, no matter how aesthetically pleasing. One might even say that the medieval preacher represented the Christian analogue to Plato's philosophical rhetor. In this regard, medieval instruction in rhetoric preserved and enhanced, albeit in an altered form, Greco-Roman rhetoric's alignment of the art with the speaker's exemplary moral goodness.

Rhetorical education reached the height of its prestige during the Renaissance as a result of the European rediscovery of Roman culture. The manifold influence of the Renaissance on modern Western culture and politics is unquestioned; the discipline of rhetoric, in so ubiquitously shaping the public and intellectual character of Renaissance life, contributed extensively to cultivating the ideal of the humanist subject according to which contemporary scholarship, civic participation, and artistic pursuits are still measured. As early as the 1370s, the Italian humanist Coluccio Salutati wrote, "[H]ow excellent, how glorious, how appropriate it is to excel in those gifts of nature which make man preeminent above other animals. The wise and the eloquent seem to me to have achieved for themselves that step of excellence above other men, which God and nature have decreed between men and creatures devoid of reason " (quoted in Struever 1970, 53).[10] The fervent intellectual worship of truth subsequently replaced the quasi-religious tincture of such testaments to eloquence. Giambattista Vico (1668–1774), the Italian humanist remembered most fondly by modern rhetoricians, similarly echoed the ancients when he asserted that, because "Truth" is the only common "aim of all kinds of intellectual pursuits," young orators "should be taught the totality of sciences and arts, and their intellectual powers should be developed to the full; thus they will become familiar with the art of argument, drawn from the *ars topica*. At the very outset, their common sense should be strengthened so that they can grow in prudence and eloquence" (1965, 9; 19). For Vico, all intellectual and civic pursuits, including "the art of argument," culminated in the revelation of "Truth."

The Renaissance humanists' promotion of the ennobling powers of speech led to the establishment of divisions between public and private life characteristic of Western modernity. Rhetorical skill allowed one to participate in civic affairs, in the esteemed *vita activa,* and thus to contribute to the improvement of humanity writ large. In 1574, Stefano Guazzo declared, "Nature herself has given man the power of speech. But certainly not in order that he converse with himself. . . . Conversation is not only an advantage but also a necessary condition for the perfection of man" (quoted in Garin 1965, 159).[11] Conversely, those who opted for the *vita contemplativa,* the pursuits of which Renaissance humanists grouped derogatorily under the rubric of "solitude," were regarded as somehow less than human and "variously described as . . . illiterate, inferior, fruitless, infertile, treasonous, inhuman, rotting in laziness, sterile, unjust, [and] vain" (Vickers 1988, 273). Taken together, Renaissance beliefs in the essentially social and linguistic nature of human beings, along with the supposedly innate human commitment to truth, reason, and civic virtue, established the modern civic precedent that one's humanity is defined by the moral and socially virtuous application of one's rhetorical abilities.[12]

Rhetorical handbooks from the Renaissance forward were also distinguished by their detailed treatments of the persuasive arousal of emotion. In Francis Bacon's (1565–1621) terms, "The dutie and Office of Rhetoricke" was "*To apply Reason to Imagination*, for the better moouing of the will" (2000, 2.18.2). By challenging the traditional Aristotelian and Ciceronian dictates concerning rhetoric's limitation to deliberative, forensic, and epideictic discourse, practitioners of the art further elaborated this attention to human sentiment throughout the eighteenth and nineteenth centuries. Such was the era in which reason, as David Hume put it, became "a species of sentiment" (2000, 103).

Modern rhetoricians often disparage these developments, claiming that at this time rhetorical education was reduced either to tedious exercises in the ornate classification of rhetorical figures or to theatrical training in elocution at the expense of the discipline's formerly substantive focus on argumentation. In either case, however, rhetorical education remained intent on the development of performative or discursive techniques that, by virtue of a sophisticated quasi-psychological understanding of human emotion, sought an entirely natural and therefore persuasive presentation of sentiment. One of the most accomplished examples of this approach was George Campbell's (1719–1796) *The Philosophy of Rhetoric* ([1841] 1992), first published in 1776. The complex rhetorical correspondence between nature and artifice in Campbell's text, and many others of the period, coalesced in the mimetic quality of the rhetorical figures. No matter how rococo they may appear to modern rhetoricians, the figures presumably replicated in speech the self-evident nature of human emotions. Although suffused with distinctively neoclassical sensibilities of taste and cognition, the rhetorical figures were thus faithful, at least in spirit, to one of the original assumptions of rhetorical training: that the orator's eloquence should reflect his or her mastery of a natural eloquence (Vickers 1988, 296).

The utility of the rhetorical figures as such conformed to a larger cultural obsession with natural language during the eighteenth century. Rhetorical theory and practice of the day reflected, in Jay Fliegelman's words, "an intensified quest to discover (or theorize into existence) a natural spoken language that would be a corollary to natural law, a language that would permit universal recognition and understanding" (1993, 1–2). The very person of the orator was understood to be the vessel of this universal language, as its suasory power derived from the speaker's gestures, tones, and expressions rather than his or her words alone. By implication, such "universal recognition and understanding" must emanate from the wells of universal human wisdom and eloquence embodied in the orator. Despite its revolutionary status in the rhetorical tradition as a whole, such an emphasis on the body of the rhetor as a conduit of pathos had classical antecedents. Perhaps most famously, Cicero advised that the body expresses emotion more vividly than language, potentially even allowing for an unmediated invocation of pathos in one's listeners. Summarizing the arguments of Thomas Sheridan (1719–1788), one of the leading figures of the elocutionary movement, Fliegelman explains the centrality of the speaker's physical performance to persuasion in the neoclassical period: "Speaking thus becomes less a form of argumentative or expository communication than a revelation of 'internal moral dispositions' and passions registered by vocal tones, physical 'exertions,' and facial expressions that are received in unmediated form by the sympathetic 'social' nature of the auditor" (30).[13] In 1783, Hugh Blair (1718–1800), who exerted a considerable influence on the development of neoclassical rhetoric, succinctly affirmed this ideal of rhetorical practice by cautioning his students that, "though figures imply a deviation from what may be reckoned the most simple form of speech, we are not thence to conclude, that they imply any thing uncommon, or unnatural. This is so far from being the case, that, on very many occasions, they are both the most natural, and the most common method of uttering our sentiments" ([1819] 1993, 132). Like his contemporaries, Blair professed this view in conjunction with his belief that, "[i]n order to be a truly eloquent or persuasive speaker, nothing is more necessary than to be a virtuous man" (338). Contrary to much modern disciplinary lore, the supposed artifice of the rhetorical figures or elocutionary exercises extended, each in their own way, the rhetorical tradition's guiding purpose of representing the natural, most essential, truths of human being in speech.[14] Blair, for one, acknowledged that avowing the supposedly unimpeachable virtue of a trained orator "was a favourite position among the ancient rhetoricians" (338). By the logic of the elocutionary movement, which presumed that one achieved eloquence in literally embodying reason and virtue, when "a speaker wishes to project a particular emotion, he must not paint it but become a portrait of it" (Fliegelman 1993, 31).

Twentieth–century rhetoricians, disillusioned by their recent disciplinary history, made Aristotelian rhetorical theory the dominant method of modern rhetorical studies (Gaonkar 1997, 28). Many shunned the bookish or theatrical airs of the belletristic and elocutionary movements while advocating an explicit return to Aristotelian rhetorical principles (Leff 1992). Others promoted a realignment of rhetoric with the humanistic practice of argumentation in general. Such influential figures as Lloyd Bitzer (1968), Thomas Farrell (1993), Richard McKeon (1987, 1998), Chaïm Perelman (1969, 1979, 1982), Robert Scott (1967, 1976), Stephen Toulmin (1964), and Richard Weaver (1953, 1970) have all defined rhetoric as reasoned and potentially egalitarian argumentation in some form. Beyond the scholarship of these individuals, the pedagogy of the field over the past century reveals an omnipresent validation of rhetoric as a species of learned and democratically responsible argumentation. Advocacy of rhetoric in this form stemmed from efforts to lend new legitimacy to the study of rhetoric by equating it with logical demonstration or public argument, with logos, rather than the perceived grandiloquence or emotional chicanery of eighteenth- and nineteenth-century preoccupations with pathos and *elocutio*.

This return to a Greco-Roman emphasis on reason, logic, and argument bequeathed to contemporary rhetoricians a disciplinary paradigm predicated upon the expression of essential truths and, as such, the refinement of human being. The discipline of rhetoric historically has flourished, not in spite of beliefs in the essential virtues of humanity, but in celebration thereof. Despite Greco-Romans' veneration of the civilizing powers of speech or modern rhetoricians' conviction in the democratic potential of rhetoric, a longer view of the tradition proves that, in practice as well as theory, it has generally reinforced, rather than subverted, exclusionary social hierarchies based on race, gender, class, religion, and nationality.[15] One of the fundamental ironies of the rhetorical tradition is that its ostensibly universal principles typically have been promoted by only the most socially and intellectually privileged individuals. Whatever its putative civic virtues, the rhetorical tradition has promulgated and preserved classical or humanist ideals that, by seeking to represent a universal human aspiration to wisdom and eloquence, represent merely a partial and privileged view of humanity.

RHETORICAL BEING

Using the foregoing historical narrative as its point of departure, this book asks: Can one conceive of rhetoric without appealing to essential notions of human being? In order to address this question, one must first consider the current status of ethos in rhetorical studies. The general twentieth-century return to logos in the field has produced few challenges to the traditional meaning of ethos. Referring to the predominance of logos in modern rhetorical instruction, Edward Corbett surmises that "training" in ethos (as well as pathos) "has been largely neglected in our schools" (1989, 202). The reigning Aristotelian conception of rhetoric, guided by rational and moral imperatives, presupposes an ethos of reason, morality, and transparency—in Aristotle's terms, an ethos reflective of "practical wisdom *[phronēsis]* and virtue *[aretē]* and good will *[eunoia]*" (*On Rhetoric*, 2.1.5). Concerning Aristotle's influence over prevailing conceptions of ethos, James Baumlin asserts that "[r]hetoric owes its technical use of the term *ethos* to him" (1994, xvi).

Aristotle's descriptions of ethos suggest that rhetorical practice should be both conducted and evaluated through an affirmation of universal human ideals. In this context, "construct[ing] a view" of oneself "as a certain kind of person" (*On Rhetoric*, 2.1.2), in Aristotle's phrasing, enhances (and perhaps even acts as a substitute for) the reason and morality of one's arguments. Aristotle's belief that an outward display of virtue corresponded to an analogous inner state was founded on more than a wager; his emphasis of ethos resonated with Plato's maxim that "the nature of justice," as Guthrie would have it, "is personified in the individual. It is a state of inner harmony, of the balance and organization of the different elements of character. Such a balanced and organized character cannot fail to show itself outwardly in the performance of the kind of action which is ordinarily considered just" (1975, 113). Thus, the rhetorical display of a favorable ethos did not merely provide compelling support for one's argument; it represented the very embodiment of wisdom and morality, of balance and harmony—in a word, justice. Throughout our heritage, this conviction in the direct correspondence between one's inner nature and its unmediated representation in outward performance has appeared in altered forms, most notably in Judeo-Christian preoccupations with testimony and confession—with supposedly fundamental affinities between truth, presence, and speech. Because of these influences, a seemingly authentic performance of human being, of its allegedly rational, moral, and truthful nature, constitutes the *sine qua non* of the rhetorical tradition.

Hence, modern scholars generally have avoided explicit interrogation of ethos, perhaps *the* controlling proof of rhetoric.[16] Even twentieth-century sociological or anthropological approaches to rhetoric, Kenneth Burke's (1966, 1969a, 1969b) foremost among them, assume an intrinsic relationship between human nature and rhetorical or symbolic processes. Without questioning that assumed relationship, however, the discipline of rhetoric will continue to accommodate a Platonic morality designed to distinguish between an authentic and a performative self, between truth and falsehood, reason and emotion, or good and evil.

In order to rethink the concept of ethos, then, one must reconsider the category of human being. Throughout the Western tradition, displaying a rhetorically effective ethos has been equivalent, in Aristotle's words, to making oneself "appear prudent and good" (*On Rhetoric*, 2.1.7), meaning that the outward appearance of one's character should reflect a reasoned and virtuous inner being. This logic manifests assumptions about the nature and expression of the self common throughout the Western heritage and taken for granted in our own time. In Richard Lanham's assessment, Western notions of the self have "from the beginning been composed of a shifting and perpetually uneasy combination of *homo rhetoricus* and *homo seriosus,* of a social self and a central self" (1976, 6). The ambiguity between these different conceptions of the self resonates with the etymological slipperiness of the term *ethos* (Corts 1968; Yoos 1979, 41). "Translated as 'character,' " Baumlin notes, "*ethos* would seem to describe a singular, stable, 'central' self. Translated as 'custom' or 'habit,' *ethos* would describe a 'social' self, a set of verbal habits or behaviors, a playing out of customary roles" (1994, xviii). Despite the apparent ambiguity between beliefs in a "social" and "central" self, the broader logic of Western values posits the central self as a controlling factor in personal expression. By this logic, one may define ethos holistically as the customary expression of one's essential character. Modern conceptions of ethos thus endorse a doubly representational logic: in verbally representing reason, truth, or wisdom, one also personifies the universal ideal of humanity.

How might one question the accepted conception of ethos that defines rhetoric according to traditional metaphysical notions of an essential human being? One can begin to do so by considering in greater detail the pedagogical confusions created by the elocutionary movement, which encompassed the rhetorical tradition's most punctilious attempt to make oneself "appear prudent and good." Although they relied on fundamental distinctions between nature and artifice, the elocutionists, in their quest to cultivate a natural language, often ended up confusing rather than distinguishing the supposedly antithetical categories of reality and performance, of the private and public self. "For all the insistence that eloquence was an art of magnifying feelings actually experienced," Fliegelman observes, "and not of deceptively fabricating feelings, to teach the code of voice and gesture—to elide the distinction between the production of natural sounds and the reproduction of them made possible through a deceptive taxonomy in the service of a mechanical science—was to equip all men to deceive, to act a role" (1993, 80). By this logic, one's presentation of a natural language or persona required considerable abilities in simulation: "Distinctions between 'sincere' and 'artful' to the contrary, 'the art of speaking' was always artful, the show of naturalness was still a show" (Fliegelman 1993, 80). In pursuing the rhetorical tradition's most meticulous effort to display a natural ethos, a transparent representation of human nature, the elocutionists repeatedly were confronted by the disquieting possibility that "[i]f the self was no more than an endless sequence of self-presentations structured for different audiences without an overarching and definable core self," then "theatricality was the essence of natural behavior" (Fliegelman 1993, 81–82). The elocutionists certainly never celebrated this possibility; it was, in fact, a source of profound anxiety for them. But if one actually endorsed this paradox inherent to distinctions between nature and artifice, or the private and public self, one would undermine the broader metaphysical logic in whose name they were established, for such distinctions reflect a philosophy committed to the differentiation of essence from appearance, truth from falsehood, good from evil. Most paradoxically of all, then, the elocutionists' obsession with the rhetorical display of an essentially natural discourse and persona ultimately revealed that rhetoric, in its orientation to an ideal human ethos, "was simultaneously intensely naturalistic and intensely theatrical: surreally mimetic" (Fliegelman 1993, 87). Nature and artifice turned out to be mutually supplemental, not antithetical, categories.

Consideration of the elocutionary movement in this regard demonstrates that rhetoricians have preserved the presumably universal truth and morality of humanist ideals only by ignoring the problematic possibilities inherent to the traditional and seemingly transparent relationship between rhetoric and human being. Chief among these is the possibility that conceiving of rhetoric beyond the representation of an ideal human ethos offers an efficacious means of disputing our culture's dominant metaphysical calculus of essence and appearance, truth and falsehood, or good and evil as it is personified and thus reaffirmed by individual rhetors. Rather than pursuing the potentially revolutionary lines of inquiry unwittingly opened up by early modern rhetorical theory, however, rhetoricians over the past century generally have avoided interrogation, not merely of traditional conceptions of ethos, but also of the classical or humanist conceptions of human being they reflect.

One notable exception to this trend is Thomas Benson, who asserted that the structure of any rhetorical interaction presupposes that the being of the agents involved, whether speaker and listeners or writer and readers, is constituted by the very process of communicative or symbolic exchange (1989, 294). Benson wished to account for the outcome of rhetorical practices in a way that affirmed the mutually constitutive agency of rhetors and audience members rather than assuming that the outcome of a given rhetorical exchange rests with either the artistry of the rhetor or the judgments of his or her audience. In those rhetorical contexts that notably influence the nature of our social relationships, he concluded, the being of rhetors and audience members does not exist prior to such discursive and symbolic exchanges but is, instead, constituted by their participation therein. Such insights led Benson to dismiss traditional metaphysical definitions of human being in favor of an alternate understanding of subjectivity that he labeled *rhetorical* being: "Rhetorical being is an action, not an essence; it is public, not private. Rhetorical being is being with, carried out through symbols. Rhetorical being is public even when it occurs as an inner reflection or a dialogue, in that it draws upon a shared system of public symbols. . . . Rhetorical being is a becoming, both the revelation of an inner condition and the ongoing creation of interacting selves. And rhetorical being is an action performed collaboratively by both speakers and listeners" (320). The elocutionists might have reached a similar conclusion about the affinity between rhetoric and being had they welcomed, rather than fretted over, the possibility that even the most apparently natural display of ethos, of emotion and reason, is actually a masterful rhetorical performance. According to Benson's more pragmatic logic, the protean nature of rhetorical exchanges dispels fixed distinctions between self and other or public and private. Such interactions reveal that our understanding of ourselves as particular sorts of beings is fundamentally influenced by the collective rhetoric of public discourse and shared symbol systems in which we participate. Within this discursive economy, the ideal of an essential or superior human nature appears to lose its previous organizing value.

Regardless of these virtues, I cite Benson's study in order to identify lingering problems with even such an innovative conception of the relationship between rhetoric and human being. Despite his stated distinction between the characteristics of "rhetorical being" and those of human being traditionally defined, problematic humanist assumptions still informed Benson's account. He retained, for instance, the following anthropological definition of the relationship between rhetoric and human subjectivity, which unmistakably echoes Greco-Roman descriptions of rhetoric as an essential human capacity: "[A]ll human being is rhetorical," he posited, "in that human personality and our awareness of it are constituted and transmitted through symbolic behavior" (294). Although Benson endeavored to replace the transcendent and hierarchical principles of human being with more contingent and revisable principles, the universality of this premise ensured that he merely replaced one essence with another, even if it was not explicitly named as such. The fundamental issue, in other words, is not how the essence of human being is defined but that it is defined as the representation of an essence at all.

Benson also retained an instrumental conception of rhetoric. Such a conception regards rhetoric as relatively unidirectional persuasion or communication between a speaker or author and a general audience of listeners or readers. In this formulation, rhetoric is merely the instrument of human intention or judgment, a product of individual artistic proficiency or political autonomy. As such, the traditional ethos of the autonomous rhetor tacitly served as the organizing principle of Benson's account. Regardless of his conviction that such autonomy alone does not dominate the outcome of rhetorical processes, rhetoric in this formulation only exists, and succeeds or fails, as the instrument by which the intentions of individual human agents are carried out. Benson's study exemplifies the traditional assumptions that implicitly hinder numerous attempts to redefine the category of rhetoric in nontraditional ways.

So long as rhetoric is defined in this manner, it will continue to be legitimated by and thus preserve essential notions of human being (even as it is used by some to counter the idealism of traditional metaphysical principles). In this book, I develop a conception of rhetoric beyond representation—one no longer organized, that is, by the representation of moral truth or transcendental reason nor representative of an ideal conception of human being, however explicit or implicit it may be. I do so, not by offering a history of the concept of ethos, but by recommending new ways in which scholars can study the affinities between rhetoric and subjectivity that implement modern philosophical insights, hitherto seldom explored by rhetoricians, concerning the relationship between discourse and the subject.

I do not propose, however, to simply replace one ontology of the subject with another. My goal is not to cast further invective at what David Simpson calls "the much-berated Cartesian subject" (2002, 205). As I demonstrate in the chapters to come, the canonical principles I have underscored thus far reflect a metaphysical value system that functions by establishing oppositions between essence and appearance, truth and falsehood, the sacred and the secular, or good and evil. Merely inverting the diametrical values according to which this system is arranged fails to counteract the organizing logic of the system itself. "[T]his disease of thinking in essences," Roland Barthes wrote, "is at the bottom of every bourgeois mythology of man" (1972a, 75).

In what follows, I do not endorse a complete rejection of the individual rhetor in favor of purely disembodied discourse, or intended meanings in favor of universal meaninglessness. Instead, I adapt, for the purposes of rhetorical inquiry, Jacques Derrida's commentary on the category of intention as it operates in his philosophy of communication. Derrida eschews the premium often placed on differentiating the original and authentic "iteration" of a discourse from its inauthentic "citation" in order to advocate "a differential typology of forms of iteration" (1988, 18). He argues, in other words, that regulating the array of meanings expressed by a given utterance across space and time solely by its originally intended sense prevents one from understanding the multiple rhetorical functions it fulfills beyond its intended purpose. In the "typology" that Derrida proposes, "the category of intention will not disappear; it will have its place, but from that place it will no longer be able to govern the entire scene and system of utterance [*l'énonciation*]" (18). By way of analogy, I devise a conception of rhetoric in which the supposedly universal ideal of an autonomous, reasoned, and virtuous subject no longer "govern[s] the entire scene and system" of rhetorical processes. The ethos of a rational, moral, and virtuous human ideal, along with the priority of human intention more generally, will still have rhetorical functions but they will no longer represent the *sine qua non* of rhetoric itself. A "differential typology" of the sort I propose will not replace the traditional ontology of the subject with another ontology; rather, it will identify methods for studying the rhetorical formation of multiple subjectivities no longer committed to promoting an allegedly universal, but actually privileged and partial, understanding of human being. It will argue for a conception of ethos no longer based on *either* "character" *or* "custom," on *either* a private *or* a public self, but generated by the discursive practices that engender such categories and infuse them with meaning and value in social, political, and ethical contexts.

Accompanying its contribution to rhetorical studies, this book ultimately advances a discourse on subjectivity that challenges the conventional criteria by which the human subject is either defended or deconstructed in a variety of disciplines. Unfortunately, even in the wake of revolutionary phenomenological, structuralist, and poststructuralist attempts to provide novel accounts of the relationship between discourse and subjectivity, many scholars continue to espouse a preferred ontology, whether traditional or avant-garde, in order to advocate a preferred form of subjectivity. Discussions of this sort typically fall back on endorsements of *either* agency *or* determinism, *either* being *or* becoming, *either* essence *or* appearance, in order to explain the nature of subjectivity. In light of the trope with which I began, such approaches are poorly equipped to consider being in its more indeterminate and potentially transformational sense, as *both* a noun *and* a gerund. In order to counteract the lingering influence of such diametrical schemas, I offer a discourse on rhetoric and subjectivity that proceeds, not on the basis of a categorical definition of being (whether it be classical, humanist, or even postmodern), but by analyzing how discursive practices engender, maintain, or transform particular forms of subjectivity without pursuing the affirmation of an ideal subject. Toward that end, I reconsider the category of ethos in terms of difference rather than identity, multiplicity instead of unity, and mutation instead of essential continuity. In this context, I demonstrate how an investigation of the rhetoric of subjectivity, of rhetoric beyond representation, yields vital ethical and political lessons concerning the academic study of subjectivity and its critical value to civic practices.

This book is divided into three parts. Part 1 is *critical* in nature. In order to critique representational definitions of rhetoric, I necessarily consider the metaphysical ontology that permeates the rhetorical tradition. Instead of critiquing that ontology by employing merely antithetical analytic categories (fiction instead of fact, appearance rather than essence), I present, in chapter 1, two accounts of the very idea of representation as it developed throughout Western modernity. Initially, I discuss the philosophical trope of the end of metaphysics, as featured in Hegel, Nietzsche, Heidegger, and Derrida, in order to clarify the critical aspirations of the present study in relation to modern philosophical critiques of foundational metaphysical categories, including reason, truth, knowledge, speech, and being. Thereafter, I use Michel Foucault's classic study *The Order of Things* (1994b) to demonstrate that those who take for granted the apparent self-evidence of representation as an organizing principle of our beliefs and values do so by ignoring the complex rhetorical history of that category. Taken together, these accounts allow me to demonstrate the long-standing affinities between rhetoric, representational thinking, and notions of a universal human identity.

These affinities are sustained fundamentally by the rhetorical tradition's valorization of human speech. In chapter 2, I question the troubling implications of retaining certain artistic and communicative ideals as the defining principles of rhetoric. I contend that definitions of rhetoric based on enduring Western assumptions about the ideal nature of speech are responsible for preserving an affinity between rhetoric and essential notions of human being. A critique of speech so conceived constitutes the most radical interrogation of rhetoric in its conventional representational form.

Part 2 is both *conceptual* and *methodological*. The task of developing a conception of rhetoric no longer based on an ideal notion of speech necessarily involves consideration of how rhetoric conventionally has been delimited according to the logic of the active voice. In chapter 3, I define the middle voice of rhetoric, which functions according to the self-enactment of discourse in a manner irreducible to the intentions of a privileged subject. In order to compose a model for this middle voice, I synthesize Michael Naas's (1995) insights on persuasion in Homeric Greece with Foucault's (1972) insights on the nature of discourse. My own conception of rhetoric in the middle voice—defined as the ethos of social, political, and ethical relations rather than a privileged subject—stems from this synthesis. In chapter 4, I employ sociologist Michel Maffesoli's (1996a) theory of style as a means of illustrating contemporary social, political, and ethical manifestations of rhetoric in this form. Over the course of chapters 3 and 4, I delineate the principles of an inquiry into subjectivity no longer beholden to the representation of universal values and imperatives but organized according to the changing discursive conditions that engender multiple forms of subjectivity.

Part 3 is comprised of two *case studies* in rhetoric and subjectivity that implement the theory and method developed in Part 2. They do so by demonstrating alternate approaches to the relationship between subjectivity and the discursive formation of time, memory, and historical experience. From Plato and Aristotle to Descartes and Kant, from Hegel and Husserl to Heidegger and Derrida, time has been one of the most elemental categories for Western understandings of subjective existence. Instead of approaching it as a transcendental or an objective category, however, chapters 5 and 6 analyze how the self is engendered by discourses constitutive of memory and historical experience. Admittedly, memory comprises only one rhetorical commonplace of subjectivity; nonetheless, in these chapters I demonstrate how an inquiry into rhetoric beyond representation vitally contributes to the more general project of accounting for subjectivity in a way that not only questions conventional notions of an essential or ideal human nature but also documents the rhetorical processes by which forms of subjectivity acquire their characteristic sense and value in response to changing social, political, and ethical conditions. Only by analyzing the rhetoric that engenders a given mode of subjectivity, I argue, can one assess the political and ethical motivations evoked by its animating discourse of self and other, individual and community, past and present, or good and evil.

In the conclusion, I underscore the ethical and political ramifications of this treatise for rhetorical studies, for research on subjectivity in philosophy, critical theory, and cultural studies, and for civic practice. Specifically, I claim that this book contributes to the study of subjectivity by altering the terms of debate according to which the very status of the subject conventionally is understood, as either centered or de-centered, as either subject or object, as either free or determined. My study provides a framework with which one can diagnose the discursive means that enable differing claims to such categories without assuming that the status of the subject itself must reflect an essential grounding in any one of them. An attunement to rhetoric beyond representation thus enables one to resist the stultifying moral uniformity of political agendas customarily justified by appeals to an ostensibly common humanity.

Reconsideration of ethos, or the performative cohesion of rhetoric and human subjectivity, must begin with an interrogation of the representational principles in affirmation of which discourse and human being traditionally have been defined. Readers conversant with Continental philosophy certainly will recognize the broad influence of the works I employ in conducting that interrogation. Yet scant effort has been made in rhetorical studies to systematically revise conventional conceptions of rhetoric in virtue of the revolutionary insights on discourse and subjectivity generated by Continental philosophers from Nietzsche forward.[17] The scarcity of such efforts likely corresponds to the mortification of some rhetoricians in the United States at the thought of a so-called invasion of Continental theory into their discipline. The oddity of such aversion is revealed, however, when one observes that the rhetorical tradition, as adopted by early North Americans, is obviously European in nature. Despite its unmistakable influence in shaping the pedagogy, politics, and culture of early American institutions, distinctively North American innovations are found wanting in the historical scope of the discipline. Thus, one might argue that the work of many modern Continental philosophers, which rigorously explores the problems and possibilities induced by customary assumptions about the nature of language and its manifold significance to human affairs, more robustly resembles, in method and terminology, the traditional forms of inquiry featured throughout the history of rhetoric than does the scholarship of those rhetoricians in the

United States who lament an invasion of French theory into their disciplinary enclave. Reconsidering rhetoric through the lens of such scholarship, I contend, not only yields a new critical orientation for scholars in rhetorical studies but also offers, for those in philosophy and cultural studies, a novel interpretation of pivotal structuralist and poststructuralist texts that underscores the hitherto undocumented value of rhetoric to the contemporary study of subjectivity.

Ultimately, my novel applications of such literature amount to merely preliminary steps in my effort to disclose the world of rhetoric beyond representation: a world in which the power of individuals to speak the unchanging logos of their own being is no longer accepted as an obvious truth but regarded as an inherited rhetorical problem. Such is a world in which the most familiar truths appear strange indeed, in which the value of truth itself is replaced by the creative powers of something like poetry as Georges Bataille described it; "If poetry introduces the strange," he wrote, "it does so by means of the familiar. The poetic is the familiar dissolving into the strange, ourselves with it" (1988b, 5). Rather than circumscribing a space outside of the familiar, the strange may be regarded as its internal dissolution, which begins slowly and at discrete points but inevitably draws even our most sacrosanct beliefs—those concerning ourselves—into its vortex. Hence our current reticence at defining being according to the conventional dialectic: as *either* a noun *or* a gerund, as objective presence or pure process, as character or custom. The dissolution of this hitherto sustaining logic, however, should not be cause for lament. It is occasion, rather, to affirm the rhetorical formation and transformation of being—being remade and made strange as it bristles forth out of the dissolution of the familiar.

Part I

Beyond Representation

Chapter 1

The Subject and Object of Representation

To date, both philosophers and rhetoricians have only superficially explored the potentially profound significance of rhetoric to contemporary reflections on the nature of language, reason, and human being. Newton Garver posits that the philosophical study of language in the twentieth century has followed what he calls "two distinct flurries" (1973, xii). "The first movement," he writes, "was naturally a reinforcement of the philosophy of language based on logic; but the subsequent movement has been an overthrow of that long tradition, the overthrow which Derrida speaks of as the closure of metaphysics" (xii). The latter movement to which Garver refers not only includes Heidegger's and Derrida's "closure of metaphysics" but Deleuze's "reversal of Platonism" as well. Despite Garver's description of this second movement as rhetorical, his implicit definition of rhetoric does not reflect the conventional principles of rhetorical theory and practice. Indeed, the revolutionary philosophical insights on language and representation to which Garver refers have, at best, only mildly unsettled canonical conceptions of rhetoric.

A brief survey of modern rhetorical studies demonstrates that the discipline has proliferated examples of a classical, essentially Aristotelian, understanding of rhetoric instead of producing systematic inquiries into the ontological status of rhetoric itself. Dilip Gaonkar gleans from disciplinary publications a partial but telling portrait of the diverse topics grouped under the ubiquitous rubric that he terms "the rhetoric of X": "assent, antitheory, doubtful authority, economics, ethnographic holism, history, human sciences, image, inquiry, interpretation, irony, motives, modernism, mourning, passivity, pedagogy, philosophy, revolution, secularism, social history, social sciences,

21

temporality, textuality, and so on" (1997, 75).[1] The organizing syntax featured here—"the rhetoric *of*"—reflects the scholarly predilection characteristic of most modern rhetorical inquiry: placing a diversity of new examples under a familiar category rather than questioning the meaning or value of that category in light of both its history and its significance to changing social and intellectual circumstances.

Questioning canonical and hitherto self-evident definitions of rhetoric necessarily involves an interrogation of the ontology that sanctions those definitions and the system of representation they maintain. Conceiving of rhetoric beyond the authority of representation, as this book proposes, obliges one to reconsider the metaphysical order reflected in representation as such. The rhetorical tradition has always valued the ontological status of the speaking subject, yet that subject has been distinguished throughout by a partisan ethos, by partial and privileged ideals of knowledge, speech, and virtue, despite conventional wisdom testifying to its representation of universal human qualities. One might retort that many rhetoricians have in fact enlarged our understanding of rhetoric and subjectivity by examining how the rhetorical activities of giving speeches, writing public letters, or signing petitions, for example, influence the subjectivity of different agents. Such studies nonetheless interpret their objects of study predominantly according to generic conceptions of rhetoric and subjectivity rather than reconsidering the classical ethos of reason, autonomy, morality, and truth that characterizes canonical assumptions about the influence of rhetoric on the subject. In what follows, I begin a process of questioning the partisan conceptions of truth, reason, and virtue represented by such an ethos—questioning the apparent self-evidence of representation itself—in order to learn from the strangeness of the being that dwells inside traditional images of rhetoric's pious practitioner.

The implications of this study therefore exceed a revised understanding of rhetoric. One can attain a conception of rhetoric no longer defined by the representation of essential reason and morality only by transmuting our inherited assumptions about categories such as truth, knowledge, and being. In what follows, I provide a context for evaluating those assumptions in light of the withering scrutiny to which they have been subjected in recent decades.

Of what does one speak when one speaks of "representation?" How can words be said to represent things? To what does one refer when speaking of "identity" and "difference"—not as attributes of particular objects but as analytic categories in and of themselves? How do these categories inform the ontological arrangements according to which our culture traditionally defines the hierarchy of being, which encompasses the divine and the mortal, the sacred and the profane? Finally, how are these arrangements relevant to an understanding of rhetoric, to the act of discursively representing such ephemera as reason, truth, judgment, and virtue?

The authority ascribed to the category of representation in our values and beliefs reflects the priority assigned to manifestations of identity throughout our heritage. "The primacy of identity," Deleuze contends, "however conceived, defines the world of representation" (1994, xix). Difference cannot be thought in and of itself in "the world of representation" because the category of *identity* holds an exclusive organizing value in traditional conceptions thereof. When one refers to an object with a given word, when one represents a phenomenon discursively or symbolically, one refers to its objective existence—to its individual identity. By this logic, two phenomena are different from one another only insofar as they possess unambiguously distinct identities. Hence, identity *in itself* is the organizing principle of representation; difference has value only as a measure of identity.

However, Deleuze (1994) suggests that notions of difference were not always subjugated to the "primacy" of identity in the Western tradition. Indeed, they were not initially subservient to this seemingly ideal and transparent category. In the following sections, I offer two distinct but complementary accounts of representation in order to demonstrate that the allegedly ideal and transparent category of identity has not always been thus. Nonetheless, I do not propose a return to pre-Socratic formulations of these concepts. Instead, I demonstrate that one must interrogate the conventional relationship between identity and difference in order to reconsider the status of rhetoric and its influence on the formation of subjectivity.

The categories of identity and difference are not matters of impractical intellectual rumination. To the contrary, the ways in which groups and individuals traditionally defined these basic metaphysical categories have shaped commonplace Western assumptions about language, reality, and communication. Such categories crucially inform classical and humanist ideals of human being, which presuppose that human beings, irrespective of time, place, and culture, are unified by an identical and transcendent essence. Adopting a revised conception of the relationship between identity and difference hastens nothing less than a fundamental transformation in predominant assumptions about the nature of human being.

Modern rhetoricians generally avoid systematic inquiry into the relationship between rhetoric and subjectivity, electing instead to conduct criticism of rhetorical appeals based on traditional ideals of reason, prudence, and eloquence—to evaluate "the rhetoric *of*," in other words. By failing to interrogate such standards, rhetorical studies typically accept as conventional wisdom the ideals of human being in whose pursuit they were first conceived. Contemporary rhetoricians habitually defend their emphasis on criticism by insisting that rhetorical inquiry ultimately must have a practical application. In relegating supposedly esoteric or impractical ontological questions to the jurisdiction of philosophy, however, modern rhetoricians continue to endorse conceptions of human being that evaluate the speech, intelligence, and even social worth of groups and individuals according to socially and intellectually prejudiced ideals.

I propose that a conception of rhetoric beyond "the requirements of representation" (that is, beyond the priority of identity) provides an indispensable means of transmuting the Platonic hierarchies that continue to shape dominant conceptions of discourse and human being. In order to surpass that ontology, however, one must first understand its guiding principles and its largely unrecognized significance to rhetorical study. Rhetoric has always been defined according to the ideal of a knowing and speaking being that personifies the fundamental values of the metaphysical tradition. Accordingly, in the next section I note the dominant objectives of that tradition and explain how they conform to processes of representation. This review of the metaphysical system also documents modern philosophical developments that threaten to transform that system by assigning unconventional value to the category of representation, thereby inaugurating a new understanding of the relationship between speech and human being.

Subsequently, I turn to Michel Foucault's *The Order of Things* (1994b), which chronicles the crucial changes in modern ways of thinking, knowing, and speaking that first made possible a discourse on subjectivity no longer organized by oppositions between words and things or subjectivity and objectivity. In this text, Foucault documents the historical processes through which representation became a governing ideal of Western thought and culture. He does so by disclosing the obscurities and mutations disguised in its appearance of transparency and transcendence. In brief, Foucault allows one to conclude that the traditional metaphysical system cannot do what it claims to do. *The Order of Things* uncovers pivotal differences and discontinuities previously obscured by the alleged transparency of a metaphysical order that presumed to represent things merely "as they are." Rhetoric, so long as it remains defined by the principles and values of that order, continues to participate in a prejudiced understanding of speech, reason, and human being, regardless of its frequently heralded value and utility to democratic life. Eventually, I use Foucault's study to explain how rhetorical inquiry might affirm a revised set of values concerning discourse and subjectivity. Taken together, these two accounts of representation illustrate the profound implications (recognized only peripherally by most modern rhetoricians) of recent challenges to traditional metaphysical principles for present and future conceptions of rhetoric.

THE CIRCLE OF METAPHYSICS

It is now commonplace to suppose that all of Western philosophy after Plato has been but a footnote to his insights. Plato (following Socrates' example) indeed established the ideals of truth, knowledge, and virtue in reference to which the majority of Western thinkers have defined their own philosophies. Socrates and Plato, that is, articulated the questions that generally have defined the task of philosophy; or, more precisely, they defined philosophy *as* a process of asking and answering certain questions—a process of discovering the *truthful* answer and accumulating knowledge in that form. The acquisition of knowledge as such, the task of philosophy in general, amounted to distinguishing the true from the false, the essence of a phenomenon from its often misleading appearance, the ideal and original forms of truth, justice, virtue, or beauty, for instance, from unenlightened approximations thereof. In this regard, one may describe the majority of Western philosophy as *meta*physical in that it has been concerned with deliberation over the existence (or denial) of ideal truths about the nature of truth, justice, virtue, or beauty that, in their transcendence of the physical world, are not immediately apparent to the senses. Guthrie writes that Greek culture during the fifth and fourth centuries B.C.E. was shaped by widespread debate over the relationship between the traditional, divine, and immutable laws of nature *(physis)* and the increasingly valued contingent laws of human convention and civic institutions *(nomos)* (Guthrie [1971] 1998, chapter 4). Socrates and Plato's formalization of the metaphysical system reflected this transitional intellectual climate. Because of the Socratic and Platonic tradition, the ontology of our culture (our inherited assumptions about the order of reality) has been characterized by a fundamental distinction between the *sensible* and the *intelligible,* between the world accessible to our deeply impressionable senses and the realm of eternal truths apprehensible only to the properly trained mind. The fundamental structure of the Christian order, with its separate human and heavenly spheres, is analogously metaphysical in nature. Thus, both the Greco-Roman and Judeo-Christian traditions so constitutive of the Western heritage exhibit patently metaphysical values and ideals.

In this section, I discuss an indispensable aspect of metaphysical thought: its supposed beginning and end. The metaphysical search for knowledge in the form of truth is equivalent to a search for origins, meaning the ideal forms of truth, justice, virtue, or beauty upon which all sensible phenomena are modeled. In discovering that origin, however, one completes the task of metaphysical inquiry because the acquisition of knowledge as such is the quintessential goal of the Socratic method. Therefore, one might say that the beginning and end of metaphysics are not located on opposite ends of a linear spectrum but are, instead, joined together in the completion of a circle.

This paradoxical logic is reflected in the founding gesture of metaphysical inquiry. John Sallis (1995) observes this gesture at work in Socrates' turn away from the method of inquiry that had shaped Greek thought prior to his innovations. Citing Socrates' own description of this turn in Plato's *Phaedo,*

Sallis explains that Socrates turned away from "that direct method of investigation which would proceed to explain certain things by referring them directly to other things" and adopted instead an "indirect way of investigating things, a way which he describes as analogous to the procedure of studying things in an image rather than looking at them directly" (5). "Hence," Sallis avers, "the Socratic turn consists in the opening of the difference between immediately, sensibly present things and those εἴδη that would be their foundation—or, more precisely and literally, those εἴδη in which the sheer unobstructed look of things would be had" (5). Socrates' novel methodology established the fundamental opposition according to which metaphysics has been structured. "The Socratic turn thus differentiates between things in their immediate, sensible presence and those things in their original truth, in their originary presence" (Sallis 1995, 5). This differentiation does not simply counterbalance the sensible with the original; more significantly, it endows sensible phenomena with a negative, chimerical value and original forms with a positive, objective value: "It shifts away from immediately, sensibly present things, away from the fragmented presence of the immediate and sensible—shifts away in order to prepare a reappropriation of those things in their originary presence" (Sallis 1995, 5–6). Sallis therefore concludes, "[T]he Socratic turn constitutes the field of metaphysics as a field of presence and metaphysics itself as the drive to presence" (6). Following this gesture, the metaphysical search for truth is equivalent to a search for "originary presence," meaning an intuitive knowledge of the unmediated and original forms of truth, justice, virtue, or beauty. The logic of this search explains the value of identity in Western philosophy. Ideal and original presence, the transcendent truth of a given phenomenon, acquires that status only if it is unified in and of itself, admitting no imperfections or ambiguities—no differences in its essential nature. As such, ideal and original presence (essential meaning or truth) is a quintessential form of identity.

The metaphysical obsession with origins indicates an equal desire for fruition. Metaphysical reflection begins by fixing a singular focus upon its desired end. Not surprisingly, the unwavering metaphysical belief in ideal forms of presence lends itself to religious applications, which led Heidegger and then Derrida to describe the history of Western ontology as "ontotheological." By this logic, inquiring into the origins of human being impels one to consider the existence of an ideal, even divine, form of Being qua Being[2]—God, in other words. In the Western tradition, this origin turns out to be the desired destiny of human beings as well: an afterlife beyond the physical realm said to give meaning to one's mortality. Investigating the category of being in this context, according to Derrida, amounts to a search for "nothing other than the metaphysical unity of man and God, the relation of man to God, the project of becoming God as the project constituting human-reality" (1982, 116). The ideal of the classical orator participates in such a project—a human "becoming God" by representing the truth of human being in speech, by personifying such Socratic ideals as reason, truth, and virtue.

The meaning of human being in our heritage, therefore, is fundamentally metaphysical or, more precisely, onto-theological. The identity of human being, its essential truth, signifies a capacity for acquiring objective knowledge of the relationship between sensible and intelligible phenomena, of the origin as well as the telos (or the purposeful fruition) of human endeavor. "The unity of these two *ends* of man," Derrida explains, "the unity of his death, his completion, his accomplishment, is enveloped in the Greek thinking of *telos*, in the discourse on *telos*, which is also a discourse on *eidos* [ideality], on *ousia* [essential substance], and on *alētheia* [truth]" (121). Accordingly, he concludes, *"The thinking of the end of man, therefore, is always already prescribed in metaphysics, in the thinking of the truth of man"* (121). Throughout the Western tradition, the category of human being incarnates the circle of metaphysics itself. It embodies humanity's search for the truth, presence, or objective identity of its own origins as well as the ultimate purpose of its own existence.

As indicated by the previous description, representation is essential to our long-standing cultural assumptions about truth and reality, as well as our ability to both know and express knowledge thereof. True to Socrates' founding metaphysical gesture, traditional ideals such as reason, truth, and virtue remain transcendent ephemera that one can represent only indirectly in language. Conventional assumptions about human nature, including its supposedly innate aspiration to wise and virtuous discourse, depend upon this representational thinking, and thus upon the metaphysical order in general. In Plato's *Phaedrus,* Socrates explains the now-commonsensical notion that one must "know the truth" of a subject by "isolat[ing] it in definition . . . until you reach the limit of division" (277b) (which is the cardinal objective of metaphysical inquiry) before one engages in discourse about it. Consequently, one's effort to critique and surpass the classical or humanist ideals of human being necessarily begins with an interrogation of the conventional ontology, the representational arrangement, of metaphysics. Such an effort might even prompt one to wonder if a non-metaphysical conception of being is at all tenable.

The Ends of Metaphysics

Throughout the Western philosophical tradition, philosophers periodically have challenged conventional metaphysical values in an attempt to reconsider the category of being or, more specifically, to conceive of the nature and origins of subjective and objective phenomena unconventionally. Brief consideration of the most recent and influential of these challenges will allow me to clarify my aim in offering related critiques throughout this study. In order to apprehend the existing precedents for such critiques, I first distinguish between the different meanings of the so-called end of metaphysics.

I have explained how metaphysical inquiry arose by anticipating its ideal end, its desired culmination. Subsequent philosophers, however, have investigated the possibility that metaphysical thought might reach a *historical* rather than a transcendental end. Such an end would mark the discontinuation of the metaphysical system's influence as our dominant conception of reality instead of its ideal and transhistorical perfection.

In order to explicate the philosophical significance of this possibility, one must inspect the paradoxical significance of history to metaphysics. On the one hand, metaphysics has run a historical course in that one can study its development as a scholastic discipline according to successive historical periods. But metaphysics was conceived, on the other hand, precisely in a disavowal of the transitory realm in favor of the transcendent, of sensible phenomena in favor of their ideal and original forms. Sallis elaborates on this defining metaphysical tension: "[M]etaphysics is taken to have a history that is not simply extrinsic to it—that is, it is taken as something which was founded, which has run a certain course, and which since Hegel has come to a kind of end, as something which cannot be defined independently of this history. And yet . . . clearly one could not indefinitely postpone taking some account of the torsion already installed within such a concept of metaphysics as historical, the torsion resulting from the fact that metaphysics is also constituted as a turning away from history" (1995, 4). The torsion of which Sallis speaks renders the metaphysical process unstable. The ideal circle of metaphysics is undone by this torsion, by this energy applied to the transcendence of a historical process that, ironically, produced the very possibility of such transcendence, the possibility of its own disavowal. This torsion creates a dilemma: either one tries to shatter the circle, to reject all notion of history as a meaningful process with an ideal beginning and end, or one attempts to escape from it, to transcend the inherent paradoxes of metaphysical thought altogether. "But of course," Sallis reminds us, "there can be no question of simply breaking with the circle any more than there can be one of simply breaking out of the circle" (xiii). Thus, one might say that the alleged circle of metaphysics is not simply constituted by the torsion that Sallis describes but is continually *re*constituted by its periodic compression and release, by repeated efforts to shatter or escape from it—or better, that it only exists *as* this reconstitution.

Because of this fundamental instability evident throughout the metaphysical tradition, one can identify many different senses in which the end of that tradition has been announced. The first such sense may be described simply as *termination*. Nietzsche augurs that two principal events will signal the termination of metaphysics: first, the death of God, the supreme ideal of Being qua Being; and, second, not merely the destruction of the ideal realm and a subsequent unleashing of the repressed sensible world but a destruction of the dialectical logic that invests both of these foundational categories with their contrasting sense and value.[3] In *Twilight of the Idols*, he famously exults, "The 'real world'—an idea no longer of any use, not even a duty any longer—an idea grown useless, superfluous, *consequently* a refuted idea: let us abolish it! . . . We have abolished the real world: what world is left? the apparent world perhaps? . . . But no! *with the real world we have also abolished the apparent world!*" (1990, 50–51). According to Nietzsche, this destruction will hasten the arrival of a new reality with new values, the nature of which cannot yet be thought. Such is "a termination so complex," Sallis writes, "that it casts its shadow over all previously established determinations, setting all sense in motion, calling not just for new determinations but for a renewal of the very possibility of determination" (1995, 19).[4] Nietzsche thus affirms a set of values radically opposed to those of traditional metaphysics. Foremost among them is our apparent inability to intuit the essential meaning of our being and the ideal fulfillment of our history, to effectively represent such forms of pure presence in discourse.

Nietzsche, however, was not the first to announce the end of metaphysics. Hegel before him is remembered for thinking most intricately the end of metaphysics in terms of its *completion*. In Hegel's philosophy, the discomfiture between the history of metaphysics and its aspiration to transcend that history is unified in the fulfillment of a dramatic entelechy. The singularity of Hegel's proclamations, according to Sallis, derives from "his awareness that the end cannot be extrinsic to the history that it completes . . . that it cannot be an end which in this sense simply negates what has preceded" (20). Rather than maintaining a tension between the historical and the transcendental, Hegel envisions history as a dialectical process that ineluctably gathers every form of otherness, difference, or the negative into a transcendental synthesis known as the actuality of spirit. In *Philosophy of Mind*, Hegel describes this synthesis according to the acquisition of ideal knowledge:

> The significance of that "absolute" commandment, *Know thyself* . . . is not to promote mere self-knowledge in respect to the *particular* capacities, character, propensities, and foibles of the single self. The knowledge it commands means that of man's genuine reality—of what is essentially and ultimately true and real—of mind as the true and essential being. Equally little is it the purport of mental philosophy to teach what is called *knowledge of men*—the knowledge whose aim is to detect the *peculiarities*, passions, and foibles of other

men, and lay bare what are called the recesses of the human heart. Information of this kind is, for one thing, meaningless, unless on the assumption that we know the *universal*—man as man, and, that always must be, as mind. (1971, 1)

The end of philosophy will be reached, Hegel prophesies, when every subjective form of knowledge, every indication of subjective difference, is gathered into absolute spirit—an ideal and original knowledge, a universal identity. "Such a gathering is thought by Hegel in the concept of *Aufhebung*," Sallis explains. "With this word—still not really translated, i.e., rethought, in English—Hegel designates a movement in which what is lower is surpassed and yet always essentially preserved by being elevated into what is higher, gathered up into it" (1995, 21).[5] Hegel does not believe that metaphysics will reach its end in simple termination. Instead, he anticipates the end of metaphysics, in a rather operatic fashion, as the actualization of its ideal form, in which diversity is sublated to the unity of an absolute identity.[6]

By foreseeing the end of metaphysics as a process either completed or terminated, Hegel and Nietzsche provide this trope with its patently modern senses. Heidegger, however, is responsible for coining its characteristically contemporary sense (Sallis 1995, 20). After Heidegger, the question of the fate of metaphysics ceases to be one of an "end" and mutates into one of *closure*. In his own fashion, Heidegger excludes the possibility of a unilateral termination of metaphysics; he admittedly anticipates its telos as a kind of completion but one fundamentally different from a process of ideal fruition. The nature of this completion may be explained by Heidegger's conception of *Aufhebung*, which is distinct from the one featured in Hegel's philosophy. Hegel's use of this term connotes predominantly a process of sublation in which what is other is gathered up into what is higher until diversity has become a unity, until all differences have been synthesized into a universal identity. But, according to a slightly different nuance in Hegel's philosophy, "*Aufhebung*" is also "the process by which what is extrinsic and peripheral is gathered to the intrinsic, the center" (Sallis 1995, 21). Thus, Hegel's *Aufhebung* more generally entails a movement of possibility into actuality, a gathering of the extreme into the center. Heidegger's complete *reversal* of Hegel's definition of this term indicates the radical nature of his philosophy. He posits that the end of metaphysics is not its perfection but "that place in which the whole of philosophy's history is gathered into its most extreme possibility. End as completion means this gathering. . . . This development looks like the mere dissolution of philosophy, yet in truth is precisely its completion" (1993, 433). In Sallis's summation, Heidegger's end of metaphysics is "a matter of gathering not to the center but to the most extreme and of gathering not into actuality but into possibility" (1995, 21).

The significance of this redefinition exceeds that of a mere semantic distinction. In fact, Heidegger's appropriation of the term helps to explain the import of his entire philosophy, which remains the most radical and ambitious reconsideration of the category of being since Plato. What does Heidegger mean, then, when he anticipates the end of metaphysics as a gathering of its history into its most extreme possibility? Simply put, the possibility to which he refers is death. For the being that understands itself by inquiring into the possibilities of its being—the being that Heidegger calls *Dasein*—death is "a possibility that cannot be outstripped, that is unsurpassable, of a possibility that withdraws all possibilities, of a possibility that closes off decisively the opening to a future" (Sallis 1995, 22). In the possibility of death, Heidegger says, *Dasein* is confronted with "the absolute impossibility of existence" (1996, 236). The extremity of this end undermines any metaphysical effort to discover the ideal origins and ultimate meaning of being because death is "an end which metaphysics cannot circumvent, get beyond, while itself remaining intact. It is an end which withdraws all possibilities—that is, an end in which metaphysics' possibilities are exhausted. And it is an end which accordingly closes off all opening to a future" (Sallis 1995, 22). Closure in this context indicates the withdrawal of the very possibility of transhistorical meaning rather than the meaningful and ideal completion of a transcendental process. What remains in the wake of this closure (if any "thing" could be said to "remain" thereafter) is not an ideally realized unity but, as Sallis describes it, "a voice speaking from the darkness . . . the darkness of enclosure" (1995, xv).[7]

In the wake of Heidegger's insights, Derrida has further elaborated the profound implications of such closure.[8] Sallis credits both Heidegger and Derrida with observing that "the figure of closure," although it is certainly a defining preoccupation of modern Continental philosophy, "can be discerned, at least retrospectively, throughout the history of metaphysics" (22). The omnipresence of this figure may be identified most easily, according to these two thinkers, in the primacy of intuition. Metaphysical ontology considers intuition to be an ideal form of knowledge through which one achieves an unmediated understanding of phenomena, not as they appear in physical form, but in the uniform and transparent presence of their essential truth or meaning.[9] This ideal, therefore, "would be a matter of sheer intuition of full presence, utterly closed off from everything else, utterly self-enclosed, a perfect figure of closure" (Sallis 1995, 23). One of the elementary premises of Derrida's philosophy is that this figure of closure is both impossible and necessary. It is impossible in the sense that metaphysics cannot simply terminate, cannot complete itself ideally, nor enclose itself with finality. It is equally necessary, however, because philosophy has reached its present condition precisely by virtue of, and can only anticipate its future through, the trope of closure— a future that it cannot effectively represent but for which it can only prepare.

According to Derrida, a philosophical method that attempts to end metaphysics based upon a cyclical model is itself caught up in a paradoxical cycle. "But all these destructive discourses and all their analogues are trapped in a sort of circle," he writes. "This circle is unique. It describes the form of the relationship between the history of metaphysics and the destruction of the history of metaphysics" (1972, 250). Derrida provides an account of the unstable metaphysical relationship between history and transcendence analogous to Sallis's description of the same dynamic. He observes that, in the cyclical logic of the metaphysical method, any effort to complete, transcend, or terminate the history of metaphysics is always already a part of that history. Such a paradox, according to Derrida, is maintained by the characteristic idiom of metaphysics: "*There is no sense* in doing without the concepts of metaphysics in order to attack metaphysics. We have no language—no syntax and no lexicon—which is alien to this history; we cannot utter a single destructive proposition which has not already slipped into the form, the logic, and the implicit postulations of precisely what it seeks to contest" (250). Metaphysics functions according to an interrogative methodology; its essential categories are sustained by an unflagging effort to interrogate its own values with the alleged transparency of dialectical reason. In seeking to end metaphysics by questioning it from a location outside of its language, one merely reproduces its desire for a neutral position of knowledge uninfluenced by the prejudices of one's senses. "For it is not possible to show that the belief in truth is an error," Barbara Johnson writes, "without implicitly believing in the notion of Truth. By the same token, to show that the binary oppositions of metaphysics are illusions is *also,* and perhaps most importantly, to show that such illusions cannot simply in turn *be opposed* without repeating the very same illusion" (1981, x). Yet what Derrida calls our "complicity" with the discursive logic of metaphysics should be a source of affirmation rather than despair: "[W]e cannot give up this metaphysical complicity," he writes, "without also giving up the critique we are directing against this complicity" (1972, 250–51). In other words, "we must remember that if we are indeed *inside* metaphysics, we are not inside it as we might be *inside* a box or a milieu. We are still *in* metaphysics in the special sense that we are *in* a determinate language" (1984, 111). In sum, one cannot reject or transcend the idiom of metaphysics in order to transform it. One must, instead, illuminate the implicit paradoxes of its sustaining logic in order to question the normative values that its defining categories engender.

Derrida thus dismisses the possibilities of attack or destruction concerning the supposed end of metaphysics because the success of such efforts would require a rejection or transcendence of the means used to carry them out. Such a claim obligates one to question the longstanding agenda (whether that of Socrates and Plato or Hegel and Nietzsche) to identify *any* determinate end of the metaphysical system, no matter how perfective or ruinous it might be. As such, one cannot view the paradox in which the so-called closure of metaphysics is caught (the "complicity" to which Derrida refers) as the symptom of an insufficiency that compromises the telos of an entire tradition; "[W]e cannot really say that we are 'locked into' or 'condemned to' metaphysics," Derrida insists, "for we are, strictly speaking, neither inside nor outside. . . . [T]he idea of the finitude and exhaustion *[épuisement]* of metaphysics does not mean that we are incarcerated in it as prisoners or victims of some unhappy fatality" (1984, 111–12). Admitting that the closure of metaphysics names neither its destruction nor its completion, but rather our complicity with it, is not an indication of failure. On the contrary, such an admission makes possible yet another, categorically different, sense of the end of metaphysics.

Heidegger provides the contemporary form of the end of metaphysics, as closure in the form of being's most extreme consequence; but Derrida pursues the ramifications of this form by putting it "under erasure." In his later writings, Heidegger (1958) underscored the inability of metaphysical terminology to objectively represent its ideal referents by literally crossing out the word *Being*, thus suggesting that language cannot actually disclose an ideal form of Being qua Being. Elaborating on Heidegger's gesture, Derrida proposes to place essential metaphysical terms such as *Being* or *presence* under erasure. In his logic, this procedure amounts to marking the discursive function of conceptual terms that we cannot transcend while simultaneously forcing them to function otherwise, to reveal the differences and contradictions disguised by their appearance of unity and transparency. Derrida's very phrase for this process dramatizes its disruption of presence: the active tense of *under erasure* suggests a form of presence defined by the activity of disappearing, a coming-to-absence taking place in the present, the familiar remaining recognizable only in its withdrawal. For Heidegger, the closure of metaphysics connotes a gathering into its most extreme possibility, into the fundamental withdrawal of meaning and presence; extending such insights, Derrida perceives in the notion of closure an opportunity to simultaneously reveal and disrupt those founding contradictions that enable the metaphysical dream of closure. Such contradictions include, most conspicuously, a history engendered by its efforts to disavow historical contingency, an origin characterized by its unity with a telos, and a drive to presence continually invoked by the absence thereof. In each case, Derrida demonstrates that, paradoxically, metaphysical inquiry cannot attain its apprehension of ideal presence without consideration of sensible phenomena. "Philosophy," he contends, "has always insisted upon this: thinking its other. Its other: that which limits it, and from which it derives its essence, its definition, its production" (1982, x). The ideal telos of philosophy, therefore, is always already deferred from the outset.

Consequently, one merely reproduces the logic of oppositions at the heart of the metaphysical system if one attempts to argue against it, to adopt a more objective stance outside of it. In Derrida's terms, "exteriority and alterity are concepts which by themselves have never surprised philosophical discourse. *Philosophy by itself has always been concerned* with them" (xiii). Derrida scrutinizes the notion of metaphysical enclosure in order to identify a form of critique that more effectively calls into question the logic and ideals of traditional ontology (or onto-theology). Because metaphysics has always sought to ground its categories in ideal forms of presence, he proposes a novel kind of "place" from which to think metaphysics differently: a place neither "inside" nor "outside" of its categories, a "place" that signifies the very refusal of such diametrical categories. Derrida calls this elusive ground of critique a "non-site, or a non-philosophical site, from which to question philosophy. But the search for a non-philosophical site does not bespeak an anti-philosophical attitude. My central question is: from what site or non-site *[non-lieu]* can philosophy as such appear to itself as other than itself, so that it can interrogate and reflect upon itself in an original manner?" (1984, 108). In Derrida's view, one must deconstruct, and thereby inhabit, defining metaphysical categories in order to challenge the metaphysical order in general; as I have indicated, the notion of closure is therefore both methodologically necessary and practically impossible. In Elizabeth Wilson's succinct phrasing, "Deconstruction has effect by inhabiting the structures it contests. . . . We are never given the luxury of simply refusing a territory . . . or accepting a territory. . . . Instead, we are forced to negotiate perpetually a position with respect to these different fields of operation" (1998, 29). The desire for an "anti-philosophical attitude" participates in the very dream of objectivity and transcendence that it ostensibly refutes. Recognizing this conundrum, Derrida submits that one can make "philosophy as such appear to itself as other than itself" by interrogating the apparently stable meaning and presence attributed to metaphysical ideals (the category of being foremost among them). Such an effort obliges one to repeatedly "place under erasure" the supposedly objective grounds of one's own propositions, to continually decenter the forms of knowledge that might otherwise acquire a normative, or central, status. Nevertheless, Johnson cautions, "[d]econstruction is not a form of textual vandalism designed to prove that meaning is impossible. In fact, the word 'de-construction' is closely related not to the word 'destruction' but to the word 'analysis,' which etymologically means 'to undo'—a virtual synonym for 'to de-construct.' . . . If anything is destroyed in a deconstructive reading, it is not meaning but the claim to unequivocal domination of one mode of signifying over another"

(1981, xiv). Regardless of insistent reports to the contrary, deconstruction does not nihilistically seek to reduce all meaning to nonsense but analyzes the discursive forms according to which meanings attain, to whatever social or political end, a seemingly self-evident authority.

In sum, Derrida regards as suspect all manifestations of closure, whether in the form of transcendent meaning, unchanging presence, or appeals to an ideal origin or telos. For him, pondering the closure of metaphysics concerns a multifaceted effort to rend open the metaphysical ideals that exhibit such closure, to reveal the irreconcilable contradictions that traditional metaphysical categories would obscure in their effort to categorize and represent essential identities. In her celebrated preface to Derrida's *Of Grammatology*, Gayatri Spivak paraphrases Derrida's logic on this point: "It is also the metaphysical desire to make the end coincide with the means, create an *en*closure, make the definition coincide with the defined, the 'father' with the 'son'; within the logic of identity to balance the equation, close the circle. Our language reflects this desire. And so it is from within this language that we must attempt an 'opening' " (1974, xx). The goal of this "opening" is, in Derrida's words, to "displace philosophy's alignment of its own types" (1982, xxiv) rather than to inaugurate an alternate alignment of ideal types. Derrida seeks to unhinge manifestations of closure, not in order to confirm a superior form of knowledge, but to keep formerly privileged meanings and referents in play, to establish "a double understanding no longer forming a single system" (xxiv). Such is a form of critique that "reads backwards from what seems natural, obvious, self-evident, or universal, in order to show that these things have their history, their reasons for being the way they are, their effects on what follows from them" (Johnson 1981, xv). Whereas Heidegger emphasizes the fundamentally meaningless and indeterminate fate of all conventional meanings and representations, Derrida deconstructs figures of closure—of uniform identity, essential meaning, or the representation of being as presence—in order to reveal and keep in play the irreconcilable metaphysical paradoxes they surreptitiously obscure.

Derrida's conception of closure evinces the irony with which he interprets the end of metaphysics. The possibility of critiquing metaphysics, he insists, entails a myriad unhinging of whatever in its system desires the appearance of closure, meaning certitude in the integrity of identities, the transparency of meanings and representations, or the uniform essence of being. This process of unhinging, moreover, is conducted without faith in a governing origin or telos because the notion of an identifiable origin and destiny for all beings suggests that history is unified by an intuitional meaning, truth, or presence that one can represent objectively in discourse. Derrida thus posits that metaphysics as we have known it ends when we realize that it cannot end as such.

THE END OF RHETORIC?

I have delineated four especially influential conceptions of the metaphorical end of metaphysics in order to refine my approach to the commonplace relationship between rhetoric and human being. I have devoted such attention to this topic not simply to draw an analogy between the philosophical and rhetorical traditions; more significantly, rhetoricians have, since antiquity, legitimated their theory and practice by assenting to the metaphysical ideals of truth, wisdom, morality, and human being central to Western philosophy from the Greco-Roman period forward. In this regard, metaphysical ontology has always dictated the intellectual and practical criteria according to which the discipline of rhetoric acquired its cultural value. By virtue of this dynamic, rhetoric traditionally has served as a preeminent pedagogical instrument used to represent metaphysical ideals in the form of conventional wisdom. Developing a conception of rhetoric and subjectivity that questions representational notions of being, that questions the alleged identity of subjects unified by a transhistorical human essence, therefore advances the contemporary project of critiquing metaphysical equations of being with continuous presence, with a privileged interpretation of being's truth.

I also cite the preceding discussion as evidence that developing a conception of rhetoric beyond representation should not amount to a simple termination of rhetoric in its conventional form. Recent efforts in rhetorical studies to establish an alternate set of rhetorical values and ideals in contrast to those of philosophy mirror the dialectical method of parsing truth from falsehood, no matter how socially constructed that truth may appear. Reversing traditional ontological categories so as to assign superior value to fiction instead of fact, culture instead of nature, discourse instead of essence, or rhetoric instead of philosophy merely rearranges those categories while leaving the metaphysical calculus of dialectical ideals intact. One cannot implement this calculus without invoking at least a tacit search for the truth of things, meaning a more objective ontology. As I have shown, one's characterization of a particular ontology as truthful, as a universal formulation of the order of things, relies on essentially Socratic values and methods. Rather than effectively terminating its traditional form, recent scholars' appropriations of the metaphysical categories by which rhetoric traditionally has been domesticated (such as appearance, deception, sentiment, and so forth) merely amplifies the significance of an existing conception of rhetoric without questioning the logic according to which it originally was formulated.

That said, other rhetoricians' contentment with maintaining separate but equal domains for philosophy and rhetoric, for *sapientia et eloquentia,* also warrants critique. I have demonstrated that the relationship between such distinct but putatively equal domains actually reflects a partial and privileged conception of both philosophy and rhetoric, albeit to the distinct advantage of the former. The canonical separation of the two disciplines, of investigation and argumentation, has assured the priority of truth, intuition, morality, and transparent discourse in their ideal forms. These ideals, furthermore, have preserved a conception of the knowing and speaking subject representative of humanity's allegedly universal identity. Like metaphysics (indeed, from *within* a metaphysical arrangement), one can maintain rhetoric in its canonical form—as reasoned, virtuous, and transparent argumentation—no more than one can abruptly terminate it.

My proposal to develop a conception of rhetoric beyond representation, therefore, should not be interpreted as an effort to "end" metaphysics, either by proposing a contrasting ontology or by ignoring the larger system of values and ideals in which rhetoric (whether one acknowledges it or not) has hitherto participated. In analogous fashion, Calvin Schrag's definition of the so-called end of metaphysics provides an apt description of my approach to developing a conception of rhetoric beyond representation: "End here is understood as a perpetual 'thinking beyond,' an ongoing dissemination of sedimented metaphysical and epistemological position-taking. It defines a task rather than a state of affairs" (1985, 166). Having defined my task as such, I propose to assign new significance to the *non*representational (rather than *anti*representational) elements of rhetoric, which have received scant attention by rhetoricians to date. Given my demonstration of the metaphysical affinity between representation and human being, I plan to investigate the influence of rhetoric on the formation of subjectivity according to the *differences* obscured by the supposed identity, the essential ethos, of human being in its classical or humanist forms. Such forms, of course, remain the models by which the knowledge, speech, and social conduct of groups and individuals commonly are measured. Ultimately, I intend to scrutinize heretofore neglected aspects of representation and human being in order to develop a nonrepresentational conception of rhetoric and subjectivity rather than to assert an ostensibly antirepresentational or antimetaphysical conception of rhetoric that inevitably endorses the metaphysical logic it was designed either to transcend or terminate. In the next section, I turn to a second account of representation, which I employ in order to reveal the analytic principles according to which one may assign an alternate, nonrepresentational sense and value to traditional notions of discourse and subjectivity.

A CRISIS OF REPRESENTATION

"Reason" in language: oh what a deceitful old woman! I fear we are not getting rid of God because we still believe in grammar...

—Friedrich Nietzsche, *Twilight of the Idols*

In *The Order of Things* (1994b), originally published in 1966, Michel Foucault presents a historical and discursive, instead of metaphysical, account of representation. He scrutinizes the ways in which individuals throughout successive periods of early modernity thought and spoke of life, labor, and language, or the fields of knowledge and experience that would become known as biology, economics, and linguistics. He thereby investigates the institutional and intellectual developments by virtue of which recent Western culture embraced representation as its organizing principle of knowledge, discourse, and, subsequently, human being. The differences between the thought and discourse of successive eras admittedly indicate changes in Western ontology, or collective assumptions about the order of things, yet Foucault interprets the significance of such changes according to their historical and discursive development rather than in the confirmation of a preferred, transhistorical ontology.

Foucault's study attends to the discursive significance of difference in itself so as to interrupt the priority traditionally given to forms of identity in histories of ideas. He proposes to leave "the problem of causes to one side" and "confine" his project "to describing the transformations themselves" that engendered particular ways of knowing and speaking (1994b, xiii). This "description" is advantageous because it avoids impressing successive historical and discursive developments with an artificial continuity (a temporal identity) that determines their individual significance without regard to the contingencies of different cultural and intellectual contexts. Accordingly, Foucault studies the development of successive forms of knowledge and speech "not from the point of view of the individuals who are speaking, nor from the point of view of the formal structures of what they are saying, but from the point of view of the rules that come into play in the very existence of such discourse" (xiv). On the one hand, Foucault devises an empirical method that avoids privileging the testimony of particular subjects as representative of an entire culture, which would assume an inherent identity between the knowledge and speech of exemplary individuals and a historical period in general. On the other hand, he refuses to deduce a uniform collective unconscious supposedly represented in the "formal structures" of an era's collective discourse as an explanation for the nature of knowledge at that time because not all forms of cultural experience, whether conscious or unconscious, are identical. Instead of appealing to an exemplary individual or to a historical unconscious as his organizing principle, Foucault argues that the very differences between discourses indicate the "existence" of tacit discursive "rules" that determine how certain forms of knowledge and speech, of representation, are made possible in one period versus another. Such rules reflect neither the subjective intentions of a privileged subject nor the objective truth of a collective unconscious but exhibit, rather, the self-germinating qualities of a given discourse. Charles Scott describes the ways in which "discursive changes take place that override traditional meanings and significations"; he avers, in agreement with Foucault, that "[t]hose changes and their consequences take on a life of their own in the sense that . . . they condition what can be said and what wants to be said" (1987, 3). One's intention to represent a given phenomenon in words is authorized by the discursive rules that "condition what can be said and what wants to be said," that endow one's statements with their characteristic meaning and value in social and historical contexts. For Foucault, the differences between modes of discourse, rather than manifestations of subjective or objective identity, engender forms of knowledge and speech without regard to a transhistorical origin or telos.

Although these discursive differences engender forms of representation, they themselves are not representational. Foucault's account of representation demonstrates how discursive practices produced changing forms of knowledge and speech throughout early modernity without himself advocating a particular set of representational principles, without endorsing a privileged type of knowledge. However, my claim that Foucault recognizes the significance of discursive differences in and of themselves, that he assigns value to the nonrepresentational aspects of representational thinking, does not mean that his stance is antirepresentational. On the contrary, Foucault traces the discursive formation of a host of related analytic categories; the notion of endowing certain categories with greater or lesser value based on some transhistorical standard of truth or objectivity is foreign to his inquiry.

I devote the following passages to *The Order of Things*, however, not simply because of its methodological features. More significantly, I elaborate on Foucault's subject matter in order to clarify the nature of representation as an analytic category. Rhetorical scholars conventionally accept as conventional wisdom that rhetoric is a representational phenomenon. Yet Foucault painstakingly demonstrates that, during recent Western culture in particular, the category of representation has been assigned different meanings and values and has been used to authorize multiple kinds of knowledge and discourse. Changeable discursive rules, in other words, presuppose a variety of meanings and uses for the category of representation, which usually is invoked by modern rhetoricians as a generic rubric. Beyond its mere recognition of intellectual differences among historical periods, Foucault's text is valuable to my study because it documents how the unquestioned truth of representation, in reaching the pinnacle of its influence as an organizing principle of Western knowledge, nevertheless became profoundly questionable.

As such, Foucault's study is not so much a history of ideas but a history of *thought* as he himself differentiates these two objects of inquiry. In his reasoning, a history of ideas presupposes that knowledge enjoys an unbroken and transparent development from the inception of an idea to its fruition, whereas a history of thought examines how the emergence of problems and discontinuities in knowledge and discourse fundamentally contributes to the development of truths, values, and conduct:

> The history of ideas involves the analysis of a notion from its birth, through its development, and in the setting of other ideas which constitute its context. The history of thought is the analysis of the way an unproblematic field of experience, or a set of practices, which were accepted without question . . . becomes a problem, raises discussion and debate, incites new reactions, and induces a crisis in the previously silent behavior, habits, practices, and institutions. The history of thought, understood in this way, is the history . . . of the way people become anxious about this or that—for example, about madness, about crime, about sex, about themselves, or about truth. (2001, 74)

Foucault's study therefore allows one to follow the emergence of a crisis in formerly self-evident truths, in accepted knowledge, practices, and forms of expression. Most rhetoricians have not yet considered how the crisis in representational thinking that Foucault documents radically challenges conventional, and generally unquestioned, assumptions about the nature of rhetoric. By drawing from his text, I underscore the nonrepresentational elements of representation, the differences obscured by its appearance of uniform transparency, in order to begin questioning such assumptions. In the end, I demonstrate that interrupting the commonplace equation of rhetoric with representation is essential to questioning the ideals of human being in which such *topoi* allegedly have been unified throughout the Western tradition.

The Order of Things reveals how initially opposed forms of knowledge and speech were united in a common identity over the course of Western modernity. Foucault's intricate inspection of Diego de Velasquez's painting *Las Meninas* sets the stage for his inquiry. He treats Velasquez's fascinating portrait of the very act of portraiture itself as a synecdoche of representation "in its pure form," made possible by "the necessary disappearance of that which is its foundation—of the person it resembles and the person in whose eyes it is only a resemblance" (1994b, 16). Foucault's text begins with this visual metonymy of representation's ideal transparency, unmarked by subjective imperfections, and ends with a radically contrasting image in which representation is doubly shackled to "man," who emerges as its simultaneous subject and object, as the person that the portrait "resembles" and "the person in whose eyes it is only a resemblance." Between these historical counterpoints, one reads the story of how representation in its modern form came to be, and also how it came to pass.

"The Empirical and Murmuring Resemblance of Things"

Resemblance was the primary organizing principle of representation during the Renaissance. "Up to the end of the sixteenth century," Foucault writes, "resemblance played a constructive role in the knowledge of Western culture" (1994b, 17). Resemblance was a form of knowledge that viewed the world as "a vast open book" (Foucault 1994b, 27). Within this *épistémé*, phenomena were represented according to their *similitude*. Similitude encompassed four main forms, in which phenomena were found in juxtaposition to one another *(convenientia)*, in emulation of one another *(aemulatio)*, analogous to one another *(analogy)*, or submerged within a play of *sympathies* (Foucault 1994b, 16–25). Foucault remarks that, by virtue of the constant movement from one form of similitude to another, "the world" of the Renaissance "remains identical; resemblances continue to be what they are, and to resemble one another. The same remains the same, riveted onto itself" (25). Such was a view of identity in which a shimmering play of resemblance traversed the sensible world.

In this ontology, a *signature* provided evidence that some form of similitude existed between two phenomena. Resemblance among things could not be expressed except by virtue of this signature, which ensured that "the system is not closed" (Foucault 1994b, 25). Because resemblance constituted the essential condition of Renaissance knowledge and discourse, its image had to be recognized, studied, and deciphered. The "buried similitudes," Foucault writes, "must be indicated on the surface of things; there must be visible marks for the invisible analogies" (26). Two elements could only enter into similitude, then, by virtue of the signature that illumined their latent resemblance.

Knowledge in this period was formulated through a continuous process of interpretation. Interpretation so conceived began with one's recognition that a signature must be distinct from the phenomena it brings into similitude; without this differentiation, "its distinct existence as a signature would then be indistinguishable from the face of which it is the sign" (Foucault 1994b, 28). The signature thus formed "*another* resemblance"; while revealing the existence of one form of similitude, it simultaneously gestured to "an adjacent similitude, one of another type which enables us to recognize the first, and which is revealed in its turn by a third" (Foucault 1994b, 28–29). One form of similitude always gestured to another in the great sliding chain of similitudes.

Because of this preoccupation with resemblance, one may describe the model of Renaissance ontology as two intertwined circles of similitude. Along the outer circle of signatures, one discerned the mark of a resemblance between two elements along the inner circle; following this discernment, one could again contemplate the outer sphere of inscriptions in order to identify visible evidence of yet another resemblance below. Knowledge, truth, and discourse were understood to be the product of this continual interpretive helix (Foucault 1994b, 29). "To know" in the Renaissance, as Foucault puts it, "must therefore be to interpret" (32). Knowledge in this *épistémé* required one "to find a way from the visible mark to that which is being said by it and which, without that mark, would lie like unspoken speech, dormant within things" (Foucault 1994b, 32).

This Renaissance preoccupation with resemblance was reflected in the contemporaneous application of rhetorical terminology to all manner of artistic endeavor. "One distinctively new application of rhetoric in the Renaissance," Vickers writes, "was to the fine arts, sculpture, architecture and, above all, painting" (1988, 340).[10] Because rhetoric "offered the only complete and integrated communication system" of the period, its artistic resources were further employed in the composition and criticism of music and poetry (Vickers 1988, 341). Renaissance humanists even coined a term in order to symbolize the fundamental resemblance between rhetoric and these other disciplines, referring to them as *sister* arts.

The foregoing description of Renaissance ontology explains the formal purity of representation to which Foucault refers in his survey of Velasquez's *Las Meninas*. Representation lit upon a thing only insofar as its appearance played a role in the representation of a larger order, an order perhaps as grandiose as the world or even the cosmos itself. Foucault describes knowledge in this form as "a thing of sand" because it relied upon a method of inquiry that "condemned itself to never knowing anything but the same thing, and to knowing that thing only at the unattainable end of an endless journey" (1994b, 30). The nature of a phenomenon was represented only as a passing blur; the continual movement of interpretation drew merely a suggestive portrait of the infinitely deferred totality of order itself. Paradoxically, Renaissance interpretation resolutely discerned the identities (resemblances) between phenomena while ensuring that one could not speak of those identities' individual significance because they always already referred to a larger play of similitude. This paradox nevertheless ensured that the purity, the transparency, of representation itself remained undiluted.

During the Enlightenment, however, the ceaseless movement of interpretation that characterized the accumulation and expression of knowledge in the Renaissance was stilled. Foucault writes that the concept of "*Order* is as essential to the Classical age as the relation to *Interpretation* was to the Renaissance" (57). Whereas representation during the Renaissance "was essentially a knowledge based upon similitude," knowledge in the early modern period was grounded in empiricism; it sought to establish an order of things "based upon identity and difference" (Foucault 1994b, 57). Identities in this context referred, not simply to the variable forms of resemblance between phenomena, but to the essential and knowable nature that unified a class of objects. Conversely, differences existed only as a means of differentiating between nonidentical objects. This relationship between identity and difference illustrates the priority that the category of identity (as Deleuze [1994] argued early in this chapter) has enjoyed over that of difference throughout much of the Western tradition. In contrast to the unending interpretive *movement* of Renaissance inquiry, representation during the Enlightenment *fixed* things in their identity so as to establish empirical orders.

In this ontology, the relationship between words and things, representations and their objects, was organized by rigid and distinct categories. "On the threshold of the Classical age," Foucault writes, "the sign ceases to be a form of the world" (58). Phenomena and the words one used to name them were categorically separated, no longer intertwined along the rich surface of nature's open book. In contrast to the connectivity of resemblance throughout the Renaissance, signs during the Enlightenment represented the essential identity of phenomena in and of themselves. "It is the sign," according to Foucault, "that enables things to become distinct, to preserve themselves within their own identities, to dissociate themselves or bind themselves together" (61). Formerly, similitude comprised the principle of representation according to which one discerned an identity between disparate phenomena. During the Enlightenment, however, knowledge and speech were based on the identity of a phenomenon in and of itself, an identity that resembled nothing other than its essential truth, either as a unique object or as the fundamental sameness according to which a group of like objects were classified.

Accordingly, modern scientific classification, organized by the ideal and opposite domains of subjective and objective phenomena, emerged in this period. Such classification was enabled by a separation of speech and analysis from the essential identities that allowed one to speak the distinctive truth of a phenomenon. Foucault observes that subjective and objective phenomena were arranged in a binary schema: "[O]n the one side, we shall find the signs that have become tools of analysis, marks of identity and difference, principles whereby things can be reduced to order, keys for a taxonomy; and, on the other, the empirical and murmuring resemblance of things, that unreacting similitude that lies beneath thought and furnishes the infinite raw material for divisions and distributions" (58). Words became fundamentally neutral as a result of this ideal arrangement. They were believed to establish knowledge by transparently rendering the essential identity, "that unreacting similitude," of a given object or group of objects. Knowledge and one's expression of it were thus dictated by ideal conceptions of truth and order, of identity as such.

The Enlightenment penchant for classification was also exemplified by rhetorical instruction of the day. The mechanical system of notation that Gilbert Austin recommended for choreographing and evaluating oratorical performances in his 1806 *Chironomia* reflected a proclivity for meticulous classification and order. Austin presented numerous tables and diagrams dissecting the modes of verbal and physical delivery by which an orator hoped to establish a transparent correspondence, a discursive identity, between his or her appeals and the minds of audience members. Austin's manual, however, was only one especially vivid example of a propensity for scientific exposition evident in commentary on the nature of language from Descartes's *Discourse on Method* of 1637 and John Locke's *An Essay Concerning Human Understanding* of 1690 to Vico's *On the Study Methods of Our Time* or *The New Science,* printed in 1709 and 1725 respectively, as well as Campbell's *The Philosophy of Rhetoric,* which first appeared in 1776.

The priority of identity at this time was precipitated by general belief in a phenomenon's essential and unchanging nature, "the infinite raw material" of its objective presence, which formed the principle of representation. Differences between phenomena were significant only to the extent that they allowed one to group objects sharing a common nature or identity. The transparency of representation annulled the impressionable nature of subjective perception. Knowledge and its expression reflected reasoned attention to the essential identities (the unchanging presence) that constituted the truth of a phenomenon.

One would be mistaken, however, in assuming that Enlightenment ontology simply eschewed the potential complications that subjective perception posed to objective reason and order. To the contrary, the ontology of this period assigned a crucial significance to the peculiarities of subjective experience in the form of madness. One's confusion of words and things, of identities and differences, was a symptom of delusion. The "madman," as Foucault puts it, was "the man of primitive resemblances . . . he groups all signs together and leads them with a resemblance that never ceases to proliferate" (1994b, 49), regardless of their empirically verifiable identities, of their inherent truth or nature. Madness personified cultural fears over the loss of reason, order, and language. Perceiving only resemblances amounted to a loss of essential identity as the transparent ordering principle of one's knowledge and speech. Subsequently, one lacked an objective origin, an unchanging nature, against which one could interpret representations and order their meanings. In contrast to its primacy throughout the Renaissance, similitude "is no longer the form of knowledge but rather the occasion of error" during the Enlightenment (Foucault 1994b, 51). The former principle of objective order and transparent identity in Western culture became a sign of subjective disorder and meaningless difference.

Foucault aptly refers to this epoch, in the French style, as the Classical period. Enlightenment knowledge was manifested by practices of classification in which phenomena were represented according to the classical principle of their essential and unchanging identity. Identity so conceived referred to the unique and objective truth or nature of an object rather than to its merely apparent and, in this context, delusional resemblance to other objects. The reasoned and transparent powers of representation traversed the space of investigation between subjective observation and the taxonomy in which phenomena were classified objectively. In the process, representation facilitated communication between subjective perceptions and objective phenomena while nevertheless ensuring their strict categorical separation according to the ideals of classical order. During the next major period in Western culture, however, this bifurcated relationship between subjectivity and objectivity was profoundly transformed.

Whereas Enlightenment knowledge classified phenomena according to the distinctive indicators of their innate identity, nineteenth-century inquiry devised ways of observing the inner workings of phenomena in order to discover the internal causes that engendered such identity. Knowledge and its expression at this time surpassed mere recognition and taxonomy of manifest identities by delving into "organic structures . . . internal relations between elements whose totality performs a function" (Foucault 1994b, 218). The notion of the organism thus became a leading explanatory principle of phenomena as small as microscopic life or as large as the workings of society. In either case, the manifest identities of phenomena reputedly corresponded to an inner system of organic processes that explained their nature and function.

According to this organic logic, one could detect the presence of an elemental law located in "the very heart of things" (Foucault 1994b, 239). Biology, for example, documented the natural laws that produced discrete forms of life. Labor was studied according to the economic laws of production and consumption as they functioned in the marketplace. Language, finally, was said to manifest the semantic and grammatical laws of meaning and communication. Nineteenth-century scientific and intellectual discourse obligated one to speak of knowledge on the basis of such laws.

The discovery of these "hidden veins" (Foucault 1994b, 239) structuring the interior workings of phenomena precipitated yet another transformation in Western ontology. The table of Enlightenment order, upon which the identities and differences of objects could be sorted so transparently and efficiently, was replaced by a radically augmented system of representation. "Withdrawn into their own essence," Foucault explains, "taking up their place at last within the force that animates them, within the organic structure that maintains them, within the genesis that has never ceased to produce them, things, in their fundamental truth, have now escaped from the space of the table" (239). As a result, representation during this era endeavored to penetrate into what Foucault calls "a sort of behind-the-scenes world" (239) where unseen hands orchestrated the inner workings of things. These inner workings formed a unity beyond the former transparency of representation, an "inaccessible store" from which "things—in fragments, outlines, pieces, shards—offer themselves, though very partially, to representation" (Foucault 1994b, 239). Whereas phenomena were known and ordered during the Enlightenment by virtue of their evident identities, the objects of observation and description during the nineteenth century were folded in upon themselves, creating a "dark, concave, inner side" (Foucault 1994b, 237) that hid their fundamental truth from the light of representation. Representation beheld only the "fragments, outlines, pieces, shards" of recondite inner natures.

This transformation in the nature of representation amounted to a transformation in the relationship between subjective observation and the empirical object. During the Enlightenment, one could not observe the nature of the observing subject; the observer himself or herself could not be represented according to the representational logic of classical order. "In Classical thought," Foucault elaborates, "the personage for whom the representation exists, and who represents himself within it, recognizing himself therein as an image or reflection, he who ties together all interlacing threads of 'representation in the form of a picture or table'—he is never to be found in that table himself" (308). The discursive rules of nineteenth-century inquiry, however, enabled one to speak of the inner nature of things; in such an *épistémé,* one might even speak of one's own internal truth. For this reason, Foucault offers a bold pronouncement: "Before the end of the eighteenth century, *man* did not exist" (308). Foucault does not mean that, prior to the end of the Enlightenment, homo sapiens did not exist in some form. Instead, he claims that the discursive conditions upon which knowledge was based during the nineteenth century first allowed one to speak of "man" as a unique form of biological existence that could be observed, measured, dissected, and classified like any other organism. "Man" is created (in its modern sense) as a form of life engendered by its own recondite and self-regulating law when one can speak of "man," not merely as a presumably rational observing subject, but as the focal point, the object, of observation as well. As such, Foucault underscores "the simple fact that man, whether in isolation or as a group, and for the first time since human beings have lived together in societies, [became] the object of science" (345). In its modern usage, "man" is the name for the observing subject able to speak of itself as the principal object of positivist inquiry, as the focus of both transcendental and empirical knowledge. The great positivist investigations of the period, in which "man" represented the apotheosis of history, nature, culture, and consciousness, provide ample evidence of "man's" newfound exemplary status in this era.

The implications of the "birth" of "man" outweigh the simple recognition that "man," in its modern sense, was spoken of as an autonomous, organic entity with its own fundamental nature, classified alongside other forms of life studied in all their dimensions as objects of scientific inquiry. More profoundly, "man" in this *épistémé* acquired a uniquely twofold existence, as *both* the subject *and* object of knowledge and discourse, of representation itself. One can only speak of knowledge in the Western tradition by virtue of an observing subject; yet the production of knowledge and its expression in the nineteenth century ultimately was motivated by the multidimensional project of discovering the unseen laws, the empirical truth, of that very observing subject. In a union of modern scientific methodology with classical metaphysical ideals, nineteenth-century positivist inquiry sought to apprehend the objective presence of "man" as an explanatory principle for beings in general. In Foucault's terms, "man constituted himself in Western culture as both that which must be conceived of and that which is to be known" (345). Accordingly, "man" became the origin and telos of knowledge, the being who generated knowledge through rational inquiry and whose objective truth represented the ideal of knowledge as such.

Throughout the Renaissance, representation functioned in its purest form, as nature's signature of a latent resemblance, or a form of identity, between similar objects. During the Enlightenment, representation facilitated classification of phenomena according to their manifest identities, their characteristic natures. In the nineteenth century, "man" became the identity of representation itself: the one for whom representation existed, in order to generate and express knowledge through observation, and the one who fell under its gaze as the privileged object of scientific inquiry. All told, these crucial changes exhibit the discursive transformations according to which conventional definitions of "man," representation, and identity central to the rhetorical tradition became questionable.

In turn, this transformation in the nature of representation, of subjectivity and objectivity, precipitated a still more profound transformation in Western ontology. The event that philosophers often describe as "the death of God" accompanied the so-called birth of "man" as the organizing principle of modern knowledge and discourse. Earlier in this chapter, I detailed the theological character of Western ontology from Socrates and Plato forward. Metaphysical reflection traditionally posited the existence of sensible and intelligible, physical and transcendental, or human and divine domains. Knowledge consisted of one's ability to distinguish representations of phenomena based on ideal and, in explicitly Christian iterations, God-like forms from false representations thereof. Truth amounted to the reflection of divine ideals, which also constituted the very purpose of human reason, morality, and conduct—of human being itself. God thus encompassed the unity of all beings, their transcendent identity, by functioning both as the authorizing subject, the prime mover, of the physical realm and as the essential and unchanging presence, the defining telos, that endowed all beings with their ultimate meaning. "In their fundamental similarity," Scott comments, "things essentially made sense and spoke, if softly, of God's continuing, undergirding, sustaining presence" (1987, 113). By the nineteenth century, however, "man" had acquired the ability to lend order to the physical realm, to name and decipher the truth of beings, while simultaneously recognizing itself as the consummate object of that process, as the pinnacle of organic life, of being as such. In *The Birth of the Clinic,* Foucault writes, "The possibility for the individual of being both subject and object of his own knowledge implies an inversion in the structure of finitude" (1994a, 197). God traditionally constituted the transcendent identity, the continuous and objective presence, represented in all manner of finite beings; during the nineteenth century, "man" emerged as the ideal subject and object of representation, and thus as the unifying presence according to which finitude was measured.

One must not assume that philosophers invoke the so-called death of God in order to claim that Judeo-Christian religion no longer influences social and political events; obviously, its influence remains a ubiquitous feature of Western culture. Nor do such philosophers wish to supplant belief in God with an equally fervent belief in "man," as if faith in the latter was more defensible than faith in the former. Nietzsche, of course, is remembered for proclaiming the death of God. Yet, Scott cautions, "[t]he death of God is not a doctrine or a belief for Nietzsche. It is an object of description. He does not particularly like it or trust it. He certainly does not believe *in* it" (1987, 39). For Nietzsche and others, the death of God may be called "an object of description" in that it dramatizes the nature of a crisis in established truths, values, and ideals. The implicit claim here is not that these truths, values, and ideals are suddenly eradicated but that, in becoming profoundly questionable, they undergo transmutation and subsequently become available for appeals to different meanings or values. Similarly, Foucault insists that the birth of "man," aside from matters of belief, "cannot be considered or treated as a phenomenon of opinion: it is an event in the order of knowledge" (Foucault 1994b, 345).

"Man" acquired its role as a unifying presence in the modern *épistémé* not simply because it personified the mere beginning and end of representational knowledge. In a more holistic sense, the ascendance of the human sciences at this time exhibited the presence of "man" throughout the very "interstices" of modern inquiry (Foucault 1994b, 347). The human sciences, Foucault explains, "proceed in accordance with models or concepts borrowed from biology, economics, and the sciences of language" (347). Such sciences were founded, therefore, as extensions of previous "models and concepts" designed to apprehend the positivist truth, immutable law, or objective presence of natural and social phenomena in general. By virtue of this process, the scientific pursuit of "man's" truth in all its manifestations eventually suffused the pursuit of every scientific truth. Hence, Foucault concludes, "man" became "at the same time the foundation of all positivities and present, in a way that cannot even be termed privileged, in the element of empirical things" (344). Invoking the metaphysical trope of closure, of a unity between the origin and destiny of being, one might say that "man," in modern parlance, embodied the omnipresent identity, the transcendental subject, in which the truth of things was enclosed.

The Reappearance of Language

I have demonstrated, however, that one must interrogate appeals to the unity of enclosure, to the ideal and objective completion of subjective processes. In the case of nineteenth-century positivism, Foucault observes that "man's" status as the subject and object of representation was shadowed by the emergence of another, less rational and transparent, discursive development. The emergence of this development would, in turn, render profoundly questionable the rhetoric of identity according to which "man" first appeared as the simultaneous origin and telos of modern representation.

In *The Birth of the Clinic,* Foucault detects the curious coexistence during the nineteenth century of "a scientific discourse in a rational form" and "a language that unfolds endlessly in the void left by the absence of the gods" (1994a, 198). In *The Order of Things,* he similarly maintains that "the entire [modern] *episteme* was bound up with the disappearance of Discourse and its featureless reign, with the shift of language towards objectivity, and with its reappearance in multiple form" (1994b, 385–86). "Man," in other words, became the subject and object of representation because language or "Discourse" became "featureless," or transparent; as such, only "man," and not language, could represent the objective identities of things and thereby represent itself. Nevertheless, Foucault detects at this time the "reappearance" of language "in multiple form," or "a language that unfolds endlessly in the void left by the absence of the gods." Such was a form of language characterized neither by transparency nor by the representation of objective phenomena but by the opacity of its existence in multiple forms as well as its self-referential quality.

Foucault explains that two developments in particular enabled the reappearance of language in multiple form. On the one hand, Foucault emphasizes the modern "importance of linguistics and of its applications to the knowledge of man" (382). Modern linguistics demonstrated that, in order to comprehend the ways in which "man" acquires and expresses knowledge, one must confront "the question of the being of language" (Foucault 1994b, 382). "Man" emerged in the nineteenth century as the unity of representation while language was reduced to transparency; yet Foucault remarks that, by virtue of modern linguistics, "we are led back to the place that Nietzsche and Mallarmé signposted when the first asked: Who speaks?, and the second saw his glittering answer in the Word itself" (382). Language was no longer "the first sketch of an order of representations of the world . . . the initial, inevitable way of representing representations" but, "[f]rom the nineteenth century," became "one object of knowledge among others, on the same level as living beings, wealth and value, and the history of events and men" (296). In this intellectual climate, language appeared to establish and disclose identities and differences, knowledge and meanings, independent of "man's" intentions. Ironically, the study of "man's" use of language placed renewed attention on the independent substance and creative powers of language itself.

Foucault also emphasizes, on the other hand, the significance of modern literature regarding such discursive substance and creativity. Modern literature, he explains, is "dedicated to language" (383), meaning that it enacts the ability of language to establish subjects and objects independent of individual intentions or external referents. In Hayden White's description, "Modern(ist) writing has its end within itself, is its own means of expression, and possesses as its 'content' nothing other than its 'form' " (1992, 180). Accordingly, Foucault calls such literature an "unsignifying region where language can find its freedom" (1994b, 383). In the works of Artaud, Kafka, Joyce, Faulkner, and others, language no longer represented the consciousness of the author or the objective presence of an external reality—it no longer represented forms of *identity* as such—but enacted its own capacities for discursively engendering subjects and objects. The function of literature, after all, is to create a reality independent of the reality we know or, in Foucault's description, to absorb "the whole world into one book" (305). Modernist literature thus exemplified the middle voice of language. It manifested the capacity of language to engender and disseminate meaning, neither as the fulfillment of authorial intention nor as the reflection of an extra-textual reality, but as a result of its own enactment in a discursive space no longer governed by a privileged consciousness or an empirical order.

The reappearance of language "in multiple form" that Foucault describes stimulated, over the course of the twentieth century, a manifold philosophical effort to reconsider the nature of knowledge, consciousness, subject-object relations, identity and difference, and even human being in light of the so-called being of language itself. Continuing preoccupations with language in this manner remain the most obvious manifestations of the crisis in representation that Foucault presaged from the outset of *The Order of Things*. This crisis is characterized by the realization that "man," rather than establishing and lending speech to the order of things, is itself merely a partial and privileged form of knowledge and speech engendered by the language over which it purports to exert such complete control. In this account, "man" is not the transcendental authorizing subject of language but a subject position engendered within its indeterminate dissemination of meaning. Questioning the alleged transparency of language, the priority of reason and meaning, and the unity of subject-object relations thus amounts to questioning the supposedly universal nature of human being.

If one can identify the origin of "man" as an organizing principle of knowledge and discourse, can one foresee its end? Commenting on the crisis in representation engendered by the nonrepresentational dimensions of language, Foucault speculates: "If this same language is now emerging with greater and greater insistence in a unity that we ought to think but cannot as yet do so, is this not the sign that the whole of this configuration is now about to topple, and that man is in the process of perishing as the being of language continues to shine ever brighter upon our horizon? Since man was constituted at a time when language was doomed to dispersion, will he not be dispersed when language regains its unity?" (386). The logic of Foucault's speculation is simple: perhaps "man" will disperse as the organizing principle of knowledge, speech, even being itself, when language has assumed the role of that same principle.

Like Nietzsche's notion of the death of God, one must not interpret Foucault's conjecture as an effort to willfully replace the "man" of representation with a more ideal ontological avatar. Instead, one must interpret Foucault's prediction that, under an emerging set of discursive conditions, "man would be erased, like a face drawn in sand at the edge of the sea" (387) as an object of description. Understood in this manner, Foucault's wager dramatizes the nature of an unfolding crisis in formerly accepted truths, values, and ideals; he identifies the "possibility" of their transformation without endorsing it or advocating an alternate ontology. The "dispersion" of "man" in this context functions as a trope according to which one can document the discursive transformation of an entire cultural ethos—the ethos of representation.

THE SUBJECT AND OBJECT OF RHETORIC

Unfortunately, many since Foucault have taken his commentary on the possibility of "man's" dispersion to be a statement of belief in the essentially discursive and subjective, rather than empirical and objective, nature of reality. Regardless of this common interpretation, Foucault refuses to identify a superior truth, value, or ideal as a means to either terminate the present order or bring it to fruition. Instead, he underscores the frequently neglected significance of discursive difference rather than the identity of an ideal subject or object. By accentuating the differences between discursive orders, Foucault renders questionable the supposed permanence and transparency of the truths, values, or ideals established therein. Derrida, of course, would likely object to the archaeological metaphor with which Foucault characterizes his methodology in *The Order of Things*. Foucault's proposal "to reveal a *positive unconscious* of knowledge" that "eludes the consciousness of the scientist and yet is part of scientific discourse" (1994b, xi), waiting to be unearthed from the textual detritus of an era's discursive practices, might appear to Derrida as a suspicious form of transhistorical presence.[11] Despite this problematic connotation, Foucault, like Derrida, inhabits normative forms of knowledge, speech, and subjectivity in order to demonstrate how nonrepresentational elements of discourse have engendered the ideals of representation, "man" being foremost among them, or how one may regard the supposedly essential identities of phenomena as manifestations of difference. Foucault, again like Derrida, does not reject a reigning *épistémé* in order to inaugurate a new ontological arrangement; such an effort would, in adopting an antimetaphysical posture, merely reproduce the dialectical procedures or metaphysical ideals of superior truth and objectivity that he set out to reject. Foucault intends, rather, to identify the discursive conditions according to which casually accepted truths, values, and ideals (all forms of identity or continuous presence) become questionable—not from a vantage external to historical or social contexts but from within the very institutions and forms of subjectivity they engender.

Understood in this manner, *The Order of Things* allows one to render questionable the unquestioned truths, values, and ideals of the rhetorical tradition. Previously, I explained the doubly representational nature of rhetoric from its classical inception to its modern form. Throughout the history of the discipline, rhetoric retained its relative practical and intellectual value because its theory and practices were based on the embodiment of supposedly universal human capacities for reason, truth, and moral conduct. By representing forms of reason, truth, and virtue in speech, one simultaneously represented the supposed truth of human being. Thus, despite its various forms, the subject and object of rhetoric has always been one and the same: an ideal conception of human being. Such is the transcendental subject of rhetoric. Since the Greek classical period, rhetoric consistently has been defined by the moral imperative that only subjects endowed with reason, truth, and virtue should be instructed in the arts of eloquence. Concomitantly, instructing individuals to enact the universal truth of human being by attaining such eloquence has remained the perennial objective, the object proper, of rhetorical education. From its inception, rhetoric has been unified by an equation of being with some form of transcendental presence, by the essential identity of the subject of rhetoric or the essential identity of its object. Whether one recognizes it or not, the assumption that rhetoric is a purely representational phenomenon necessarily, even if unwittingly, endorses an essential notion of either subjectivity or objectivity.

The axiomatic status of rhetoric's traditional reduction to representation may be a symptom of the dangers occluded by such definitional clarity rather than an indication of its correctness. As Scott contends, "the danger is *greatest* when we are secure in our communities, assured in the meanings that hold together our best sensibility, and clear about our responsibilities" (1996, 85). The clandestine danger of representation as such is manifested in the traditional humanist ideals—namely, the unflagging belief in universal reason, morality, and eloquence—that rhetoricians have, at best, insufficiently questioned and, at worst, happily celebrated.

The texts reviewed in this chapter have allowed me to clarify the relevance of basic metaphysical categories (such as identity and difference or being and representation) to any argument about the nature of rhetoric. Such texts also allow me to clarify the nature of my proposal to develop a conception of rhetoric beyond representation. To begin with, a conception of rhetoric beyond representation does not rely on an antimetaphysical stance. Establishing an opposite or even hostile rhetorical ontology to that of traditional metaphysics merely reproduces the quintessentially dialectical search for a superior truth or ideal. I propose, rather, to investigate the nonrepresentational (rather than antirepresentational) aspects of rhetoric, which amounts to asking how one can use the ideals of representation to engender unconventional values and modes of discourse that resist habitual appeals to transparent truth and reason or transcendent morality and being. In the context of rhetorical theory, this deconstruction of representation will yield a conception of rhetoric engendered by discursive difference rather than categorical identity—engendered, that is, by differences between discourses, which establish the changing values and meanings of multiple subject positions, rather than the allegedly universal identity, truth, or presence of human being.

Subsequently, the organizing principle of rhetoric beyond representation will be neither the identity of a given subject nor the objective identity of a given referent but an attunement to *rhetoric in the middle voice.* By way of analogy with modern literature, the self-enactment of discourse, rather than individual intentions or the objectivity of an extra-discursive reality, defines rhetoric in this mode. In identifying the middle voice of rhetoric, I do not intend to eliminate altogether the rhetorical significance of intention or appeals to objectivity. I nonetheless insist that one must assign such *topoi* a radically different sense and value if one is committed to developing a conception of rhetoric that no longer represents a partial and privileged definition of human being. A conception of rhetoric beyond representation scrutinizes the nonrepresentational dimensions of discourse in order to give priority to the discursive differences that engender, maintain, or transform modes of subjectivity instead of preserving the essential identities, truths, or forms of transcendental presence that define the subject according to the representation of a supposedly universal human nature.

In the next chapter, I scrutinize the ideal medium of rhetoric: human speech. Since the inception of rhetoric, the disciplinary value of this ostensibly ideal and original form of discourse has preserved definitions of rhetoric based on the principles of representation and essential notions of human being. In order to eventually develop a conception of rhetoric in the middle voice, I devote chapter 2 to questioning the traditional sense and value of its supposedly ideal and original medium.

Chapter 2

The Ideal of Rhetoric

Even commonsensical notions of language and communication presuppose critical, but frequently unexamined, assumptions about their value to human affairs. In our heritage, one can trace the presumed value of language as merely a transparent conveyance of objective meaning to the influence of early Western philosophy, which asserted the sovereignty of the knowing and speaking subject over the domain language. Nietzsche's interpretation of language, however, rendered questionable the traditional transparency of philosophical knowledge and discourse. Foucault refers to Nietzsche as "the mad philosopher" (1977, 44) in order to underscore Nietzsche's cultivation of a philosophical discourse irreducible to reason and truth. In contrast to the dialectical language of philosophy, with which the philosopher speaks confidently of objective knowledge and inherent identities, Foucault describes the discovery "of another language that also speaks and that he [the philosopher] is unable to dominate, one that strives, fails, and falls silent and that he cannot manipulate, the language he spoke at one time and that has now separated itself from him" (42). In Foucault's estimation, "this is not the end of philosophy, but rather, the end of the philosopher as the sovereign and primary form of philosophical language" (42). The emergence of this non-dialectical language in the wake of Nietzsche's insights suggested a speaking subject no longer governed by transparent reason and identity. "This experience," Foucault concludes, "forms the exact reversal of the movement which has sustained the wisdom of the West at least since the time of Socrates, that is, the wisdom to which philosophical language promised the serene unity of a subjectivity which would triumph in it, having been fully constituted by it and through it" (43–44). Because of its implications for the status of the knowing and speaking subject, Nietzsche's non-dialectical perspective on language might allow one to question, beyond traditional philosophy, the "serene unity" often ascribed to subjectivity in general. For this reason, I briefly scrutinize his interpretation of language for its potential insights on the relationship between rhetoric, truth, and human being, which, in turn, will establish a useful framework for the analyses featured in this chapter.

In his 1873 essay "On Truth and Lying in an Extra-moral Sense," Nietzsche advances an interpretation of the relationship between language, "man," and truth powerfully resonant with contemporary commentary on such topics. He asks, "What is truth?" and answers: "a mobile army of metaphors, metonyms, anthropomorphisms, in short, a sum of human relations which were poetically and rhetorically heightened, transferred, and adorned, and after long use seem solid, canonical, and binding to a nation" (Gilman et al. 1989b, 250). Throughout the Western tradition, knowledge and speech have always been measured according to standards of truth, according to the accurate representation of an objective meaning or presence. Nietzsche underscores the moral imperative that characterizes this conception of knowledge and speech. In Socratic fashion, the rectitude demanded by one's apprehension of truth compels one to testify to its nature as if that truth were "solid, canonical, and binding." A lie is not merely a factual error but a deviation from right conduct. In Plato's account of Socrates' legendary trial, not even the threat of a death sentence deters Socrates from his commitment to the expression of truth; instead, he receives the ultimate punishment by mocking those who would advise him to speak falsely in order to escape his fate. "I would much rather die as the result of this defense," Socrates avows, "than live as the result of the other sort" (*Socrates' Defense (Apology)*, 38e). Not coincidentally, Michael Naas observes, "[w]ords having to do with persuasion occur close to forty times in this short dialogue, often associated . . . with forgetting and deception" (1995, 223).

Nietzsche contends that the elevation of truth to an ideal status, and the martyrdom that constitutes its most extreme consequence, amounts to a denigration of life itself. "Nietzsche does not criticise false claims to truth," Deleuze explains, "but truth in itself and as an ideal. . . . If someone wills the truth it is not in the name of what the world is but in the name of what the world *is not*," for that person "makes life an 'error' and this world an 'appearance'. He therefore opposes knowledge to life and to the world he opposes another world, a world-beyond, the truthful world" (1983, 95–96). The transcendent value with which Western philosophy has invested the category of truth manifests a nihilistic impulse. Metaphysical ontology negates the sensible world—life itself—in order to affirm an ideal and original form of being, a "*moral origin*" (Deleuze 1983, 96).[1]

Nietzsche nevertheless discovers a suppressed irony: the supposedly ideal nature of truth, along with our moral obligations to it, is actually a semblance of "metaphors, metonyms, [and] anthropomorphisms," of poetics and rhetoric. He insists that the ideal and original ethos of apparently fixed, canonical, and binding truths is actually a poetic or rhetorical formulation rather than the objective representation of a transcendent form. Nietzsche's thesis obviously resembles contemporary claims that the most fundamental truths are, in essence, products of discourse. Indeed, modern scholars often invoke his insights in order to justify ontological arguments about the so-called socially constructed nature of reality. Yet the unreflective use of Nietzsche's philosophy to recommend yet another universal principle structuring the order of things carelessly enlists him in the inauguration of a new objective truth while overlooking the most radical component of his critique.

This component is evinced by Nietzsche's further commentary in "On Truth and Lying." He continues: "Truths are illusions about which it has been forgotten that they *are* illusions, worn-out metaphors without sensory impact, coins which have lost their image and now can be used only as metal, and no longer as coins" (Gilman et al. 1989b, 250). Some today are satisfied to cite Nietzsche's proclamations on truth in order to justify an alternate ontology of fiction rather than fact, appearance rather than essence, body instead of mind, or subjective perception instead of objective representation. Nietzsche, however, promoted an unrelenting revaluation of *all* values based on such dialectical categories. His analogy between metaphor and coinage therefore promotes a different valuation of truth. Language loses its metaphorical embossing, its "sensory impact," in order to become a transparent conveyance of truth as it is worn down into a cold and inert representation of ideal and immaterial value. The pristine value of truth is forged concurrently as the distinctive metaphorical, poetical, or rhetorical sense and value of language is negated. This Socratic conversion of metaphor, poetics, and rhetoric into the transparent currency of an inherently rational and moral idiom amounts to a denigration of "life itself," as Deleuze would have it, meaning a sublimation of the sensible (language) to the intelligible (truth). Like Foucault's account of representation, Nietzsche's genealogy of the antithetical moral values attributed to truth and falsehood reveals the method by which one might assign to those categories a nonmoral value. His delineation of a moral economy governing the use of language in our heritage warrants an alternate interpretation of the origin and nature of truth. In turn, this new interpretation assigns to the category of truth a contingent and discursive, rather than a transhistorical and intuitive, value.

However, Nietzsche's most penetrating insight regarding language and truth concerns, not the illusory nature of any truth-value, but the process of *forgetting* that engenders it. In proclaiming, "Truths are illusions about which it has been forgotten that they *are* illusions," Nietzsche does not advocate a mere reversal of categories. Instead, he initiates a fundamental displacement of the moral dialectic that initially opposed truth to falsehood based on an ideal and original meaning or presence. "[U]ntil now," Nietzsche posits, "we have heard only of the obligation which society, in order to exist, imposes: to be truthful, i.e., to use the customary metaphors, or in moral terms, the obligation to lie according to an established convention, to lie collectively in a style that is mandatory for everyone. Now, of course, man forgets that this is his situation; so he lies in the designated manner unconsciously and according to centuries-old habits—and precisely *by this unconsciousness,* by this forgetting, he arrives at his sense of truth" (Gilman et al. 1989b, 250). Ironically, one lies "in the designated manner" when one speaks in the name of truth. Such an account does not simply invert the priority of truth over lies but undermines their metaphysical sense and value altogether. It allows Nietzsche to assert that "man" becomes the moral arbiter of truth, or speaks of truth at all, only because of an "established" process of "forgetting" the nature of "his" being in relation to language, meaning, and truth.

Nietzsche does not deny that truth, moral imperatives, or "man" exist in some form. Rather, he discloses the discursive inception of an apparently ideal moral economy that first endowed such phenomena with their traditional sense and value. In revealing the rhetorical conditions that initially engendered the putative permanence and transparency of categories such as truth, morality, and "man," Nietzsche simultaneously identifies in those conditions the means by which their ideal ethos can be made available for the creation of new values.

Nietzsche thus provides a lucid and philosophically revolutionary interpretation of the relationship between language, truth, and human being; however, his implicit definition of rhetoric in "On Truth and Lying" is more ambiguous. Nietzsche's initial description of rhetoric as an intensification or embellishment, as "a movable host" of linguistic devices, suggests that rhetoric is an instrument or tool used by a speaker to fulfill his or her intentions. But Nietzsche simultaneously and unequivocally argues that when one expresses a truth, one speaks, in *"unconsciousness"* and "forgetting," a "centuries-old" truth, as if the rhetoric of that truth used the unwitting speaker for its instrument or medium. In a more refined version of this notion, Hans-Georg Gadamer posited that "language is not only an object in our hands, it is the reservoir of tradition and the medium in and through which we exist and perceive our world" (1976, 29).[2] One can therefore detect two competing senses of rhetoric at work in Nietzsche's essay. The first reflects a classical, instrumental conception of rhetoric that conforms to the artistry and intentions of a speaking subject. The second suggests an inverse view in which rhetoric exists as a transcendent, objective presence of which one's consciousness and intentions are only effects. In the former sense, rhetoric is an action one performs, a linguistic or symbolic phenomenon one creates; in the latter, rhetoric creates the one who uses language, creates possibilities for the knowledge and expression of truth and error, good and evil.[3] Contemporary definitions of rhetoric as the articulation of ideological frameworks most directly exemplify this latter sense of rhetoric.

Neither definition is acceptable in and of itself, nor can they be combined in order to account comprehensively for all conceivable dimensions of rhetorical processes. Both conceptions of rhetoric are governed by an active voice. Whether rhetoric is an action performed by an individual or that individual is a subject ideologically determined through rhetorical processes, rhetoric remains defined by a linear, cause-and-effect model in which an object receives some intended, meaningful action. Whichever the case, the active voice of these formulations dictates that rhetoric either originates or culminates in the manifestation of an essential identity, a form of being as essential presence, a representation of subjective intention or objective meaning. In classical or instrumentalist conceptions of rhetoric, the active voice privileges a transcendental subject unaffected by the art, a subject whose speech is assumed to be rational, autonomous, and transparent. But, in the contrasting Althusserian view, the active tense is preserved while one simply reassigns the position of causal agent to a universal ideology, an ideal meaning or consciousness, reflected in rhetorical phenomena (Charland 1987; McGee 1975, 1980; McKerrow 1989; Wander 1984). The character of rhetoric in this form presupposes that a transcendental structure of essential meaning inevitably surmounts all differences between subjective representations or individual utterances.

These competing senses of rhetoric are, of course, somewhat anomalous to Nietzsche's general revaluation of all values, which boasts a critique of all forms of transcendental identity, whether subjective or objective. Taken together, one may nevertheless regard them as representative of defining tendencies in contemporary arguments over the status of rhetoric. Neither tendency decisively interrogates, as Nietzsche does, the essential truth-value upon which their respective senses of rhetoric are based, either according to the humanist identity of an autonomous agent or ideological determinations of rhetoric itself. In this chapter, I argue that our failure to question such active voice formulations of rhetoric, in all their classical and contemporary iterations, prevents a thorough deconstruction of the representational logic (the logic of subjective and objective meaning) by which rhetoric invariably has been defined. These active voice formulations preserve the value of an essential truth or identity represented in rhetorical processes.

My critique of the active voice in this chapter will allow me to develop a conception of rhetoric in the middle voice in chapter 3. Such a conception assigns an alternate sense and value to the categories of truth, morality, and identity because these categories have preserved rhetoric as the representation of a universal human condition from its classical inception to the current period. However, I must explain briefly the nature of the middle voice so as to differentiate it from the active voice analyzed in this chapter.

The middle voice implies that a subject is somehow implicated in the occurrence of an action, though neither as its active subject nor its passive object. The action neither originates nor culminates in the subject. To say "I marry" indicates that an object (the spouse) is acted upon by a subject exterior to the event; to say "I wed," however, suggests an action in which the condition of the subject is interior to, and actually constituted by, the event (White 1992, 186). One would be mistaken in supposing that the middle voice merely rendered the subject passive. Citing the example of writing, Hayden White explains: "The middle voice is, if anything, doubly active, at once productive of an effect on an object (for example, on language) and constitutive of a particular kind of agent (namely, the writer) by means of an action (specifically, writing)" (1992, 181). In the middle voice, that is, "only in writing and by writing [can] the writer be said to exist at all. The 'writer' is what exists in the interior of the activity of 'writing' " (White 1992, 182). This example illustrates how the middle voice connotes the discursive formation of a subject in which he or she neither intends the action nor receives it.

The grammar of the middle voice interrupts the dialectical logic of cause and effect or subject and object essential to the primacy of representation and identity in Western ontology. White stresses that, in the middle voice, "actions and their effects are conceived to be simultaneous; past and present are integrated rather than dirempted, and the subject and object of the action are in some way conflated" (185). In expressing a meaning irreducible to the intentions of a subject, the middle voice undermines the presumption that meaning originates in reason alone. Meaning subsequently gains an autonomous, self-engendering capacity that places in question the essential identity suggested by a supposedly direct correspondence between action and effect, subject and object. The middle voice expresses the occurrence of meaning without identifying it as either cause or effect. This self-engendering capacity of the middle voice places in question the identity of the speaking subject as well as the object to which he or she refers. Its grammar subverts the ethos of a transcendent human subject exterior to discursive events. The most dramatic ramification of the middle voice, therefore, is its ability to undermine the dialectical logic opposing subject to object upon which basic metaphysical ontology is predicated.[4]

To develop a conception of rhetoric in the middle voice is to develop a conception of rhetoric in which the rhetorical agent is not a subject exterior to the order of discourse but a form of subjectivity that is itself discursively engendered, maintained, and transformed. Edward Corbett unwittingly indicated the need for such study when he argued that modern rhetorical scholars have devoted only slight attention to "discussing how an impressive *ethos* is created and maintained in speaking or writing" (1989, 204). Whereas Corbett likely intended his words to justify discussion of how one's effective *use* of discourse creates a favorable ethos, I cite them to justify my investigation of the ways in which the enactment of discourse itself engenders discursive practices constitutive of one's subjectivity.

I explicitly develop a conception of rhetoric in the middle voice in chapter 3; in the present chapter, however, I first offer a critique of the ideal of rhetoric, meaning its supposedly ideal and original form: human speech. In expounding on the virtues of "eloquence," Emerson asserted that foremost among "the great triumphs of the art are, when the orator is lifted above himself; when consciously he makes himself the mere tongue of the occasion and the hour, and says what cannot be said" (1964a, 49). The orator's speech facilitates "his" effacement because its alleged transparency discloses "what cannot be said"—namely, truth or meaning in its ideal and original form. As in Nietzsche's analysis of language, speech in the rhetorical tradition has been endowed with an ideal status because it appears to facilitate one's desire for an effacement of the human realm in pursuit of transcendent, purely intelligible truth. Despite modern research into increasingly diverse forms of rhetoric, including (for example) literature, visual media, music, and architecture, human speech retains an exclusive value in rhetorical studies as the commonplace truth, the apparently original, authentic, and therefore ideal manifestation, of rhetoric in general. Deconstructing the value of this ideal, I contend, is necessary in order to undermine the existing authority of an active voice (or representational) formulation of rhetoric and endorse one that accounts for its middle voice.

LOGOCENTRISM AND RHETORIC

The premise that speech is the ideal form of rhetoric in relation to which all other forms are defined requires little demonstration. One would be hard-pressed to identify a more commonsensical and apparently innocuous premise regarding the nature of rhetoric. My argument in this chapter is not historical; there is no question that the body of theory and practice known as rhetoric originated in classical Greece as a codification of oral practices. My argument, rather, concerns the value that rhetoricians habitually accord to speech as the original and supposedly authentic form of rhetoric. Conventional wisdom in rhetorical studies, for example, differentiates between an oratorical performance and its preservation in print or electronic media, between the immediate audience gathered to hear that performance and those that listen to, see, or read it in countless other circumstances after the fact. The meaning and effects of a given address are subsequently evaluated according to this temporal and spatial calculus.

Rhetoricians who seek to identify alternatives to oral rhetoric, moreover, nevertheless preserve its ideal value by interpreting phenomena not traditionally described as rhetorical according to the communicative principles of speech. Some rhetorical scholars, for example, posit that scientific discourse, images, gender, or even silence (the putative opposite of speech) can be said to communicate, persuade, or argue. Efforts to establish alternatives to the traditionally ideal form of rhetoric—oral address—ironically preserve its status by preserving interpretive paradigms or critical vocabularies originally suited to the study of oratory. Naturally, the widespread embrace of logos in recent decades as the organizing proof of our discipline has ensured that such paradigms or vocabularies are predominantly Aristotelian.

In what follows, I demonstrate that the retention of this ideal is chiefly responsible for preserving the dominant representational conception of rhetoric, despite modern disputes over its nature and scope. Conventional notions of speech assume an identity between one's intentions, a speech act, and its reception in the minds of listeners. Defined in this manner, speech acts represent forms of presence (reason, meaning, truth, and subjectivity) that exist prior to the order of language. The ideal value assigned to speech in rhetorical studies accordingly preserves a conception of rhetoric defined by its representation of objective presence.

Not surprisingly, the discipline of rhetoric lacks a comprehensive critique of the metaphysical values manifested in conventional notions of speech. I remedy this shortcoming by employing Derrida's reflections on that topic as a critical template. Although Derrida critiques conceptions of speech commonly found in literatures outside of rhetorical studies, such conceptions are also foundational elements of rhetorical theory and practice. I therefore use his critique as an instructive model with which to perform an analogous deconstruction of conventional assumptions about the nature of rhetoric and its affinity with categories such as representation, meaning, and communication. Before doing so, however, I summarize the approaches to language that Derrida critiques as a way of delineating the longstanding assumptions responsible for preserving ideal notions of speech in modern scholarship, rhetorical or otherwise.

"Only Differences"

Ferdinand de Saussure's view of language is one of Derrida's most famous critical targets. Saussure's *Course in General Linguistics* (1974), taken from his lectures on language at the University of Geneva from 1907 to 1911, is considered to be one of the principal sources of semiotics. His widespread influence on twentieth-century studies of language is explained by his departure from the reigning philosophies of language at the turn of the century. In brief, he devised a social or institutional, rather than a metaphysical, account of language formation. On the one hand, he disagreed with positivists, who held that society is the sum of individual subjective realities representing nothing more than an aggregate social fiction. He also disagreed, on the other hand, with German idealists who argued, as Hegel did, that social conventions, laws, or even the state itself are only manifestations of spirit. Offering a novel middle way between these alternatives, Saussure proposed that society must be regarded as a reality unto itself. Concomitantly, he maintained that one must explain the nature and function of linguistics according to the conventions that shape social institutions.[5]

One can most efficiently examine Saussure's interpretation of language according to three related distinctions. The first is a distinction between *synchronic* and *diachronic* linguistics. Saussure defines synchronic linguistics, which he recommends, as the study of "logical and psychological relations that bind together coexisting terms and form a system in the collective mind of the speakers" (1974, 99–100). Diachronic linguistics, in contrast, emphasizes "relations that bind together successive terms not perceived by the collective mind but substituted for each other without forming a system" (100). Synchronic or "static" linguistics reconstructs language as a functional whole in a given context whereas diachronic or "historical" linguistics follows the formal evolution of language over time. By drawing this distinction, Saussure does not intend to dismiss diachronic linguistics altogether; language, he admits, is subject to mutation by virtue of "external" influences that occur temporally. Nevertheless, Saussure maintains that synchrony is the hitherto neglected dimension of linguistics and, in his words, "generally much more difficult than the study of historical linguistics" (101).

Saussure's methodological preference for synchrony reflects his attention to the social qualities of language. According to Saussure, a simple speech act requires a certain linguistic competence, which he likens to the game of chess. "Language is a system that has its own arrangement. Comparison with chess will bring out the point. In chess, what is external can be separated relatively easily from what is internal. The fact that the game passed from Persia to Europe is external; against that, everything having to do with its system and rules is internal" (22). Such is, perhaps, the structural analogy par excellence in Saussure's text. His comparison of language to a game exemplifies his effort to identify the universal conditions that enable a speaker's potential for adaptation or innovation within a finite set of conventional linguistic possibilities. Language, like chess, requires a comprehension of its internal elements, its inherent "system and rules"; knowledge of its external composition or historical evolution is essentially irrelevant to its usage.

Saussure's synchronic frame thus underscores one's natural aptitude for the comprehension and use of language as a functional whole, as a social institution. This approach to language assigns an exclusive value to the living dynamism of speech over the taxonomies of comparative philology: "[I]n the lives of individuals and societies," Saussure proclaims, "speech is more important than anything else" (7). The "exclusively comparative method" of philology, he insists, cannot document the nature and function of speech because it has "no basis in reality, these notions simply could not reflect the facts of speech" (4). In all, Saussure's initial distinction between *synchronic* and *diachronic* linguistics emphasizes an immanent, rather than a historical, perspective on language.

Following this initial distinction, Saussure differentiates between *langue* and *parole,* or language and speech. Saussure claims that one cannot adequately document his privileged object of study, *parole* (speech), without a methodology that somehow organizes its cacophonous nature. He insists that *"from the very outset we must put both feet on the ground of language and use language as the norm of all other manifestations of speech"* (9). According to Saussure, "[S]peech is many-sided and heterogeneous; straddling several areas simultaneously—physical, physiological, and psychological," whereas "[l]anguage, on the contrary, is a self-contained whole and a principle of classification. As soon as we give language first place among the facts of speech, we introduce a natural order into a mass that lends itself to no other classification" (9). *Langue* (language) thus performs a crucial function in Saussure's system, lending a "principle of classification" or "natural order," by which to study and classify the otherwise "heterogeneous" and dissonant activity of speech.[6]

Saussure elaborates on the relationship between *langue* and *parole.* He describes language as a virtual entity actualized in speech and made whole in its adoption by a community of speakers. He likens it to "a storehouse filled by the members of a given community through their active use of speaking, a grammatical system that has a potential existence in each brain, or, more specifically, in the brains of a group of individuals. For language is not complete in any speaker; it exists perfectly only with a collectivity" (13–14). In this account, the relationship between language and speech appears to be reciprocal in nature. On the one hand, language is "a collection of necessary conventions that have been adopted by a social body to permit individuals to exercise that faculty" (9). "Language," Saussure reasons, "is comparable to a symphony in that what the symphony actually is stands completely apart from how it is performed; the mistakes that musicians make in playing the symphony do not compromise this fact" (18). But, on the other hand, Saussure also asserts that language is "a social product of the faculty of speech" (9). He explains that "speaking is what causes language to evolve: impressions gathered from listening to others modify our linguistic habits" (19). "Language and speaking," Saussure concludes, "are then inter-dependent; the former is both the instrument and the product of the latter" (19). According to this description, one experiences language as an existing collection of linguistic resources upon which a speaker draws. Yet the preex-istent quality of language is simultaneously a function of the conventions produced by speakers who engage in "a sort of contract signed by the mem-bers of a community" (14). Such is the reciprocal interplay that engenders the separate categories of *langue* and *parole*.[7]

Saussure's distinction between *langue* and *parole* corresponds to his con-ception of the most elemental linguistic units. His simple claim that "[t]he bond between the signifier and the signified is arbitrary" (67) is the signature statement of the *Course in General Linguistics*. Taking its most basic unit—the sign—as the defining element of language, Saussure declares that words do not function according to an essential bond of resemblance with that to which they refer. Instead, "every means of expression used in society is based, in principle, on collective behavior or—what amounts to the same thing—con-vention" (68). Arbitrary convention, or unstated collective agreement, engen-ders the apparent semantic bond that joins a word to its referent. As such, Saussure appears to identify the origins of language in its use by groups and individuals rather than in the representation of essential meaning or ideas.

Saussure's entire account ultimately devolves upon his valuation of differ-ence in language. "Everything that has been said up to this point," he states, "boils down to this: in language there are only differences. . . . Whether we take the signified or the signifier, language has neither ideas nor sounds that existed before the linguistic system, but only conceptual and phonic differ-ences that have issued from the system" (120). These differences are not derivative of or secondary to stable linguistic meanings or identities—"posi-tive terms between which the difference is set up" (120), as Saussure would have it. Instead, they emerge from the reciprocal and arbitrary interplay of *langue* and *parole,* and thus as "differences *without positive terms*" (120).[8] Saussure's account appears to offer a model of language no longer governed by meanings or identities that transcend the social context of speech acts. Such an account does not deny that groups and individuals use language in a representational manner, in order to refer to "ideas" as if they "existed before the linguistic system." It does, however, propose that such usage is based on social conventions rather than on the essential truth or meaning of representations. For Saussure, signification appears to be a social activity rather than a metaphysical process.

Saussure claimed that "semiology" offered a preferable methodology for linguistic analysis because it eschewed the metaphysical ideals characteristic of previous philosophies of language. Derrida's *Of Grammatology* (1974), first published in 1967, argued that Saussure's tacit but fundamental investment in a series of classical assumptions about the nature of *langue* and *parole* compromised his ostensible departure from traditional approaches to language. As such, Derrida's critique of Saussure is remembered for signaling, in part, the emergence of a *post*structuralist approach to language, speech, and signification.[9]

Derrida objects primarily to the priority that Saussure, despite his proposal to treat language as a system of "differences *without positive terms*," assigns to *parole* over other manifestations of language. Saussure identifies the proper object of his study by stating, "The linguistic object is not both the written and the spoken forms of words; the spoken forms alone constitute the object" (23–24). The derivative status that Saussure accords to writing indicates his concomitant view of speech as a more natural, ideal, or original manifestation of language. Derrida argues that, in Saussure's view, writing is "[d]erivative because *representative:* signifier of the first signifier, representation of the self-present voice, of the immediate, natural, and direct signification of the meaning (of the signified, of the concept, of the ideal object or what have you)" (1974, 30). In sum, Saussure retains a representational understanding of *parole:* writing merely *re*presents the more ideal and immediate meaning, object, or truth first and most transparently presented in speech.[10]

Saussure's conception of the qualitative difference between speech and writing reflects a long-standing preference in Western philosophy for the representation of ideal, original, or transparent meaning. Derrida notes that Saussure's description of writing, as an impoverished representation of speech, resembles Aristotle's definition of writing (1974, 30). In the *Phaedrus,* furthermore, Plato dramatizes a classical suspicion, echoed in Saussure's definitions of *langue* and *parole,* that one's use of writing impaired one's ability to acquire knowledge intuitively, in an unmediated apprehension of essential meaning or truth. Plato has Socrates relate the tale of Thamus and Theuth, during which Thamus, an Egyptian god and king, chastises Theuth for boasting of his latest invention, writing. As narrated by Socrates, Thamus proclaims:

> If men learn this [writing], it will implant forgetfulness in their souls; they will cease to exercise memory because they rely on that which is written, calling things to remembrance no longer from within themselves, but by means of external marks. What you have discovered is a recipe not for memory, but for reminder. And it is no true wisdom that you offer your disciples, but only its semblance, for by telling them of many things without teaching them you will make them seem to know much, while for the most part they know nothing, and as men filled, not with wisdom, but with the conceit of wisdom, they will be a burden to their fellows. (275a–b)

Writing, in other words, produces forgetfulness, the semblance of knowledge, and thus ignorance, whereas speech enjoys a direct correspondence with memory, conforms perfectly to reason, and thereby engenders wisdom.

According to metaphysical ontology, speech is a uniquely valued mode of communication because it most transparently represents meaning, truth, or wisdom in their essential identities and therefore facilitates one's intuitive apprehension of such ideal forms.[11]

These enduring assumptions about the transparency of speech originate in the rich connotations of the Greek *logos*. In his concise delineation of the term, Heidegger states that "*logos* as speech really means *dēloun,* to make manifest 'what is being talked about' in speech" (1996, 28). He draws out the relationship between truth and perception evoked by logos: truth as *alētheia,* in which truth is "seen as something unconcealed *(alēthes),*" or as *aisthēsis,* which involves "the simple sense perception of something" (29).[12] Heidegger admittedly interprets the affinity between logos and presence in a manner contrary to much of the metaphysical tradition (particularly in his distinctive interpretation of concealment and unconcealment); nevertheless, his summary of the term's classical sense highlights its predominant meaning from that epoch forward. By definition, logos manifests presence in speech. As such, an ideal conception of speech is one of the most vital components of the metaphysical system because it constitutes a medium of transparent communication between the sensible and the intelligible realms, between human reason and ideal truth.

Logocentrism is Derrida's name for the exclusive value with which the Western heritage has endowed logos, and thus speech. According to Derrida, the entire history of Western philosophy has been unified by logocentrism, "which has," he writes, "in spite of all differences . . . always assigned the origin of truth in general to the logos: the history of truth, of the truth of truth, has always been . . . the debasement of writing, and its repression outside 'full' speech" (1974, 3). The conventional assumptions on which Saussure's treatise is based reflect such logocentrism. Specifically, he debases the ontological value of writing in order to compound that of speech, and thus of an original truth. Although Saussure acknowledges that diachronic approaches to language are somewhat valuable, their value is always secondary. He insists that a diachronic analysis of factors external to the dynamic and integrated whole of speech has "no basis in reality, these notions simply could not reflect the facts of speech" (1974, 4), meaning the ideal form of language. By implication, diachronic studies of language merely document linguistic residue left over time by the passing propinquity of speech.

The notion that one medium better represents meanings or ideas suggests that such phenomena exist in an objective state prior to the order of language. The question here concerns, not the objective existence of those meanings or ideas, but how best to disclose them. In this context, speech acquires an especial value in metaphysical ontology because of its reputed transparency as a mode of representation. "There is an unfailing complicity here," Derrida observes, "between idealization and speech *[voix]*. An ideal object is an object whose showing may be repeated indefinitely, whose presence to *Zeigen* is indefinitely reiterable precisely because, freed from all mundane spatiality, it is a pure noema that I can express without having, at least apparently, to pass through the world" (1973, 75). Speech, in other words, is said to represent phenomena as objectively and transparently as possible, allowing things to show themselves instead of using physical signs to approximate and thereby distort them. As in Plato's *Phaedrus*, speech itself represents an ideal medium of meaning and wisdom.

These presuppositions concomitantly endow the human voice with an ideal status. "The ideality of the object," Derrida explains, "which is only its being—for a nonempirical consciousness, can only be expressed in an element whose phenomenality does not have worldly form. *The name of this element is the voice*" (76). The voice, as a medium of signification, lacks substance and thereby appears to transcend every physical context while providing the semblance of immediate presence. "The 'apparent transcendence' of the voice thus results from the fact that the signified, which is always ideal by essence, the 'expressed' *Bedeutung*, is immediately present in the act of expression. This immediate presence results from the fact that the phenomenological 'body' of the signifier seems to fade away at the very moment it is produced; it seems already to belong to the element of ideality" (Derrida 1973, 77). The transparency of the voice, the fact that "its substance seems to be purely temporal," consequently preserves the metaphysical priority of consciousness over the production of meaning: "[I]f one is heard by another, to speak is to make him repeat immediately in himself the hearing-oneself-speak in the very form in which I effectuated it" (Derrida 1973, 80). Intuition governs this system of meaning and communication because speech appears to ensure a perfect transparency of consciousness to consciousness, unmediated by the obfuscations of language.

Modern equations of *voice* with *ethos* comprise perhaps the most conventional manifestation of this presumed transparency. Literary studies in particular presume that the so-called "voice" of a text represents the character of the author. Despite the fact that the Latin *vox* can be traced to *verbum*, meaning simply the spoken "word," contemporary discourse, in the wake of this literary influence, tends to conflate speech with the speaker (Baumlin 1994, xxiii)—most conspicuously, as Derrida points out, with the speaker's consciousness.[13]

From the beginning, Saussure's assumptions about the transparency of speech compromise his effort to define the relationship between signifier and signified as arbitrary, supporting a system of "differences *without positive terms*." The sign cannot be arbitrary if its natural medium is speech. Defined as the allegedly ideal and original form of language, speech represents things in their essential identity. As a result, "[n]ot only do the signifier and the signified seem to unite, but also, in this confusion, the signifier seems to erase itself or to become transparent, in order to allow the concept to present itself as what it is, referring to nothing other than its presence" (Derrida 1981b, 22). Governed by the transparency of speech, signifier and signified assume an appearance of seamless closure. Derrida observes that Saussure's understanding of the relationship between signifier and signified consequently reflects an investment in the most fundamental metaphysical opposition—that between sensible and intelligible phenomena: "The semiological or, more specifically, linguistic 'science' cannot therefore hold on to the difference between signifier and signified—the very idea of the sign—without the difference between sensible and intelligible, certainly, but also not without retaining, more profoundly and more implicitly, and by the same token the reference to a signified able to 'take place' in its intelligibility, before its 'fall,' before any expulsion into the exteriority of the sensible here below. As the face of pure intelligibility, it refers to an absolute logos to which it is immediately united" (1974, 13). The signified, in other words, is present prior to the order of signification; one may call the linguistic term by which it is named arbitrary but such a description cannot infringe upon the essential identity of the signified. As such, the signified is located in a realm of "pure intelligibility," a transcendental order of "absolute logos" where meaning subsists in ideal form. The putatively arbitrary nature of the sign in Saussure's account is therefore predicated upon the inherent identity of what Derrida calls "a 'transcendental signified,' which in and of itself, in its essence, would refer to no signifier, would exceed the chain of signs, and would no longer itself function as a signifier" (1981b, 19–20). The forms of objective presence, absolute logos, or essential identity upon which the order of signification is founded in Saussure's account fundamentally undermine the priority that he assigns to the category of difference. Difference so conceived is always already secondary to the essential identity of "*a concept signified in and of itself,* a concept simply present for thought, independent of a relationship to language" (Derrida 1981b, 19).

Intention and Representation

Despite his intended departure from traditional philosophies of language, Saussure's inquiry nevertheless hinged upon offering a more accurate, scientific account of its fundamental nature. Saussure's belief in this fundamental nature prevented his study from developing conclusively an interpretation of language no longer reliant on transcendent forms of presence. One can observe such unexamined premises at work throughout influential treatises on language that more closely resemble rhetorical approaches to the subject.

The very title of J. L. Austin's *How to do Things With Words* (1962), for example, succinctly expresses an attention to the pragmatic functions of language hospitable to rhetorical methods. Austin explores the "performative," which he calls a neglected linguistic category. In such a locution, "the issuing of the utterance is the performing of an action" rather than a description of factual circumstances, as in other kinds of statements (6). Nonetheless, Austin has difficulty separating these categories as he attempts to identify the criterion by which one might conclusively distinguish "constatives" from "performatives." The performative dimensions of language prove more pervasive than even Austin initially suspected, suffusing other linguistic forms. He consequently insists that the cardinal task in linguistic analysis must be "to consider from the ground up how many senses there are in which to say something *is* to do something, or *in* saying something we do something, and even *by* saying something we do something" (94). In this sense, the performative dimension of language refers to its capacity to carry out actions instead of neutrally conveying meanings. Aristotle, of course, provided a persuasive justification for the disciplinary distinctiveness of rhetoric when he defined it as a practical art, an art of doing, in contrast to a productive or speculative art. Thus, one might reasonably describe this aspect of language as its rhetorical dimension.[14]

In order to apprehend this dimension of language, one must attend to the context or "*circumstances*" of a speech act. Although he was not a rhetorician, Austin's discussion of this point in Lecture I belies an essentially Aristotelian sensitivity to the influence of social conventions on rhetorical practice. He emphasizes that standards of propriety inform the nature of statements in a given circumstance: "The uttering of the words is, indeed, usually a, or even *the*, leading incident in the performance of the act (of betting or what not), the performance of which is also the object of the utterance, but it is far from being usually, even if it is ever, the *sole* thing necessary if the act is to be deemed to have been performed. Speaking generally, it is always necessary that the *circumstances* in which the words are uttered should be in some way, or ways, *appropriate*" (8). When he advances this argument again at the end of Lecture IV, Austin stresses that such an approach to language amounts to a critical transformation in its study: "In conclusion, we see that in order to explain what can go wrong with statements we cannot just concentrate on the proposition involved (whatever that is) as has been done traditionally. We must consider the total situation in which the utterance is issued—the total speech-act—if we are to see the parallel between statements and performative utterances, and how each can go wrong. So the total speech act in the total speech situation is emerging from logic piecemeal as important" (52). Austin argues that, instead of utilizing scientific principles foreign to a speech act in order to understand the nature of language, one can best apprehend the linguistic function of statements by scrutinizing their relative success or failure in specific circumstances. In his estimation, such a change signifies nothing less than "a revolution in philosophy" (3).

Despite his announcement of this methodological revolution, Austin nevertheless relies on a fundamental affinity between speech, consciousness, and context. His account of the performative embraces traditional forms of presence. The perfomative fulfills an action insofar as it carries out the intentions of a speaking subject. Speech, in Austin's analysis, is the transparent medium in which the intentions of a speaker are enacted immediately, in his or her presence. Austin admittedly stipulates that the performative should not refer to an ideal or original content; but Derrida nonetheless argues that Austin maintains a transparency between consciousness, meaning, and speech. "Thereby," he writes, "performative communication once more becomes the communication of an intentional meaning, even if this meaning has no referent in the form of a prior or exterior thing or state of things" (1982, 322). The spatial and temporal transparency of intention to meaning, and of speech to action, presupposes that the performative expresses a form of content prior to the order of language.

The ground of such presence is even reflected in the ideal teleology with which Austin judges the success of a performative. A successful performative realizes its telos in the enactment of the speaker's intentions; a performative fails and its meaning is compromised if the connection between intention and action is somehow disrupted. Derrida explains how the totality of context as such secures the primacy of intention: "Through the values of 'conventionality,' 'correctness,' and 'completeness' that intervene in the definition, we necessarily again find those of an exhaustively definable context, of a free consciousness present for the totality of the operation, of an absolutely full meaning that is master of itself: the teleological jurisdiction of a total field whose *intention* remains the organizing center" (1982, 323). A performative, in other words, is semantically or communicatively successful only if it performs its *intended* action. This intention is predicated on the existence, prior to the order of language, of "an absolutely full meaning that is master of itself," which originates in reason alone. Consequently, the fulfillment of a performative relies upon a transparency between consciousness, speech, and action. The spatial and temporal context of such an utterance is unified completely in the sense that its outcome is dictated by the intentions of the speaker. The meaning of a performative utterance, therefore, is reliably grounded in a form of presence—intention—exterior to language.

Despite their efforts to relinquish patently metaphysical approaches to language, both Saussure and Austin's projects ultimately recoil upon traditional assumptions about the ideal nature of speech. Until now, my treatment of this recoil has merely implied the existence of similar issues concerning the affinities between rhetoric and traditional notions of speech. In what follows, I employ the foregoing interrogations of speech in its ideal and original form as a means of questioning its commanding status in rhetorical theory and practice.

RHETORIC IN THE ACTIVE VOICE

Neither Saussure nor Austin dealt with the topic of rhetoric in their respective treatises. Both thinkers, however, relied on assumptions about language, speech, and the pragmatic functions of discourse equally valued in rhetorical studies, whether in its classical or modern incarnations. Austin's notion of the performative in particular suggests the problematic entailments of defining rhetoric as a strictly practical art, as an art of doing.

To date, rhetoricians have evinced little aspiration to systematically interrogate ideal notions of speech fundamental to the theory and practice of their discipline. I have reviewed Saussure and Austin's treatises on language and, more importantly, Derrida's critiques of their so-called logocentrism in order to facilitate my own critique of the ideal status accorded to the category of speech throughout rhetorical studies. More generally, the present and previous chapters together illustrate that modern rhetoricians profess seemingly axiomatic, and therefore value-neutral, definitions of rhetoric as a species of representation only by ignoring the complex conceptual history of representation itself, including the occasionally regrettable values and interests it has served.

Since its disciplinary codification in the Greek and Roman classical periods, rhetoric has been defined by a spatial and temporal logic much like that reflected in Saussure and Austin's inquiries. Similar to Saussure's emphasis of the synchronic study of language, or Austin's emphasis of the immediate context of a performative utterance, the discipline of rhetoric traditionally has valued the place and time of the oratorical performance as the ideal manifestation of rhetorical activity. Aristotle defined rhetoric as "an ability, in each [particular] case, to see the available means of persuasion" (*On Rhetoric,* 1.2.1). By this logic, one's skill in rhetoric amounted to an ability to recognize and perform whatever appeals would prove most persuasive in a specific moment and forum. Such skill required sensitivity to both *kairos* and *phronēsis,* to the prudential moment for judgment or action.

At the other end of the rhetorical tradition, Lloyd Bitzer's (1968) notion of the rhetorical situation reflected Aristotle's continuing influence on the field. Bitzer's now-canonical treatment of the topic attempted to discern the principles with which one could distinguish truly rhetorical situations from other types of social situations. The principle of urgency is especially pivotal in Bitzer's theory; one's rhetorical response to an exigence is more likely to be successful if offered without imprudent delay. Although Bitzer did not equate rhetoric explicitly with traditional oratory, his model, because of its debt to an Aristotelian conception of rhetorical practice, is most ideally realized in oratorical performances, in a spatially and temporally unified rhetorical situation (Biesecker 1989).

Whether in its classical or modern forms, rhetoric inevitably has been characterized by appeals to its situated nature, by a presumption of spatiotemporal unity and singularity.

The spatiotemporal unity and singularity featured in rhetorical theory and practice lends priority to speech. Even in recognizing the persistence of a rhetorical act in subsequent textual or electronic forms, rhetoricians habitually describe such forms as mere approximations of, or even derivations from, an original rhetorical event. Myriad collections of public address or rhetorical criticism presuppose that a rhetorical act must be evaluated in two forms: first, as an address spoken before an audience and, second, as printed, audio, or visual copies of the original performance (for example, Reid 1995, 6–7). In its ideal and original incarnation, rhetoric refers to a speaker's efforts to persuade an audience in a common time and place. Based on this definition, an oration's subsequent effects achieved in textual and electronic form, at a later time and in different forums, are somehow less authentically rhetorical than whatever effects it first produced. Granted, many rhetoricians undeniably argue for the valuation of alternate rhetorical forms and functions. Yet the dominant, classical terminology retained by the field presupposes that one may regard other media as rhetorical only if one can characterize it as purposeful communication between rhetors and audiences. Despite the fact that modern rhetoricians now regard communication between writers and readers as equally rhetorical as that between speakers and listeners, one can draw such a parallel only by expanding the logic of oral communication to account for textual discourse. Rhetorical accounts of images, music, bodily performances, architecture, even silence, rely on further expansion of the traditional model of public address to classify their objects of study as rhetorical. Efforts to transcend oral address as a privileged form of rhetoric thus implement interpretive paradigms and critical vocabularies that preserve the primary value of oral communication.

Hence, the classical model of rhetoric as public address has never been supplanted, only supplemented. A Platonic logic of representational copies based on original forms implicitly suffuses basic assumptions about the nature of rhetoric. Modern rhetoricians customarily disregard Plato's identification of the Socratic philosopher as the ideal rhetorician, dismissing it as an intellectually misguided and exceedingly conservative view of rhetorical practice. Yet the fundamentally unquestioned model of public address in modern rhetorical studies reflects Plato's association of speech with ideal knowledge in the *Phaedrus*. Following the dialogue's parable about the invention of writing, Socrates and Phaedrus eventually agree that writing is permissible if governed by "no dead discourse, but the living speech" (276a)—that is, if one has written a discourse "with a knowledge of the truth . . . and can demonstrate the inferiority of his writings out of his own mouth" (278c). As in Nietzsche's analysis, the denial of writing's value as an independent, tangible form of language enhances the ideal and original value of transcendent knowledge and truth. As in modern public address, furthermore, a supposedly authentic form of rhetoric governs the value of all other forms.

Most significantly, Plato endows speech and writing with these asymmetrical values in order to enshrine a superior form of human being. Socrates reasons, with tongue in cheek, that the "man" who uses speech and writing in the prescribed manner should not be called "wise" because that "epithet is proper only to a god. A name that would fit him better, and have more seemliness, would be 'lover of wisdom' " (278d), meaning (according to the very etymology of the term) a philosopher. One's use of speech therefore represents the quality of one's human virtue. According to Plato, Socrates' preeminence in the use of dialectic proved his moral standing. The title character of Plato's *Phaedo,* in recalling Socrates' death, laments "the end of our comrade, who was, we may fairly say, of all those whom we knew in our time, the bravest and also the wisest and most upright man" (118a). The philosopher represents the apogee of human virtue, endowed with slightly less wisdom than God, because "he" can express ideal truths and knowledge transparently in speech. In Nietzsche's terms, identifying the expression of ideal truth as the objective of language implies a moral evaluation of the one who uses it.

Plato's evaluation of speech and writing, of truth and human being, is integral to his account of rhetorical instruction. One of the interlocutors' central preoccupations in the *Phaedrus* is "by what means and from what source can one attain the art of the true rhetorician, the real master of persuasion" (269c–d). While giving his first speech on love, Socrates covers his head in order to avoid "breaking down for shame" (237a) because the speech is an imitation of Lysias's written discourse and thus severs the transparent bonds of truth that should join the speaker with his or her speech. Socrates offers his second oration "no longer veiling my head for shame, but uncovered" (243b) because he finally speaks on the basis of truth. In terms of the *Phaedrus's* underlying logic, one cannot acquire knowledge of rhetoric through written instruction because knowledge or wisdom cannot be passed on in that form. This belief likely motivates Socrates' pithy rebuke of "books on rhetoric" for aggrandizing the mere "niceties of the art" (266d) and perhaps explains, by implication, Aristotle's asides in his own instruction on rhetoric concerning "other writers" presumably unschooled in philosophy (*On Rhetoric,* 1.1.11). Only a philosopher can disseminate knowledge and truth, and only through dialectic (an oral *techné*).

Consequently, the superior value afforded to speech throughout the Western tradition, and its persistent association with truth, transparency, and unvarnished wisdom, preserves an intellectually conservative and rigidly moral interpretation of pedagogy, communication, and civic conduct. In Plato's philosophy, one can only acquire sound knowledge of rhetoric by literally becoming an idealistically privileged kind of human being: the philosopher. In the introduction to this book, I showed how Plato's insistence that one's speech must represent truth and virtue differed more in degree than in kind from the sophists' typical endorsement of those same standards. Although rhetorical education before and after Plato did not consistently identify the philosopher as an ideal rhetor, the values and ideals associated with that figure, particularly the philosopher's reverence for wise and virtuous speech, nonetheless retained a privileged status throughout the majority of the rhetorical tradition. Aristotle's overwhelmingly influential teachings on rhetoric preserve the spirit of Plato's directive that dialectic must govern one's use of rhetoric. Despite the fact that he initially defines rhetoric as "an *antistrophos* to dialectic" (*On Rhetoric,* 1.1.1), thereby suggesting that the two arts enjoy an equal status, dialectical inquiry in Aristotle's system is always preliminary to, and therefore determinative of, rhetorical practice. Aristotle's later remark that "rhetoric is a certain kind of offshoot *[paraphues]* of dialectic" (1.2.7) better expresses the unequal values with which he endows the two arts. Above all, his claim that "character is almost, so to speak, the controlling factor in persuasion" (1.2.4) resonates with Plato's conviction that virtuous rhetorical practice follows from the virtuous character of the dialectician. Cicero's more colloquial, yet equally influential, premise that sound rhetorical practice requires *sapientia* as well as *eloquentia* (*De Inventione,* 1.1.1) permanently crystallized classical assumptions about the ideal nature of speech, wisdom, and human virtue into central features of rhetorical theory and practice.

Despite the apparent diversity and sophistication of modern rhetorical studies, oral address, whether implicitly or explicitly, remains the ideal of rhetoric. Even if rhetoricians do not intentionally promote Socratic notions of truth, wisdom, or virtue as the leading standards of rhetorical theory and practice, they preserve a fundamentally Platonic reduction of rhetoric to the representation of essential truth or meaning by preserving the ideal and original value of oral address. The primary sense and value assigned to speech throughout the history of rhetoric reflects the same metaphysical values that Saussure tacitly endorsed in his emphasis of *parole.* Hugh Blair's declaration that "[s]peech is the great instrument by which man becomes beneficial to man" ([1819] 1993, 9) synthesizes the rhetorical tradition's reverence for *parole* with its celebration of moral virtue: one personifies the ideals of humanity when one applies the ideal medium of human expression to unassailable reason. As I have demonstrated, speech is an especially valued form of communication in the Western tradition because it appears to represent phenomena most transparently and immediately, in their objective presence. In so doing, speech maintains the most fundamental metaphysical opposition:

that between sensible and intelligible phenomena. Wherever speech is endowed with an ideal status, a speaker embodies (represents) the defining ideal of human being: the ability of such a subject to realize its own essential truth by knowing and speaking of truth as such. For this reason, the unity between speech and transcendental presence has, until now, comprised the very essence of rhetoric.

Additionally, Austin's study unwittingly demonstrates that one cannot retain the traditional sense and value of speech without giving priority to the category of intention. The category of intention governs the discipline of rhetoric much as it governed Austin's account of performative utterances. In either case, language performs an action ideally realized in speech. Speech allegedly establishes a transparency between the consciousness of speaker and listener. In this ephemeral space of communication, the meaning conveyed between individuals exists in a state of essential identity, undiluted by the properties of language. Defined as the performance of an action, communication hinges on the transparent expression of a speaker's intended meaning.

The practices by which rhetoric has been defined—overwhelmingly as persuasion or argumentation—reflect its original basis in these metaphysical assumptions about speech, communication, and meaning. The goal of persuading or arguing is inexplicable without some notion of persuasive or argumentative intent. Perfect conformity with one's intentions is seldom, if ever, achieved in rhetorical practice; yet it remains the ideal possibility upon which notions of persuasion or argumentation are predicated. The more one's listeners agree with the logic of one's appeals, the more they have been persuaded. Because of the equivalence between intention and persuasion or argumentation, rhetorical criticism invariably evaluates either the immediate or delayed outcome of a rhetorical act in relation to the critic's estimation of its intended effects. In 1925, Herbert Wichelns's (1993) assertion that rhetorical criticism must measure the effects of a discourse rather than its literary qualities, regarded as a crucial innovation by contemporary rhetorical scholars, oriented the modern study of rhetoric according to the success or failure of persuasive intent. By this logic, delayed rhetorical effects are essentially compensatory, typically falling outside the purview of the rhetor's persuasive, and seemingly transparent, intentions. Whether one defines it as persuasion or argumentation, rhetoric functions essentially as an extension of subjective intentions, which, in turn, depend upon the notion of a concept or meaning independent of language.

The extent of these remarks can be reduced to the observation that the active voice dominates conceptions of rhetoric even in the present day. The categories of persuasion or argumentation suggest the activity of a subject upon his or her listeners, of objects that receive the intended action of a subject. The exclusive value of speech in the rhetorical tradition presupposes that such processes are organized by the supposedly inherent reason, virtue, and identity of a speaking subject whose speech represents forms of presence exterior to the order of language.

In order to counter traditional conceptions of rhetoric, some have proposed an inverse logic in which rhetorical phenomena reflect ideological structures that determine the reason, virtue, or identity of the speaking subject (or of any meaning at all, for that matter). Early in this chapter, however, I used Nietzsche's essay on moral definitions of truth and lying to demonstrate that simply reversing the traditional values accorded to truth and language nonetheless preserves a conception of rhetoric predicated on the active voice. Following such a reversal, rhetoric assumes the role of a transparent medium that produces identities and differences, truths and lies, as manifestations of a transcendent ideological order. In such a formulation, all semantic or symbolic differences inevitably are incorporated into a transhistorical unity of absolute meaning. As either instrument or ideology, rhetoric is defined by the representation of ideal and original presence.

Representational accounts of rhetoric thus depend on the accepted priority of the active voice in our heritage. In order to develop an account of rhetoric beyond representation, I propose to dissociate rhetoric from its conventional affinity with speech and intention. To be clear, I do not argue that one should disregard the significance of speech and intention in rhetorical processes. But I do insist that they must be given a different sense and value in order to formulate a conception of rhetoric no longer governed by a transcendental subject, namely, human being as such. Neither do I offer an opposing ideal to that of oral address. Instead of dispensing with this ideal, I argue for the benefits of assigning it an alternate sense and value. Doing so obligates one to devise a conception of rhetoric in the middle voice—a conception of rhetoric defined neither by the supposed truth of character nor that of custom (neither by an essential nor social self) but by the self-enactment of discourse in which such apparently antithetical categories acquire sense and value as constitutive features of subjectivity. An attunement to such enactment, instead of representing an essential identity, lends priority to discursive difference, to the nonrepresentational elements of representation traditionally obscured by appeals to the transparency of speech, reason, or intention. Throughout Part 2, I develop conceptual and methodological principles with which we may finally begin to listen to rhetoric in this voice.

Part II

Being Otherwise

Chapter 3

Rhetoric in the Middle Voice

Plato's *Gorgias* and *Phaedrus* typically are linked in disciplinary narratives concerning the classical Greek origins of rhetoric. Such narratives couple these dialogues in order to present an ostensibly complete portrait of Plato's thinking on rhetoric and his related concerns over truth, knowledge, and virtue. Plato's scathing critique of sophistry in his *Gorgias* is balanced by his veneration for philosophical rhetoric in the *Phaedrus*. When read together, these dialogues conveniently exhibit Plato's commitment to preserving speech, truth, and human being in their ideal forms.

The preservation of these ideal forms assigns central philosophical and rhetorical significance to the active voice, to the priority of intention as the governing principle of speech. Disputation throughout the *Gorgias* predominantly concerns confusions over the meaning of rhetoric, speech, persuasion, knowledge, and virtue. The *Phaedrus* systematically dispels such confusions by asserting the priority of reason over meaning through the practice of dialectic, through speech guided by intuition. In the end, Plato bases his admonitions for responsible rhetorical practice on a hierarchy of human virtue in which one's probity is measured by one's ability to speak in conformity with dialectical reason.

In this chapter, I build upon my previous critiques of representation, speech, and the active voice in order to define rhetoric in a nonrepresentational sense. I begin with a reading of Plato's *Sophist* that uses the very transcendental categories of Platonic philosophy to subvert his reduction of rhetoric to principles of intention, truth, and essential virtue. Such a reading discloses the inchoate forms of persuasion (evident throughout classical literature and philosophy) that Plato suppressed in formulating his own conception of rhetoric, the influence of which remains constant throughout the rhetorical tradition. Thereafter, I examine a modern analogue to those inchoate forms of persuasion in order to define rhetoric in the middle voice. Such maneuvers concomitantly enable me to underscore the implications of rhetoric beyond representation concerning the philosophical, political, and moral prejudices elemental to the history of rhetorical theory and practice.

RHETORIC MADE STRANGER

The considerable significance of Plato's *Sophist* to rhetorical theory and practice generally has been overlooked in rhetorical studies because of the common pedagogical juxtaposition of his *Gorgias* and *Phaedrus*. The *Sophist* exhibits compelling traces of Plato's efforts to repress the middle voice of rhetoric in order to preserve the categories of speech, truth, and human being in their putatively ideal and original forms. Deconstructing the means by which Plato represses this middle voice, instead of offering a critique based on opposite ontological principles, allows one to annul the moral conceptions of truth and human being that pervade assumptions about the nature of rhetoric even today.

The *Sophist* commences with the Stranger and Theaetetus's agreement to "begin by studying the Sophist and try to bring his nature to light in a clear formula" (218b–c). "Judging the Sophist to be a very troublesome sort of creature to hunt down," the Stranger muses, "let us first practice the method of tracking him down on some easier quarry" (218d). The interlocutors decide to pursue the Sophist by deliberating on the kind of art he produces and the kinds of practices in which he engages. They are preoccupied initially with the nature and origin of sophistic knowledge. The Stranger describes the Sophist's profession as "a merchandise of the soul which is concerned with speech and the knowledge of virtue" (224c–d). The Sophist is a "trader in virtue" (224c); he "sells the knowledge of virtue" (224e) to those who have not learned how to intuit that knowledge themselves. More disturbing still, he barters the knowledge of virtue without having acquired such knowledge himself. The interlocutors wonder whether a "man who has no knowledge," whose speech does not reflect an essential truth or meaning, is capable of refuting "one who does know" (233a). If so, then a mere semblance of knowledge would not simply contradict, but insidiously supplant, dialectical knowledge (knowledge based on categorical meaning, truth, or presence).

In this manner, sophists apparently cause even virtuous individuals to mistake shows of virtue for actual wisdom. The Sophist's unique skill, the Stranger claims, belongs under the rubric of "imitation." By "skill in the region of discourse," sophists "impose upon the young who are still far removed from the reality of things, by means of words that cheat the ear, exhibiting images of all things in a shadow play of discourse, so as to make them believe that they are hearing the truth and that the speaker is in all matters the wisest of men" (234c). Because of its capacity to furtively produce a convincing appearance of wisdom, sophistic skill in speech, "in the region of discourse," threatens to usurp dialectical knowledge.

The notion that "a shadow play of discourse" might produce conviction based on mere imitation raises a related anxiety over the category of being. In Plato's philosophy, knowledge is derived from one's intuitive apprehension of ideal and original forms, of transcendent being. The Stranger and Theaetetus wonder whether, in the Sophist's discourse, one can separate the categories of being and appearance, of being and nonbeing, if that discourse functions without knowledge of ideal and original forms, regardless of its convincing appearance to the contrary. They wonder whether "what is not, in some respect has being, and conversely that what is, in a way is not" (241d). If the Sophist produces the semblance of truth, knowledge, or virtue through speech, then does the falsity of such referents, the fact that they *appear to be* when they really *are not,* give to certain forms of nonbeing a being all their own? To answer in the affirmative is to admit that what *is,* ideally and originally, also *is not.* In such a formulation, Deleuze observes, the category of the negative loses its traditional capacity to define the positive value of being (1994, 63). If the distinction between being and nonbeing is blurred, the category of being relinquishes its ideal and original value. Being, therefore, would no longer denote pure and uniform presence or meaning.

The Sophist thus represents a prodigious threat to the dialectician's ability to distinguish between sensible and intelligible phenomena. For this reason, the Stranger seeks to define being once again by its categorical "unity" and "wholeness": "Whenever a thing comes into being, at that moment it has come to be as a whole; accordingly, if you do not reckon unity or wholeness among real things, you have no right to speak of either being or coming-into-being as having any existence" (245d). Phenomena, that is, cannot both exist and not exist. Plato's principal standards for defining and classifying beings are unity or wholeness, essential presence or identity. Based on these standards, being and nonbeing or existence and nonexistence are mutually exclusive categories.

But the source of this confusion between being and nonbeing remains. The Sophist's skill in imitation continues to produce the semblance of knowledge without knowledge, the mere illusion of wisdom based on ideal and original meaning or presence. Confusions over the true and false forms of knowledge and being will persist until the Sophist's authentic nature is defined. The Stranger and Theaetetus presume that one can judge the veracity of a speaker's discourse only by apprehending the integrity of his or her reason and virtue. They consequently realize that, in order to define the Sophist's cryptic art, they must measure it against its established opposite, the method of the philosopher. "Or—good gracious, Theaetetus," the Stranger exclaims, "have we stumbled unawares upon the free man's knowledge and, in seeking for the Sophist, chanced to find the philosopher first?" (253c). In the Stranger's description, the "free man's knowledge" consists of the following practices: "Dividing according to kinds, not taking the same form for a different one or a different one for the same—is not that the business of the science of dialectic?" (253d). Dialectic is an art of division and classification. By definition, it is a "science" designed to parse the true from the false, being from nonbeing. The "mastery of dialectic," furthermore, belongs solely to "the pure and rightful lover of wisdom" (253e). Only the philosopher, an individual endowed with laudable wisdom and virtue, can master dialectical inquiry. Besides allowing one to discriminate between sensible and intelligible phenomena, the practice of dialectic allows one to distinguish between philosophers and sophists, between superior and inferior human beings. The question of the Sophist's true nature is a fundamentally moral question.

Whereas the art of the Sophist threatened to collapse the distinction between knowledge and ignorance, or being and nonbeing, the art of the philosopher preserves the integrity of those distinctions. It does so by revealing the imitative qualities of sophistic discourse so unapparent to others. Through the art of dialectic, the philosopher preserves the fundamental separation of sensible and intelligible phenomena. The Stranger and Theaetetus agree that dialectic is a divine art because it is based on knowledge of ideal and original forms; conversely, the Sophist's art is all too human, and therefore unwise, because it is based on semblances. The Sophist's art must be negated because it represents the most fallible elements of human nature. The philosopher's art must be affirmed because it represents the ideal virtues thereof.

The truth of the Sophist finally is disclosed through dialectical reason. Having defined and classified the many forms of imitation, the Stranger identifies the art and nature of the Sophist as follows: "The art of contradiction making, descended from an insincere kind of conceited mimicry, of the semblance-making breed, derived from image making, distinguished as a portion, not divine but human, of production, that presents a shadow play of words—such are the blood and lineage which can, with perfect truth, be assigned to the authentic Sophist" (268c-d). In revealing the truth of the Sophist's "mimicry," "image-making," and "shadow play of words," the dialectician restores the category of truth to its ideal and original status by providing an account of the sophistic techniques that threatened to undermine it. In so doing, the philosopher isolates the truth of human virtue by contrasting it to the duplicity of the Sophist. "[T]he philosopher," in Derrida's words, "is the man of man" because the philosopher's speech reflects the inherent identity of meaning or being: "Whoever does not subject equivocalness to this law is already a bit less than a man: a sophist, who in sum says nothing, nothing that can be reduced to a meaning" (1982, 248).

Although Theaetetus and the Stranger never use the term, one may interpret Plato's *Sophist* as an effort to neutralize the perceived discursive excesses
or distortions of rhetoric. Hence Theaetetus and the Stranger's recurrent
description of their inquiry as a hunt, as an attempt to ensnare the truth of
their prey, the Sophist, so as to tame it.[1] Plato's motivations for ensuring the
subservience of rhetoric to dialectic are particularly evident in this dialogue.
The practice of rhetoric must be governed by dialectic because the deceptive,
yet inexplicably convincing, tendencies of rhetoric obfuscate categorical distinctions between truth and error, good and evil, identity and difference, or
being and nonbeing. Despite its semblance of erudition, rhetoric produces
a fundamentally monstrous representation of reality in which "what is not,
in some respect has being, and conversely . . . what is, in a way is not"
(*Sophist,* 241d). For this reason, Deleuze describes the Sophist as "the one
who raises everything to the level of simulacra and maintains them in that
state" (1994, 68). In such a state, ideal and original forms of truth or being
relinquish their privileged status. Rhetoric, the characteristic method of the
Sophist, thus threatens to topple the very distinctions upon which basic
metaphysical ontology is predicated.

Faced with this threat, Plato expropriates rhetoric into the science of
dialectic. Deleuze calls Plato's encounter with the simulacrum of rhetoric at
the end of the *Sophist* "the most extraordinary adventure of Platonism": "[A]s
a consequence of searching in the direction of the simulacrum and of leaning
over its abyss, Plato discovers, in the flash of an instant, that the simulacrum
is not simply a false copy, but that it places in question the very notations
of copy and model" (1990, 256). Plato's swift sublimation of rhetoric to
dialectic preserves the inviolable distinction between the sensible and intelligible domains, between a transcendental truth or meaning and its illusory
representations. By preserving the distinction between these domains, Plato
also preserves his moral hierarchy of human being. Such a hierarchy is reflected
in Plato's contrast between the reasoned and transparent speech of the philosopher, the personification of virtue par excellence, and the equivocal or
polysemous speech of the Sophist, the consummate personification of vice.

Plato absorbs rhetoric into dialectic in order to negate the middle voice
of rhetoric. In the speech of the Sophist, things come into being as an
enactment of discourse, not as a representation of transcendental being;
meanings are enacted out of language itself, not as the reflection of an ideal
and original referent. Sophistic discourse produces meanings or representations that cannot be measured against dialectical reason, against an intuitive
knowledge of phenomena fully present and intelligible prior to the order of
discourse. Rhetoric in this form is semantically monstrous because it cannot
be governed by intention. Plato must suppress the middle voice of rhetoric
in order to retain the discrete positive and negative values of intelligible and
sensible phenomena, of truth and error or virtue and vice.

Plato's suppression of rhetoric in the middle voice, however, only draws attention to what he intends to conceal. It offers an opportunity from within cardinal metaphysical categories to assign those categories an alternate sense and value. Deleuze proposes an ironic reading of the *Sophist* that parodies Plato's philosophy from within his own text. Referring to the dialogue's opening passages, in which Socrates relinquishes his usual role as the principal dialectician to the Stranger, Deleuze observes: "Socrates distinguishes himself from the Sophist, but the Sophist does not distinguish himself from Socrates, placing the legitimacy of such a distinction in question. Twilight of the *icônes*" (1994, 128). Instead of Socrates, the unnamed Stranger guides the dialogue toward the truth of the Sophist's deceitful nature. In so credibly fulfilling the Socratic role, the Stranger produces a convincing simulacrum of Socratic virtue and inquiry. "The Eleatic Stranger," Deleuze comments, "gives a definition of the sophist such that he can no longer be distinguished from Socrates himself: the ironic imitator who proceeds by brief arguments (questions and problems)" (68). Irony of ironies: the Stranger is the very Sophist feared by philosophers such as Socrates because he commands the souls of virtuous men, *even Socrates himself*, with a "shadow play of words" instead of knowledge or virtue.

The Stranger, it appears, has produced a semblance of Socratic knowledge and virtue that cannot be distinguished from that of Socrates himself. In doing so, the Stranger's speech not only blurs distinctions between ideal forms and their representations, between knowledge or truth and their counterfeits; more profoundly, it inverts the Platonic hierarchy of human being governed by Socrates himself. The ambiguous, and therefore ironic, status of the Stranger suggests that the dialectician's exemplary intuition and moral sense may be a product of sophistry rather than the philosopher's learned refinement of human virtue. Despite Plato's efforts to contain its excess or monstrosity, the allegedly lowest form of human being may engender the very pinnacle of humanity in Plato's philosophy. Deleuze's reading does not simply oppose the lowest form of humanity to the highest, the Sophist to the philosopher, or the false copy to the ideal form, but disrupts the dialectical logic of opposites altogether. In this manner, he posits that Plato himself was "the first to overturn Platonism, or at least to show the direction such an overturning should take" (1994, 68).[2] The Stranger's speech, no matter how dialectical it may appear, reveals that Plato's supposedly categorical hierarchy of being depends for its alleged truth and transparency on the rhetorical skills of the one who professes it, whether it be the Stranger or Socrates himself.

Beings no longer hold categorically superior or inferior value in Deleuze's interpretation of the *Sophist*. One can no longer measure them according to their identity with, or representation of, ideal and original forms of being, truth, or virtue. Deleuze invalidates traditional appeals to such ideal and original forms based on principles of identity or representation. Instead, he insists that, after the Platonic hierarchies of being have been dismantled, only simulacra remain—only the unending differences that continually engender and transform the sense and value of beings without origin or telos, without model or copy, without positive and negative value. By undermining the priority of identity in this way, one begins to establish a concept of difference *in itself.* Affirmation of such a concept emphasizes the discursive creation and mutation of truths and values instead of merely taking for granted the ideal and original truth of Platonic ideals. It also enables recognition of multiple modes of being and valuation of their inevitable mutation rather than an unexamined insistence upon the superior and unvarnished value of privileged forms of being.

In Plato's own dialogue, the speech of the Sophist precipitates this overturning of Platonism. The Stranger may be Socrates' faithful copy or his deceitful double. The meaning of his speech therefore functions independent of a discernable intention, of a knowable source of reason or virtue. He disseminates meaning without assurance of meaning at all. His rhetoric invokes the grammar of the active voice in order to disrupt it. Meaning is allowed to multiply and divide of its own accord. Consequently, the Stranger's discourse does not reflect, but actually engenders, the sense and value of the very category of being. At every turn, the active voice of the Stranger's rhetoric is undermined by rhetoric in the middle voice.

In the most general terms, rhetoric in the middle voice connotes the formation and dissemination of meanings prior to individual intentions or utterances. It functions as discursive simulacra, overturning the hierarchies of positive and negative value expressed in dialectical speech so as to engender new values no longer based on transcendent ideals. Rhetoric in the middle voice connotes the capacity of discourse itself to engender and transform meanings and values, to lend priority to discursive difference, rather than to maintain an identity between speech governed by intention and the transcendent meanings or values it represents. Rhetoric in the middle voice cannot be suppressed or domesticated by appeals to essential truth, knowledge, virtue, or being. The striking resemblance between Socrates' speech and that of the Stranger confirms that the apparently ideal and original nature of such categories, and the active voice that speaks of them, is merely one of the discursive modes through which rhetoric in the middle voice engenders contingent meanings and values irreducible to subjective intentions.

Plato had to suppress rhetoric in the middle voice in order to preserve the integrity of his ontology. Meaning or truth could attain their ideal and original status only if they were said to exist prior to the order of discourse, in a purely intelligible or transcendental state. Meaning or truth had to originate in reason, not speech. Only through the transparency of speech could one accurately represent such transcendent phenomena. In Plato's philosophy, dialectic allowed one to distinguish truth from error, good from evil, identity from difference, and being from nonbeing. In turn, the moral obligation to express categorical meaning or truth represented the ideal and original truth of human being—a being that realized its own essential truth, that is, in naming the transcendent origin and meaning of its existence. The discipline of rhetoric has yet to renounce these Platonic values.

The foregoing interpretation of Plato's *Sophist* represents a necessary first step in doing so. The dialogue demonstrates that an alternate conception of meaning, being, and discourse has been suppressed by basic Western ontology. How could one conceive of such categories independent of Platonic philosophy? What earlier senses of the affinities between meaning, being, and speech does Plato suppress when he defines rhetoric as we know it, based on principles of representation, identity, and the active voice? In order to address these questions, I now turn to a provocative account of the very concept of persuasion as it operated in Greek culture prior to the codification of rhetoric during the fifth and fourth centuries B.C.E. This account will enable me to tell a different story about the origins and nature of rhetoric than the one conventionally narrated by way of Plato's *Gorgias* and *Phaedrus*. As a result, it will also enable me to redefine contemporary rhetorical theory and practice in order to accommodate the middle voice of rhetoric.

THE MIDDLE VOICE OF PERSUASION

Before *rhêtorikê*, terms such as *logos* and *peithō* (speech and persuasion) were used to describe the activities of public address in classical Greece. In chapter 2, I noted the connotation of showing, of making visible or present, associated with logos. Such notions of illuminating explain the classical association of logos with truth as *alētheia,* as unconcealment. In contrast, the meaning of *peithō* was more obscure (at least from a contemporary perspective). Throughout its history in ancient and classical Greek culture, persuasion was viewed as a process that one could neither master nor completely resist. Its effects could not be subjected to reason; they were unpredictable, potentially beneficial or harmful (if not both). The synthesis of *logos, peithō,* and *rhetor* into *rhêtorikê* in Plato's time suggests that the formulation of rhetoric as we know it represented an effort to transform the middle voice of persuasion into the active voice of dialectical speech.[3] One could fix meaning, classify it in discrete categories, and represent it according to a principle of identity between speech and idea when one subjected meaning to categorical reason or intention. Thus, instead of amounting to a wholesale deviation from the history of rhetoric, my effort to analyze rhetoric in the middle voice, to devise a conception of rhetoric beyond representation, is warranted by the profound significance of a hitherto neglected dimension of early public address.

The manifold intellectual and cultural significance of persuasion to early Greek history is best illustrated by Greek drama and Homeric poetry. In his

assiduous reading of Homer's *Iliad,* Michael Naas cites the conclusion of
Aeschylus's trilogy the *Orestes* as "[p]erhaps the most dramatic moment in
the 'history' of persuasion" (1995, 1). The goddess Athene acquits Orestes
in an Athenian court (*Eumenides*, 750–68). Her acquittal incites the vengeance of the Furies; the forces of violence and disorder subsequently threaten
the law and order of the polis (792–888). The wrath of the Furies is quelled
and civil order is restored only when Athene invokes Peitho, the goddess of
Persuasion (893–909). Where reason and law are opposed by vengeance and
disorder, an ambiguous and seemingly magical means of resolution is invoked to end the stalemate—"a mysterious third term that is properly neither overt, physical force nor reasoned, lawful judgment and compromise"
(Naas 1995, 2).

Prior to and during the fifth and fourth centuries, persuasion connoted
a multifaceted process traversing self and other, past and present, law and
transgression. This process was simultaneously formative of and irreducible
to either natural or human law. "At once rational and irrational, harmonious
and violent, this persuasion before the law takes part in the measured logic
of argumentation as well as in the excesses of bewitchment and seduction;
it can both serve rational discourse and undermine it, both serve the law and
threaten it" (Naas 1995, 4). For the Greeks, persuasion was as politically
necessary as it was ontologically ambiguous. Naas observes that persuasion,
as exemplified at the end of the *Oresteia,* prevents either reason or vengeance,
law or violence, from dominating civic order—indeed, prevents them from
instituting *an* order. The victory of one over the other would signal the end
of civic *agon,* of democratic practice. It would signal the end of politics itself,
for all political contests would be resolved. Persuasion therefore keeps these
forces in tension for the sake of robust and meaningful civic engagement.
"Without persuasion," Naas posits, "there would be no political space" (3).

To be clear, persuasion in this formulation referred to a *process* rather than
an intention or effect. Naas calls persuasion a *topos* in that it enacted the
formation and transformation of thought, speech, action, and intersubjective
relations. Thus, one could not define persuasion according to an objective
identity or essential content. One could not master persuasion because, as an
ambivalent third term, it did not refer to a noun, to a stable referent. "It is
as much good counsel and confidence as seduction and flattery, as much
masculine rhetoric as female beguilement, as much the turning-toward of
order and recollection as the turning-away of separation and forgetfulness"
(Naas 1995, 9–10). More precisely, then, persuasion originally referred to a
gerund instead of a noun, to the very process of *turning (tropos)*. It did not
refer to any one form of turning but to turning itself. Consequently, in order
to appreciate fully the *topos* of persuasion one must attend to its middle
voice. In an apt parallel to Derrida's notion of *différance* (1982, 1–27), Naas
observes that "turning will prove to be neither a word nor a concept, neither

simply active nor passive, neither a verb nor a noun, since it will be shown to disrupt the spontaneous identity or self-presence of both the object and the individual" (12). Persuasion could not be expressed in the activity of a subject upon an object nor did it culminate in a single, determinate effect. An individual did not persuade another individual. Rather, persuasion simply happened, neither actively nor passively but somewhere in the middle.

The *topos* of persuasion was hardly a topic of obscure scholarly debate. To the contrary, Naas argues, it held crucial intellectual and cultural currency in the fifth and fourth centuries: "From tragic drama to philosophical dialogue to lyric poetry, discourses and arguments about the nature of persuasion can be found just about everywhere. Praised here, condemned there, allied with subversion and rebellion in one place and with harmony and accord in another, persuasion is one of the most elusive and, yet, significant 'concepts' or 'activities' in classical Greek literature and philosophy" (8). The very concept of persuasion, therefore, incited vigorous and widespread debate over the nature of law, justice, and virtue. Plato's unremitting suspicion of persuasion likely reflects the fact that, as a ubiquitous public preoccupation, its power of fascination posed an intellectual and cultural obstacle to one of the guiding aspirations of early philosophy: namely, to dictate universal standards of moral and civic conduct.

Indeed, the middle voice of persuasion was inimical to this defining task of metaphysical inquiry. Plato's *Gorgias* commences with Socrates asking the title character "Who he is" (231, 447d), meaning how his person is defined by his craft. Because Gorgias is an acclaimed orator, this line of questioning leads to the interlocutors' disputations on the nature of persuasion. Socrates' questions presuppose that phenomena such as persuasion enjoy a fundamental essence or objective nature. None of Gorgias's answers satisfy Socrates because persuasion connotes a process rather than an outcome, a gerund instead of a noun.

Derrida describes the "What is . . . ?" question, so indispensable to Socrates' method, as the inaugural question of philosophy (1982, 1–68). The logic of the question presupposes that the truth or essence of a phenomenon exists prior to the order of discourse. This presupposition explains the metaphysical equation of being with continuous presence, with a complete and uniform truth or essence available exclusively to one's intuition. It also explains the metaphysical insistence on separate intelligible and sensible domains, on a fundamental division between subjective and objective spheres of existence. Assumptions of this kind authorize notions of truth, morality, and human nature common throughout the Western heritage. By this logic, asking "What is . . . ?" presupposes the ability of a subject to identify the objective truth of a phenomenon.[4] Being is thereby defined by a principle of identity between its objective (ideal and original) form and its subjective representations. Being supposedly has an essential meaning, an ideal and original form. In meta-physical ontology, being is the transcendental signified par excellence.

The middle voice of persuasion, however, defies the logic of the "What is . . . ?" question. Persuasion so conceived provides an account of thought, speech, and action that emphasizes processes or relations instead of subjects and objects, difference rather than identity, ambiguity instead of transparency, and enactment rather than representation. Such an account suggests a conception of being as an occurrence, not an essence; as an event without origin or telos; as a phenomenon without essential meaning—a phenomenon, therefore, that cannot be evaluated according to categorical notions of truth or moral rectitude. The history of classical Greek philosophy and culture shows that persuasion could accommodate the inaugural "What is . . . ?" question only when, as Naas observes, it was "idealized and restricted to the human subject or agent, such that any talk of 'persuading' objects or 'turning' minds will, from then on, be deemed 'merely metaphorical' " (10).

Metaphorically defined, persuasion no longer enacts thought, speech, or social relations out of its own occurrence. Instead, persuasion only occurs to the extent that a rhetor successfully communicates his or her command of ideas or objects, meaning or truth. Successful persuasion therefore amounts to a fusion of subjective intention and conceptual identity, to a correspondence between a rhetor's persuasive intent and an audience's acceptance of his or her intended meaning. Persuasion so defined makes the speaking subject an object of tacit moral evaluation: sound persuasion reflects moral intentions, whereas faulty persuasion reflects immoral intentions.

For those like Socrates and Plato, the notion of providing instruction in the arts of persuasion was at least somewhat counterintuitive. How could one purport to instruct students in the mastery of such a potentially unruly process, fundamentally resistant to reason and intention? Fifth and fourth century discourse on rhetoric is characterized by efforts to neutralize and domesticate persuasion, its master *topos*. I have already examined some of Plato's most conspicuous attempts to do so, as featured in his *Gorgias, Phaedrus,* and *Sophist*. In their own fashion, both Isocrates and Aristotle contributed to this purification of persuasion in order to identify a legitimate organizing principle for the study of rhetoric. As an academic discipline, rhetoric was conceived on the basis of categorical distinctions between reason and emotion, form and content, sensible and intelligible, subject and object. The foundational teachings of Isocrates, Plato, and Aristotle all insist that rhetorical practice must be based on sound analytical reflection. In Plato and Aristotle's texts especially, the use of dialectic, a method designed to define and classify phenomena based on a principle of essential identity, must precede rhetorical practice. "No longer thought in terms of a turning that precedes law or philosophy," Naas writes, "persuasion had become a tool or practice in the service of law and philosophy. Persuasion had thus become understood, localized, and seemingly mastered by philosophy, such that one could distinguish and separate good persuasion from bad" (5). Purified and redefined in this manner, persuasion allowed one to carry out the quintessential mission of metaphysical reflection: to define and classify phenomena according to their intrinsic identities and to provide a convincing logos of knowledge as such.

As Naas indicates, the standards of truth with which one evaluated the practice of persuasion in early metaphysical inquiry further facilitated a moral definition of the art. Rhetorical practice was evaluated by differentiating good persuasion from bad, moral from immoral appeals. Because persuasion became a matter of either virtuous or deceitful intention, of wisdom or ignorance, good persuasion reflected the rhetor's reason and virtue while bad persuasion represented the rhetor's ignorance and vice. Taken together, the reductions of *tropos* to *ethos,* of gerund to noun, of polysemous meaning to uniform content, of difference to identity, of turning to representation, meant that rhetoric (despite the fact that it was often derided as the opposite of philosophy) was institutionalized as the civic activity through which narrow metaphysical beliefs about truth, morality, and human nature became widely accepted moral, political, and cultural standards. Even today, when one defines rhetoric in an ostensibly neutral manner, as persuasion or argumentation, one unwittingly invokes a definition of the art consistent with the fifth- and fourth-century delimitation of persuasion to inflexible notions of human nature and moral truth.

Nevertheless, I do not argue that the middle voice of persuasion in classical Greek literature and philosophy encompassed a more original and authentic form of rhetoric. I do not advocate a return to a putatively ideal origin in order to dispel the exclusionary implications of rhetoric in its traditional, representational forms. Such a return would either negate or transcend the entire history of rhetorical theory and practice. Replacing the current ideal and origin of rhetoric with a supposedly more authentic ideal and origin would merely preserve the metaphysical notions of an essential truth and an authentic mode of communication in radically altered form. Replacing our dominant ontology of rhetoric with another ontology would preserve the assumption that one may intuit an objective order of things. Such an assumption would preserve belief in an ideal and original form of rhetoric while merely referring to it by a different name.

Returning to what one might call the prehistory of rhetoric in order to identify a more authentic ideal for contemporary rhetorical theory and practice is therefore untenable as a method of critiquing the dominant representational conceptions of rhetoric. Instead, I argue that consideration of the middle voice of persuasion demonstrates conclusively that rhetoric in its presumably natural form—as the representation of universal reason, intention, truth, or human being—is the work of a socially prejudiced and intellectually partisan set of interests. Consideration of this middle voice has proven that those who define rhetoric exclusively according to traditional standards of reason, transparent speech, and moral intention unwittingly align themselves with definitions of the art based on allegedly universal, but actually privileged and partial, notions of wisdom, communication, and moral conduct. Above all, the middle voice of persuasion reveals that rhetoric's supposed refinement and expression of a transcendent human nature initially was proclaimed in order to radically curtail, not universally enhance, the egalitarian potential of persuasive processes to human and civic endeavors. I invoke the classical middle voice of persuasion, therefore, in order to justify the premise that one can conceive of rhetoric in a manner irreducible to principles of representation, to speech in its ideal sense, or to a grammar of the active voice that preserves transcendent reason, intention, or subjectivity. Invoking this middle voice also indicates that a conception of rhetoric beyond representation would illumine the philosophical, political, and moral prejudices inherent in conventional, representational forms of rhetoric, including those that promote its apparent value to the project of liberal democracy.

Having identified this warrant for an account of rhetoric beyond representation, I do not propose to replace one set of prejudices with another. In what follows, my account of rhetoric in the middle voice is not intended to eliminate rhetoric in its active tense. My account of rhetoric beyond representation, in other words, is not intended to eliminate all affinities between rhetoric and representation. The elimination of such elements would also indicate an effort to transcend the history of rhetorical theory and practice in order to establish a new rhetorical ideal. Nevertheless, I question the very habit of formulating rhetorical theory and practice according to ideal or transcendent categories. Consequently, I do not oppose the nonrepresentational elements of rhetoric to its representational forms, fragmented meaning to the ideal transparency of speech, the middle voice of persuasion to its active grammar, or rhetorical being to being metaphysically defined. Rather, in identifying the nonrepresentational elements of rhetoric, forms of meaning irreducible to reason or intention, and subject positions engendered by discourse, I assign an unconventional sense and value to the categories of reason, speech, and being. My affirmation of rhetoric beyond representation, of rhetoric in the middle voice, recognizes that individuals think and speak according to principles of representation but denies the categories of representation, speech, and being their conventionally ideal sense and value. Identifying the middle voice of rhetoric thus invalidates the philosophical, political, and moral prejudices elemental to conventional definitions of rhetoric by accounting for the formation and transformation of truth, knowledge, morality, and subjectivity as enactments of discourse rather than as representations of transcendental subjects or ideals.

Because a return to the classical middle voice of persuasion is unfeasible, I turn in the following section to one of the most influential accounts of discourse in late-twentieth-century philosophy. Despite its manifold implications for the categories of representation, speech, and being, rhetoricians still have yet to confront the challenges that Foucault's definition of discourse poses to conventional rhetorical theory and practice. Consideration of such challenges, I argue, amounts to a necessary final step in my effort to identify the middle voice of rhetoric.

DISCOURSE, FORM, AND ETHOS

In "The Discourse on Language," his appendix to *The Archaeology of Knowledge,* Foucault muses, "Ever since the exclusion of the activity and commerce of the sophists, ever since their paradoxes were muzzled, more or less securely, it would seem that Western thought has seen to it that discourse be permitted as little room as possible between thought and words" (1972, 227). Earlier in this chapter, I revealed how the "paradoxes" of the sophists "were muzzled" in Plato's *Sophist.* Such founding gestures of "Western thought" dissipated the self-engendering region of discourse once located between "thought and words," between intuition and its transparent expression, between intention and its verbal realization. The muzzling of discourse at the inception of philosophy and rhetoric, Foucault suggests, amounted to a repression of discourse in its middle voice and a veneration of discourse in the active voice, of discourse *as* representation. As I have shown, this valuation of the active voice concomitantly established the ideals of a transcendental speaking subject, an objective referent, and transparent speech.

Foucault's musings in "The Discourse on Language" concerning what he calls the "profound logophobia"[5] of Western society (229) indicate that one can read his infamous methodological treatise as a scrupulous effort to apprehend the substance of discourse in itself, of discourse in its middle voice. The effect of this effort is to invalidate the longstanding authority of intention, meaning, or being over the production of discourse. Therefore, *The Archaeology of Knowledge* (originally published in 1969 but generally ignored by modern rhetoricians) offers an indispensable methodological template with which to identify the middle voice of rhetoric because it calls into question the same logic of the active voice used to repress persuasion in the middle voice and codify rhetoric into its accepted form.[6]

In chapter 1, I noted that the very differences between orders of discourse constitute the object of Foucault's inquiry in *The Order of Things.* Therein, he stresses the formative role of these differences in the production of discourse so as to undermine the priority traditionally given to essential continuity, identity, or presence in histories of ideas. Discursive differences, discontinuities, and transformations engender discursive orders instead of transcendental reason or meaning. Such differences constitute the nonrepresentational elements of discourse that engender forms of representation. By emphasizing these differences, Foucault cultivates the middle voice of discourse: discursive transformations are not intended effects of speech but merely occur in the formation of truth, knowledge, and speech. Simply put, discourse *occurs* as the conditions according to which truth, knowledge, and speech become possible.

The Archaeology of Knowledge represents Foucault's effort to elaborate his methodology in the wake of criticisms concerning his earlier characterization of discursive formations. Colloquially defined, discourse is the means by which a speaking subject expresses his or her intended ideas, by which he or she refers to objects beyond the order of language. Yet Foucault asserts that what we call objects of thought, knowledge, or speech are not antecedent to, but formed as a result of, discursive processes (1972, 45). If discourse is not governed by intentions or objective referents, however, one might reasonably conclude that it comprises a transcendent ground of meaning, a formal structure, which would thus reintroduce a form of essential continuity into histories of ideas. How can one conceive of discourse neither as an intended form of speech nor as the formal structure of a collective consciousness?

Foucault circumvents these alternatives by treating "discourse itself as a practice" (46). Discourse produces ideas instead of neutrally representing them. Hence Foucault's continual refrain in *The Archaeology of Knowledge:* discourse is productive. Discourse produces the *objects* to which statements refer; the *forms of speech* in which such reference occurs; the *concepts* that constitute knowledge in a given era; and the *strategies* by which individuals can implement that knowledge (Foucault 1972, part II). It suggests, in Charles Scott's succinct description, "a complex interplay of speaking, doing, and knowing" (1987, 92). As a practice, discourse is irreducible to the thoughts or statements of an individual subject and therefore exceeds the reason or intention of a single speaker. Discourses reflect neither consciousness alone nor ideal representations of collective understanding or experience. Discourse is neither the intended statement of an individual nor an aggregate of individual statements.

Nevertheless, discourse does not exceed the individual subject's reason or intention in the sense of transcendence. As a practice, discourse is characterized by its historicity, by its emergence, maintenance, or transformation in successive stages. "[I]t is, from beginning to end, historical" (Foucault 1972, 117; see also 164–65). Thus, the only continuous element of discourse is its discontinuity. In Foucault's estimation, this premise compels one to regard forms of identity or continuity as products of discourse instead of ideals transparently represented therein: "[T]he identical and the continuous are not what must be found at the end of the analysis; they figure in the element of a discursive practice; they too are governed by the rules of formation of positivities; far from manifesting that fundamental, reassuring inertia which we like to use as a criterion for change, they are themselves actively, regularly formed" (Foucault 1972, 174). Rather than representing the origins and ideals of discourse, manifestations of fundamental identity or notions of objective presence are continually fashioned and refashioned from discursive practices. The nature of discourse is therefore historical rather than transcendental. This feature of discourse in particular explains Foucault's insistence on attending to the very differences between orders of discourse as a methodological principle for discerning their formation and functions.

I also noted in chapter 1 that Foucault attends to the rules of formation peculiar to a given mode of discourse. Discourses are not invented *ex nihilo;* they do not produce objects, ways of speaking, concepts, and strategies ideally or objectively. As a practice, discourse is engendered out of existing orders of truth and knowledge. It does not transcend present discursive conditions that determine what can be thought, known, and said in a given era. By the same token, such conditions or rules of formation do not determine what can be thought, known, or said by *constraining* knowledge and speech. "[D]iscourse has not only a meaning or a truth, but a history, and a specific history that does not refer it back to the laws of an alien development" (Foucault 1972, 127). The "truth" of a discourse, therefore, is not categorical but historical. It is engendered by the rules or conditions of possibility that define whatever beliefs or premises can attain the status of truth in a given social or historical context.

Such rules enable—*produce*—capacities for thinking, knowing, and speaking. They constitute, not an artificial constraint on otherwise plentiful forms of thought, knowledge, and speech, but the practical, historical conditions of possibility from which thought, knowledge, and speech emerge. They are, in Foucault's description, "a body of anonymous, historical rules, always determined in the time and space that have defined a given period, and for a given social, economic, geographical, or linguistic area" (117). In *The Order of Things,* Foucault demonstrated that one can neither trace knowledge and speech to an ideal origin nor ascribe to them an ideal status. To the contrary, knowledge and speech in early Western modernity developed in accord with specific practices of representation (the unstated and anonymous discursive rules) that produced hermeneutic knowledge during the Renaissance, classificatory knowledge during the Enlightenment, and positivist knowledge during the nineteenth century. As the implicit rules definitive of a discourse changed, the very nature of the objects that could be identified, the ways in which they could be described, the concepts according to which they could be interpreted, and the modes of conduct they enabled changed as well. Discourse, therefore, is neither the sum of a given form of inquiry nor the medium of individual thought (Foucault 1972, 63). It encompasses the historical conditions of possibility, or practical rules of formation, that enable both the emergence and transformation of modes of thought, knowledge, and speech (Foucault 1972, 34).

By this definition, "discourse" (like *peithō*) does not refer to an object but a *process*. As such, one cannot reduce a given discourse to an objective form, to a specific text or set of utterances. Discourses comprise possibilities for thinking, knowing, and speaking of which specific texts and utterances are merely symptoms. Because they are historical practices, discourses are simultaneously manifested in, yet irreducible to, discrete statements or texts. In *The Birth of the Clinic* (1994a), Foucault observed that the categories of knowledge and forms of speech that justified the creation of the modern clinic engendered an early modern discourse on life and death. In *Discipline and Punish* (1979), he similarly observed that the categories of knowledge and forms of speech used to justify the modern prison system engendered an early modern discourse on crime and punishment. Foucault posited that one should regard the moral, political, and legal arguments that sanctioned these institutions; the scientific or criminological concepts that warranted their existence; the normative practices adopted therein; and the subject positions that populated them as the heterogeneous manifestations of a particular *discursive formation* (either that of life and public health or of crime and punishment).

Discourse refers, not to statements uttered by the representatives of these institutions, but to the possibilities, the tacit rules or conditions, for thinking, knowing, and speaking that bring them into being. It refers to "relations among things, among bodies, words, rules, professions, principles, buildings, habits, ways of perceiving, stating and asking" (C. Scott 1987, 93). Consequently, Foucault insists that a discursive formation, including the so-called rules that enable its production, is not a uniform configuration; it is not "an ideal, continuous, smooth text that runs beneath the multiplicity of contradictions, and resolves them in the calm unity of coherent thought" (1972, 155; see also 35, 119). To study the formation of a discourse, rather, is to study the *dispersion* and *transformation* of specific institutional practices relating to thought, knowledge, and speech—in Foucault's words, "to maintain discourse in all its many irregularities" (156). By proposing to treat discourse as a process rather than a product, Foucault assigns priority to discursive differences, to the transformations from which new discursive formations emerge, rather than basing the production of discourse on the existence of an essential identity. The object of his analysis is to "discover" how certain statements, based on particular modes of thought or knowledge, "can reappear, dissociate, recompose, gain in extension or determination, be taken up into new logical structures, acquire, on the other hand, new semantic contents" (Foucault 1972, 60). Foucault emphasizes, not the stability of a given mode of thought, knowledge, and speech, but its "anonymous dispersion through texts, books, and *œuvres*" (60). Such is "[a] dispersion that characterizes a type of discourse" (Foucault 1972, 60; see also 175). In this way, forms of dissociation, recomposition, dispersion, or transformation gain priority over forms of identity, continuity, similitude, or transcendence in the production of discourse.

Foucault thereby establishes a methodology for apprehending discourse in the middle voice. Discourse in this conception interrupts the representational relation between thoughts and words, the effect of which has been to privilege forms of identity (such as transcendental reason or essential meaning) while negating the formative powers of language itself. Discourse neither reflects a transcendent human consciousness nor transparently mediates essential meaning. One cannot reduce its functions, that is, to the logic of the active voice. This conception of discourse rejects all whispers of transcendence in that one cannot conceive of a discourse, including the truths, values, and meanings it engenders, apart from its defining discursive practices.

Perhaps the most innovative aspect of Foucault's treatise is that it formalizes possible explanations for the production of subjectivity much like those that Plato suppressed in his *Sophist*. Foucault maintains that the discursive conditions for thought, knowledge, and speech in a given *épistémé* engender subject positions (50–55). In *The Birth of the Clinic,* he showed that an early modern discourse on the medical investigation of disease and its treatment engendered the subject positions of doctor and patient in their modern forms, endowed with institutional meaning and value. In *Discipline and Punish,* he similarly showed that the early modern discourse on the nature of crime and punishment engendered the subject positions of the criminal and his or her rehabilitators in their modern forms. As new possibilities for thought, knowledge, and speech emerge, so do the subject positions that carry out such thinking, knowing, and speaking. Discursive formations are comprised of institutional practices to the extent that those practices engender subject positions endowed with institutional authority to enact them. The subject position of a doctor is defined by the possibility of acquiring, lending speech to, and acting upon knowledge of life and death, symptom and cause, disease and cure. The subject position of a criminologist is defined by the possibility of acquiring, lending speech to, and acting upon knowledge of crime and punishment, sin and rehabilitation, virtue and vice.

Of course, such subject positions acquire their meaning and value by virtue of institutional *relations*. A discourse constitutes "a field of regularity for various positions of subjectivity" (Foucault 1972, 55). The subject position of a doctor is constituted by the authority to treat the patient, to define the nature of life and death, disease and cure. The subject position of a criminologist is constituted by the authority to analyze the criminal, to define the nature of crime and punishment, sin and rehabilitation. Discursive formations engender subject positions by engendering institutional relations. Ultimately, such relations define (in these instances) the space of the clinic or the prison. The clinic is designated as the space in which physicians treat patients for the purposes of public health. The prison is designated as the space in which state authorities rehabilitate criminals for the purposes of social control. These institutions, and the relations that define them, came into being as a feature of specific discursive practices concerning life and death or crime and punishment.

By emphasizing that discursive formations produce these relations, Foucault provides the framework for a novel form of social critique. Clearly, such relations acquire an ethical or political character. Instead of evaluating them in light of universal ethical or political standards, however, Foucault suggests that one must evaluate conceptions of life and death or crime and punishment, for example, according to the quality of the institutional relations they produce. The object of this evaluation is not the confirmation of an ideal or universal standard for thought, knowledge, and speech, but the cultivation of discursive conditions in which all such seemingly ideal or universal standards become questionable and thus subject to transmutation. If such critique represents an especially valuable outcome of Foucault's methodology, how might one diagnose the discursive means by which such relations are formed and attain institutional meaning and value? A revised conception of *ethos*, I argue, provides an answer to this question.

An Ethos in the Multiple

A conception of ethos compatible with Foucault's archaeological method constitutes the defining principle of rhetoric in the middle voice. Foucault necessarily emphasizes the ontological characteristics and functions of discourse. The vocabulary of rhetorical theory, however, offers additional terms with which one can apprehend the self-engendering rhetoric by which discourses acquire a recognizable *form* out of their own enactment. Here I do not wish to invoke a traditional, literary distinction between form and content. Nor do I wish to define form in terms of discursive uniformity. Instead, I argue that, because a discourse consists of discursive practices, its form encompasses the heterogeneous ways in which those practices are related to one another. One cannot reduce the relations between such practices to intended, rational justifications for how and why they should be organized. Instead, such practices are affiliated according to a logic and coherence invoked by the institutional meaning and value of those very practices. Foucault himself points to this additional line of analysis without pursuing it. "[W]hat properly belongs to a discursive formation," he writes, "and what makes it possible to delimit the group of concepts, disparate as they may be, that are specific to it, is the way in which these different elements are related to one another" (1972, 59–60). One may attribute the formal distinctiveness of a discursive formation to the characteristic way in which the practices of thought, knowledge, and speech that it produces are related to one another.

Foucault necessarily emphasizes *that* transformations in institutional practices engender a discursive formation. Despite his preoccupation with discontinuity and intentions to the contrary, such an emphasis might lead one to regard this "formation" as an outcome rather than a process, as a noun instead of a verb. A rhetorical perspective, however, emphasizes *how* a discursive formation is engendered by transformations in institutional practices, which presupposes that one regard the "formation" of discourse as a process without origin or telos, as a verb rather than a noun. The *form* of a discourse here is taken as its condition of discursive production rather than its principle of stability or uniformity, as its condition of mutation rather than its principle of identity. A discursive formation acquires the form, the characteristic logic and coherence (however illogical and incoherent), through which it produces discursive differences and transformations out of the very enactment of such phenomena.

In order to emphasize the productive capacities of form in this sense, one can profitably describe the characteristic configuration of a discursive formation as its *ethos*. A discursive formation is engendered by difference, by its continual articulation (or *dispersion,* to use Foucault's term) throughout institutional practices. It is defined principally by its ability to carry out institutional functions, not by its ability to represent a fundamental truth or universal essence. In *The Birth of the Clinic,* Foucault showed that an early modern discourse on life and death, on disease and cure, enabled the establishment of the clinic as an institution of public health. In *Discipline and Punish,* he showed that an early modern discourse on crime and punishment, on social deviance and legal rehabilitation, enabled the establishment of the prison as an institution of civic order. The value and utility of a discursive formation is maintained by its symbolic authority over, and relevance to, immediate social, political, or ethical interests (in these cases, public health and civic order). Out of discursive differences and discontinuities, a discursive formation engenders truths and ideals, beliefs and commitments, desires and motivations, laws and transgressions. The rhetorical currency of such phenomena, their character and authority, derives from their apparent usefulness and appropriateness for generating knowledge and speech in specific institutional environments. The ethos of a discursive formation refers to its rhetorical value and utility as the manifestation of a desirable social order. Out of discursive differences and transformations, a discursive formation engenders accepted truths, apparently transparent representations of empirical and metaphysical orders, and putatively natural forms of speech. The continual implementation of these truths, representations, and forms of speech in response to changing historical, political, or cultural circumstances indicates the rhetorical currency of that discursive formation. In turn, the accrued value and utility of the formation manifests its ethos, its reputation for fulfilling social and political functions.

From this perspective, the reputation of a discursive formation does not denote its uniformity. Indeed, Foucault stipulates that a characteristic dispersion manifests the form of a given discourse (60). *Its reputation is engendered by its dispersion* throughout a variety of institutional practices, artifacts, and statements, throughout established modes of thought, knowledge, and speech. As such, the ethos of a discourse does not reflect the inherent reason or virtue of a transcendental human subject, nor on a transhistorical essence. Its ethos is produced by discursive differences rather than the representation of an essential identity.

The characteristic configuration of discursive practices, meanings, and values through which a discourse acquires its self-engendering form, however, is only the most general manifestation of its ethos. Ultimately, its ethos is exhibited in the array of subject positions it establishes as articulations of those practices, meanings, and values. Discursive formations engender subject positions based on the production of social, political, and ethical relations. Such subject positions do not precede the articulation of these relations but are engendered by them; the ethos of a discursive formation finds its consummate manifestation in their symbolic value. The discursive practices, or conditions for thinking, knowing, and speaking that define a discursive formation, engender, maintain, and transform relations between self and other, native and foreigner, individual and community, healthy and diseased, or citizen and criminal (to name but a few examples).

Such conditions, the rules of formation peculiar to discursive practices, become consubstantial with or embodied in the individual ethos of specific subject positions. Because they are productions of discursive practices, however, one cannot view subject positions as autonomous states of being. To the contrary, they emerge from a matrix of social, political, and ethical relations. The institutional authority or reputation, the symbolic meaning and value, of a single subject position is engendered, maintained, or transformed by virtue of the social, political, and ethical relations constitutive of a discursive formation. These heterogeneous relations themselves exhibit an ethos that informs, in the fullest sense of that term, the individual ethos of a single subject position. They consist of an institutionalized sense and value—an established *character*—for founding, maintaining, or transforming social, political, and ethical orders, for securing commitment to, and action in the name of, the very ethos of established truths and ideals in their many symbolic forms and manifestations.

This revised conception of ethos authorizes a rhetorical account of subjectivity no longer based on the presumption of a universal human nature. Throughout the history of rhetorical theory and practice, rhetoricians have justified the value and utility of rhetoric to civic affairs by celebrating its capacity to refine and express supposedly categorical human virtues and abilities. By this reasoning, the category of ethos became *the* defining—or, in Aristotle's terms, "controlling"—feature of rhetoric. Sound persuasion was based on the moral integrity of a speaker guided by reason and truth. Such integrity reflected the presumably fundamental virtues of human nature— namely, reason and eloquence. Deficient persuasion indicated an immoral character, and thus a perversion of universal human virtues. The conception of ethos that I propose, however, does not seek to represent an allegedly universal human essence, truth, or virtue. It eschews any pretension to represent a transcendent form or presence. The ethos of a discursive formation denotes the changing sense and value that its characteristic social, political, and ethical relations obtain in specific institutional contexts. Such sense and value is engendered by transformations in discursive practices constitutive of those relations instead of any transhistorical meaning or worth. Before one can claim to represent a universal human nature, existing discursive practices (established forms of thought, knowledge, and speech) must enable such a claim to be recognized as meaningful or useful in the negotiation of social, political, and ethical relations. In Lawrence Grossberg's summation, "The notion of a transcendental subject, of a universal human nature, is itself a historically determined self-understanding, but one which does not exist outside of the codes of differences" (1979, 247).

From this perspective, one should view institutionalized claims to a universal human nature as symptoms of the conditions for thought, knowledge, and speech characteristic of a given discursive formation. The sense and value acquired or maintained by such claims in institutional settings derives, not from their authenticity (not from their representation of categorical truth in language, that is), but from the rhetorical currency they obtain as discursive practices in social relations. As the defining feature of rhetoric beyond representation, then, ethos refers to the heterogeneous sense and value of social relations themselves, to the different meanings and values of multiple subject positions affiliated in particular social, political, or ethical orders, instead of the normative authority of an ideal and original subject position.

This definition of ethos, furthermore, does not dispense with, but assigns alternate meaning to, its traditional senses. As I noted in the introduction, ethos conventionally has been rendered as either "character" (meaning a central self) or "custom" (referring to one's performance of a social role). Instead of abrogating these definitions altogether, ethos as I define it here refers to the coalescence of meanings and values that make possible notions of an essential and aesthetic, or authentic and performative, self. In other words, it undermines the dialectical logic according to which the self has been conceived in our heritage. With this redefinition of ethos, I intend to nullify the traditionally controlling influence of a presumably essential or ideal self in Western culture by emphasizing the elusive middle space *between* "character" and "custom," between a central and social self. As the defining feature of rhetoric beyond representation, the ethos of a discourse refers to the discursive formation of symbolic relations (social, political, and ethical) without which specific senses of self and other, just and unjust, or good and evil would not exist. Such a process neither originates nor culminates in either "character" or "custom" (in either self or other, in either an essential or aesthetic subject) but occurs, rather, in the middle, as these antitheses gain discursive meaning and value as organizing principles of social relations and subject positions.

Notions of ethos distinctive of different historical and cultural periods exemplify how the changing meanings and values constitutive of social relations engender the very meaning and value of the self. Aristotle's lengthy discussion of character in Book 2 of his *Rhetoric* reflects the importance of drama in classical Greek culture as an embodiment of social roles, institutional relations, and the cultural values that sponsored them. For him, ethos held a distinctively theatrical connotation. By contrast, individuals in Republican Rome considered one's ethos to be, at least partially, an inheritance; one possessed a "civil *persona*" because one's rights as a free citizen were secured by family name, an option unavailable to slaves (Baumlin 1994, xix, xvi; Mauss 1985; May 1988). In this social and political milieu, the category of the self exhibited a patently legal sense and value. The contrast between these conceptions of ethos suggests, however briefly, that the very idea of self and other emerges from the divergent symbolic practices and customary relations that comprise different orders of discourse.

The ethos of a discursive formation accordingly invalidates definitions of subjectivity based on principles of representation because such ethos reflects the discursive production of subject positions, the affective production of subjectivities, rather than the representation of a universal humanity. In previous chapters, I noted that identity is the foremost such principle in metaphysical ontology. Conventional claims that human beings are modeled on a universal human essence, that their reason and speech represent transhistorical truths or meanings, presume that forms of representation disclose an essential identity between individual beings and an ideal, original being qua being, or between human expressions of truth or meaning and objective forms thereof. The ethos of a discursive formation, however, does not represent the intrinsic identity of human nature; it does not represent universal human virtues for the purpose of intended persuasion. The sense and value that defines such an ethos is engendered, rather, by discursive differences, by transformations in discursive practices. It represents, not the character of an ideal subject, but the sense and value acquired by a variety of social, political, and ethical relations. *Ethos here refers to the discursive production of subject positions through transformations in ways of thinking, knowing, and speaking rather than to the representation of an essential human identity, of an ideal and original human nature or virtue.* It defines subjectivity as a discursive practice rather than the expression of an essential state of being.

From this perspective, manifestations of ethos are not representative of reason or intention. Ethos so defined resists the logic of the active voice. It is not an essential characteristic conveyed transparently in speech. The ethos of a discursive formation is engendered by discursive practices that produce the heterogeneous character and quality of social, political, and ethical relations—*the capacity of those relations themselves to produce forms of thought, knowledge, and speech out of their own symbolic enactment.* By way of contrast, if Edwin Black's "second persona" (1970) refers to the model subject that a rhetor wishes his or her audience members to become, then the ethos of a discursive formation refers to the mutually constitutive personae made possible by discursive practices themselves. As such, one can neither reduce ethos to the representation of intended meaning nor to the manifestation of an ideal or objective content. Only the middle voice can express the ethos of a discursive formation because ethos in this form comes to pass precisely as a production of discursive differences, as a manifestation of discourse itself.

In this context, appeals to reason, intention, or the active voice admittedly retain sense and value. Their sense and value, however, emerges from, and is sustained by, discursive practices instead of transcendent meaning or truth. Such claims enjoy a discursive and historical, rather than an essential and transcendent, sense and value. Defined as the multiform ethos of different subject positions, one does not "use" rhetoric; instead, rhetoric itself occurs in the changing symbolic meanings and values of those subject positions, as the discursive conditions that make possible particular kinds of statements or forms of address.

That said, I do not seek to oppose one conception of ethos with another. The ethos of a discursive formation, of its characteristic social, political, and ethical relations, is not the opposite of ethos traditionally defined, as the representation of essential human virtues. The ethos of an individual subject is symptomatic: it manifests traces of the characteristic configuration of discursive conditions for thinking, knowing, and speaking in which claims to such an ethos attain symbolic value and utility in the management of social, political, and ethical relations. Conversely, the ethos of a discursive formation is engendered by the many forms of ethos articulated through individual subject positions, for the character of those subject positions derives from their institutional authority to enact the practices of thought, knowledge, and speech constitutive of a discourse itself. Such a definition of ethos, therefore, refuses the dialectical logic supporting conventional accounts of human being by affirming that subject positions are produced as a function of ongoing discursive differences and transformations rather than as representations of a continuous human essence or virtue. I advocate a definition of ethos as multiplicity rather than singularity; as a production of difference rather than a representation of identity; and as an aggregation of discursive practices instead of an objective referent. In this conception of ethos, being is both noun and gerund, both product and process, both character and custom.

Ethos in this form, as manifested in the character and quality of social, political, or ethical relations, engenders *a rhetoric of subjectivity*—a system of truths and ideals, beliefs and commitments, desires and motivations, or laws and transgressions—concerning the relations among institutional subject positions. This rhetoric of subjectivity is irreducible to a series of rational arguments or persuasive appeals. The ethos produced and maintained by social, political, and ethical relations engenders the *affective* means by which individuals symbolically enact the character of particular subject positions. Analyzing this affective rhetoric of subjectivity allows one to account, not simply for what individuals said, but for the discursive conditions that enabled them to do so. It allows one to account for the ongoing discursive production of subjectivity, for what Foucault himself calls the *dispersion* of the subject, rather than the autonomy of a subject position or the categorical being of an ideal agent.

In his conclusion to *The Archaeology of Knowledge,* Foucault explains the purpose of his approach to the category of the subject. He does not intend "to discover laws of construction or forms that could be applied in the same way by all speaking subjects, nor . . . to give voice to the great universal discourse that is common to all men at a particular period" (1972, 200). Instead, his "aim was to show what the differences consisted of, how it was possible for men, within the same discursive practice, to speak of different objects, to have contrary opinions, and to make contradictory choices" (200). One can cite Foucault's commentary here as a way of rebutting those critics who seek to upbraid him for denying the subject an essential and autonomous agency. One cannot be deprived of an ontological status that one never possessed in the first place. "[I]t is vain," Foucault contends, "to seek, beyond structural, formal, or interpretative analyses of language, a domain that is at last freed from all positivity, in which the freedom of the subject, the labor of the human being, or the opening up of a transcendental destiny could be filled" (112; see also 121). In scrutinizing the discursive formation of subject positions, Foucault scrutinizes the emergence, maintenance, and transformation of specific *capacities* for agency—the existing discursive conditions that allow individuals "to speak of different objects, to have contrary opinions, and to make contradictory choices." Ideally, the study of a given discursive formation allows one to evaluate the capacities for agency that it either cultivates or forecloses. In Foucault's reckoning, a definition of discourse as "merely a thin transparency" reflecting the inherent reason and will of a transcendental subject lacks political consequence (209). For him, investigation of a given discourse enables one to diagnose the capacity of institutional relations to produce different ethical and political conditions rather than to promote universal ethical or political prescriptions.

Equipped with the vocabulary of rhetorical theory, I argue, one can diagnose precisely the affective or symbolic conditions according to which individuals are given to speak, form opinions, and make choices by participating in common discursive practices. The mutable sense and value of established truths and ideals, beliefs and commitments, desires and motivations, or laws and transgressions enables every such form of speech and judgment, every such capacity for agency. Discursive practices, rather than one's transcendental reason or autonomous will, engender agency so defined. One may therefore regard the multiple capacities for agency produced by a discursive formation as symptoms of the rhetoric of subjectivity—the ethos of social, political, and ethical relations—without which one could not conceive of the contingent sense and value of the self.

Such a perspective stems from Foucault's attempt to define the subject in its dispersion, without recourse to categorical being. By way of his archaeological method, Foucault proposed "to define the positions and functions that the subject could occupy in the diversity of discourse" (200). A conception of ethos as I have devised it allows one to identify *how*, in institutional contexts, subjects come to occupy those positions and functions, to identify how the rhetoric of subjectivity exhibited by a discursive formation produces social, political, and ethical relations as well as the capacities for agency that define them.

Although this conception of rhetoric augments Foucault's insights, it also offers a radical new gloss on one of the most cherished commonplaces of the rhetorical tradition. For centuries, rhetoricians have justified instruction in rhetoric by citing its supposed refinement and expression of innate human virtues. My own account of the relationship between rhetoric and subjectivity emphasizes the significance of rhetoric to social affairs, but does so in a manner that undermines the representational logic that has dominated conceptions of the art since the Greco-Roman period. Ethos is the defining element of rhetoric as I have described it here, albeit a conception of ethos that comprises the sense and value of multiple subject positions, as well as the character of the institutional relations in which they function, rather than the intrinsic virtue of an ideal subject. Ethos so conceived refers, not to *an* ethos, but to the ethos of multiple subject positions, of multiplicity itself. Rhetoric as such does not represent categorical truths or meanings, much less universal reason or virtue. Speech is not its ideal medium, nor is it governed by intention. Rhetoric in the middle voice is affective in that it constitutes the dynamic symbolic matrix of truths and ideals, beliefs and commitments, desires and motivations, or laws and transgressions in affirmation of which individuals enact, sustain, and transform social, political, and ethical relations. It does not seek to negate definitions of rhetoric based on public address and traditional humanist values but offers an alternate account of the discursive practices by which public address and humanist values acquire and maintain their distinctive institutional authority. This alternate account is preferable because it analyzes the discursive production of multiple subject positions according to the quality of the institutional relations that sustain them and in which they participate instead of measuring all forms of speech and judgment against the standard of a presumably ideal and original human essence or virtue.

§

Having developed, in Part 1 of this book, a critique of rhetoric traditionally defined, I offered in this chapter a nonrepresentational conception of rhetoric in the middle voice. Initially, my reading of Plato's *Sophist* demonstrated that thinkers such as Plato, Isocrates, and Aristotle repressed, in their teachings, the middle voice of persuasion during the fifth and fourth centuries B.C.E. in order to institute rhetoric in its now-traditional form. My subsequent commentary on the middle voice of persuasion proved that contemporary rhetoricians who define rhetoric in presumably neutral terms, as persuasion or argumentation, endorse (however innocently) socially prejudiced and intellectually partisan values once used to restrict, not universally enhance, rhetoric's dynamic role in maintaining a robust social and political *agon*. Such commentary also demonstrated that my proposal to identify the middle voice of rhetoric, rather than amounting to a radical deviation from the history of the discipline, provides an opportunity to explore the profound significance of a hitherto neglected dimension of early public address. Yet the prospect of casually replacing modern conceptions of rhetoric with ancient notions of persuasion suggests that one can simply transcend the historical or institutional development of the discipline in order to apprehend a more ideal and original form of rhetoric. Instead of opting for such transcendence, I have argued that Foucault's *The Archaeology of Knowledge* offers the most serviceable framework produced by late-twentieth-century philosophy with which to identify the middle voice of rhetoric.

By way of Foucault's treatise, I have formulated a conception of rhetoric no longer dominated by intention, identity, or an essential human nature. My purpose is not to negate canonical definitions of rhetoric, as persuasion or argumentation, but to offer a mode of inquiry with which to apprehend the ways that rhetoric simply happens, in the middle voice, out of its own enactment. The characteristic configuration of a discourse does not simply produce *what* is said but conditions *how* and *why* it is said. One may identify the reasons for the emergence, maintenance, or transformation of this configuration without reducing such motivations to effects of reason or intention alone. The subject positions established by conditions for thinking, knowing, and speaking, and subsequently articulated through the social, political, and ethical relations that define them, embody the characteristic ethos of a discursive formation. Such a definition of ethos allows one to account for the creation of authority, judgment, and agency as a series of discursive practices rather than representations of categorical human attributes. The middle voice of rhetoric, manifested in the ethos of social, political, and ethical relations, discloses the affective means by which discursive practices emerge in response to changing exigencies. An attunement to rhetoric in the middle voice does not simply assert that a discursive formation coalesces around the authority of particular truths, values, and commitments but examines *how* discursive practices engender such coalescence through the symbolic management of social, political, and ethical relations.

Like the vast majority of the rhetorical tradition, this conception of rhetoric beyond representation underscores the centrality of ethos to rhetorical theory and practice. *Unlike* the vast majority of that tradition, it denies the centrality of ethos as such any grounding in supposedly universal, but actually privileged and partial, notions of human being. It inquires into the discursive practices that engender different subject positions. From this perspective, the subject is not a representation of inherent identity but a manifestation of discursive differences—a product of mercurial institutional relations as well as the nature of the social, political, or ethical influences they invoke. The subject is thus understood to be a discursive practice, not an essential state of being—a manifestation of differences and discontinuities, not a principle of identity or unity. Of course, one must acknowledge the institutional value and utility of rhetoric in its representational sense, as an instrument of reason. Yet that value and utility derives from the ethos of discursive formations in which accepted discursive practices—established ways of thinking, knowing, and speaking—endow public address with its characteristic cultural authority. Rhetoric in the middle voice occurs as the ethos of a discursive formation (its defining social, political, and ethical relations) affects capacities for agency and modes of judgment, whether they're manifested in the activities of public address or in a host of other discursive practices.

In sum, a conception of rhetoric in the middle voice does not oppose traditional conceptions of rhetoric. Instead, it insists that the truths, ideas, laws, and values that individual rhetors seek to represent in their appeals are available for such appeals precisely because discursive practices irreducible to the reason or intention of an individual rhetor engender, maintain, or transmute them. A conception of rhetoric in the middle voice provides rhetoricians with the option of analyzing, not only what individuals said, but, more significantly, the discursive conditions (the rules for thinking, knowing, and speaking) that made their statements at all possible within a specific historical or social context. My nonrepresentational definition of ethos—as the sense and value of multiple subject positions, of fluctuating social, political, and ethical relations—does not deny the existence or effectiveness of intention, reason, truth, and even human being as bases for persuasive appeals. It does insist, however, that their existence or effectiveness manifests the distinctive ethos of an institutional discourse, an accepted and valued aggregation of ideas, truths, and subject positions, rather than essential virtues or transcendent categories.

Ultimately, the chief contribution of rhetoric in the middle voice is an account of the rhetoric of subjectivity—the symbolic genesis, maintenance, or transformation of subject positions—as manifested in the material conditions for thought, knowledge, speech, and judgment definitive of social, political, and ethical relations. Such an account assumes the centrality of rhetoric to social affairs, and of ethos to rhetoric itself, while denying rhetoric its previous subservience to traditional metaphysical ontology (in the form of categorical distinctions between the sensible and the intelligible, human being and ideal being, truth and error, or good and evil). In not simply opposing new ontological values to the old ones, but in assigning an altogether different sense and value to traditional ontological categories, rhetoric in the middle voice facilitates inquiry into the relationship between rhetoric and subjectivity without reducing that inquiry to the endorsement of an ideal or original subject, to a supposedly universal (but actually privileged and partial) definition of human being. Simply put, the study of rhetoric beyond representation scrutinizes the rhetoric of multiple subject positions by accounting for the ethos—the characteristic sense and value—engendered and maintained by the social, political, and ethical relations that produce such subject positions out of their discursive enactment.

Chapter 4

Style without Identity

In the previous chapter, I provided a rationale for, and conceptual outline of, rhetoric in the middle voice. Not surprisingly, explorations of theoretical questions often raise subsequent methodological considerations—in this case, questions concerning how, exactly, one should analyze the ethos of a discursive formation to more incisively disclose the political and ethical ramifications of existing discursive practices and subject positions. By what heuristic principles can one apprehend this ethos? What are its characteristic discursive or symbolic features? On what basis, finally, can one make critical judgments about the social, political, and ethical relations that it engenders?

In this chapter, I argue that one can study the ethos of a discursive formation according to its *style*. Style so defined does not indicate superficial formal qualities; nor does it suggest either artistic or political autonomy. To the contrary, the defining discursive practices, or social, political, and ethical relations, of a given epoch exhibit a style that manifests, neither formalism nor autonomy, but what Foucault would call the very *dispersion* of multiple conditions for thought, knowledge, speech, and judgment—subjectivity itself—throughout public settings. In the following, I therefore advocate a revised definition of style that offers both an interpretive principle for analysis of rhetoric in the middle voice (as the ethos of social, political, and ethical relations) and a demonstration of such analysis on the characteristic style of so-called postmodern culture.

STYLE AND HUMANISM

Modern rhetoricians habitually avoid the canon of style. The reasons for this avoidance should be familiar to those versed in the disciplinary lore of rhetoric.

Since the fifth and fourth centuries B.C.E., when oratorical virtuosos such as Gorgias proclaimed that "[s]peech is a powerful lord, which by means of the finest and most invisible body effects the divinest works" (*Encomium of Helen*, 8), the suspicion that rhetorical style amounts to irrational verbal excess has dogged those who would argue for the moral integrity of the art. Most recently, twentieth-century rhetoricians, Toulmin (1964) and Perelman (1969, 1979, 1982) in particular, realigned rhetoric with the study of argumentation after its apparent reduction during the eighteenth and nineteenth centuries to innocuous matters of form and taste by the elocutionist and belletristic movements. Consequently, the aesthetic capacities of rhetoric have received scant attention from modern rhetoricians, who generally resign considerations of style to supposedly regrettable episodes in the history of the discipline. For better or worse, then, modern rhetorical theory lacks a contemporary rationale and methodology for the study of style.[1]

Beyond unfortunate equations of rhetoric with grandiloquence, this scarcity in recent rhetorical scholarship corresponds to general humanistic and social scientific prejudices against the topic of style. Robert Hariman posits, "Established academic conceptions of style hardly prepare one to take seriously the aesthetic dimension of political experience" (1995, 7). As evidence for this claim, Hariman cites Stuart Ewen's reflections on the "frustration" peculiar to research on style: "It seemed to be a universal category," Ewen observes, "transcending topical boundaries, an accolade applied to people, places, attitudes and things . . . a subject that was, at best, amorphous" (1988, 2). Yet the social ubiquity of style—"[o]n news magazines, sports magazines, music-oriented magazines, magazines about fashion, architecture and interior design, automobiles, and sex"—indicates that it offers "a key to understanding the contours of contemporary culture" (Ewen 1988, 2). Hence, the paradox of style as an analytic category: that which exhibits its cultural importance makes it seem intellectually vacuous.

Hariman's treatise on political style offers the most noteworthy attempt in contemporary rhetorical studies to remedy these trends; brief consideration of his insights will suggest further objectives for the study of rhetoric and style.[2] In Hariman's estimation, "style ultimately is a significant dimension of every human experience" because "relations of control and autonomy are negotiated through the artful composition of speech, gesture, ornament, decor, and any other means for modulating perception and shaping response. In a word, our political experience is *styled*" (3, 2). The distinctive contribution of rhetorical inquiry into political style involves "understanding the dynamics of our social experience or the relationship between rhetorical appeals and political decisions" rather than merely "cataloging discursive forms in the artistic text alone" (Hariman 1995, 8).

Accordingly, Hariman acknowledges that one must recognize the substantive social and political influences of style apart from its traditional connotations of individual artistic performance. "In this context," he explains, "although style still highlights aesthetic reactions it no longer enforces artistic autonomy. Style becomes an analytic category for understanding a social reality; in order to understand the social reality of politics, we can consider how a political action involves acting according to a particular political style" (9). Thus, for Hariman, rhetorical choices in political style need not amount to a valorization of "artistic autonomy": "[E]ach political style draws on universal elements of the human condition and symbolic repertoire but organizes them into a limited, customary set of communicative designs. . . . Each is thoroughly conventional, yet the means for personal improvisation and intelligent, innovate responses to unique problems" (11–12). His treatise therefore appears to dissociate style from its quainter definitions while recommending the utility of rhetorical principles to the study of political culture.

What Hariman calls the "cautious postmodernism" (6) of his project, however, hinders its innovative aspirations. The postmodern portion of his work endorses the study of style according to the aesthetic dimensions of social relations rather than "artistic autonomy" alone; but its "caution" refers to his reliance on a classical, patently Aristotelian, definition of rhetoric. For Hariman, the rhetoric of a political style functions, by definition, as "a catalog of the means of persuasion characteristic of a particular political culture that could be used by anyone attempting to secure advantage" (4). Regardless of his stated distaste for the equation of style with "artistic autonomy," one cannot employ the hermeneutic principles of classical rhetoric without invoking the artistic autonomy according to which rhetoric originally was defined. Inquiry into the rhetoric of political style as such inevitably reduces diffuse and heterogeneous aesthetic phenomena to the reasoned (in Hariman's terms, "intelligent") decisions of a humanist agent: "it equips the reader to act skillfully within characteristic situations" (4). Rather than questioning the classical, predominantly rational, ethos of autonomous rhetorical action, this definition neutralizes the aesthetic and affective capacities of style by regarding it merely as one available means of persuasion, thereby reducing rhetoric to the individual mastery of persuasive conventions, to skill in matters of "decorum" (Hariman 1995, 177). Both rhetoric and style in Hariman's account remain essentially rational and purposeful communicative resources. As a result, neither category substantively complicates the priority of subjective intention or "the intelligibility and rationality of social practices" (Hariman 1995, 181). Such cautious, yet unquestioned, valuation of a rationally governed political agent limits consideration of the radical interpretive possibilities raised by Hariman's recognition of style as an organizing feature of social and political relations.

My commentary on Hariman's study is intended to identify critical themes according to which the relationship between rhetoric and style should be further interrogated. Is style always chosen? Does style not shape our social relations through communicative or symbolic dynamics irreducible to the reasoned choices of a single agent? Does the aesthetic expression of certain political values not influence the character of civic life by *contradicting* conventional democratic ideals? How might rhetorical inquiry orient itself to account for the affiliations between such phenomena and thereby enhance present insights into the aesthetic dimensions of social and political practices?

Rhetorical inquiry offers an invaluable means of disclosing, not merely the importance of style as an organizing feature of social and political relations, but more significantly the ways in which it engenders, maintains, or reconfigures them. However, in order to avoid reducing the dynamic aesthetic patterns of communal life to an available battery of persuasive choices, or to the intrinsic rationality of humanist ideals, one must document the rhetorical function of style without exclusive reliance on an Aristotelian conception of rhetoric. The opportunity to redefine the canon of style by emphasizing its significance to social and political relations warrants an augmentation of the domain of rhetorical inquiry to better account for present and future changes in the interplay between collective discourse and cultural aesthetics.

French sociologist Michel Maffesoli's "Treatise on Style" in *The Contemplation of the World* (1996a) provides an account of style and communal values attuned to the social, political, and aesthetic transitions currently shaping the so-called postmodern era. Although his innovative redefinition of style, as the crystallizing sentiment of an epoch, cogently elucidates the aesthetic dimensions of contemporary Western culture, it has received little scholarly attention in the United States and none in rhetorical studies. The applicability of this revised definition to the study of specific cultural contexts, however, will benefit greatly from additional reflection on the ways in which style so conceived functions rhetorically, through its public communication (though, as I will demonstrate, not in the conventional sense of that term).

Maffesoli's treatise on style advances his larger research agenda. In other works, namely, *The Shadow of Dionysus* (1993) and *The Time of the Tribes* (1996b), he has argued that, as analytic tools, the modernist social and political ideals of reason, production, and order insufficiently account for the nature of postmodern society and politics. This emerging epoch appears to be informed by a spirit of collective excess, of shared passions and rituals, which evinces what Maffesoli calls a postmodern tribalism in contrast to the characteristically modernist faith in individual agency. Recognizing these developments, he contends, allows us to trace the present and future transmutation of our defining social and political values into other forms. Accordingly, I contend that revised rhetorical principles enhance such study by revealing the modes of communication that engender these forms and thereby typify contemporary social and political interactions.

In what follows, I initially summarize the key tenets of Maffesoli's "Treatise on Style," emphasizing its advantages for the study of contemporary style, culture, and politics. Thereafter, I demonstrate that such insights require further elaboration by way of rhetorical inquiry. In so doing, I explain how Maffesoli's redefinition of style allows one to not only eschew, but productively challenge, enduring intellectual commitments to the sanctity of artistic or political autonomy common to classical conceptions of both style and rhetoric.

STYLE *REDUX*

Few would dispute the claim that, for some time, Western culture has been experiencing a complex transition from one set of dominant values, beliefs, and practices to another, still inchoate, cultural paradigm commonly and imperfectly known as postmodernism. Many, however, disagree on the meaning of this transition. Such disagreement stems from the fact that, within the experience of unprecedented social, economic, and geopolitical change, the nature of the current *épistémé* is provisionally defined at best, and its final shape (if any) is uncertain. Faced with this interpretive dilemma, some argue for the maintenance of established values, beliefs, and practices, while others argue for the inauguration of new paradigms.

Michel Maffesoli argues that, whatever our predilections for a given paradigm might be, recent cultural events indicate the emergence of values and ideals whose social and political importance, whether we like it or not, one can no longer deny. "The diverse religious fanaticisms, the ethnic resurgences, the linguistic claims or other attachments to territories," Maffesoli writes, signal the advent of a postmodern tribalism (1996a, xiii). This tribalism is sustained by "enthusiasms of whatever order they may be—sporting, musical, or festive," which lend "the great megalopolises the appearance of a perpetual bazaar where unprecedented conspicuous consumption is being celebrated" (Maffesoli 1996a, xiii). Based on the modernist values of order, reason, and economy, these "fanaticisms," "resurgences," or "enthusiasms" represent an irrational celebration of wasteful excess. Yet, Maffesoli cautions, one cannot deny that, in contrast to "irrationalism," the "nonrational or the nonlogical" currently enjoy an undeniable "social import," producing new social orders through their putatively unproductive ethos of excess and disorder (viii). In Maffesoli's description, "[t]he languishing civilization of an economic and utilitarian modernity is being succeeded by a new culture in which the sense of the superfluous, the concern for the useless, and the search for the qualitative all take on paramount importance" (12). The traditional values of "individualism, instrumental reason, the omnipotence of technique, and the 'everything is economics' no longer arouse the adherence of former times, and they no longer function as founding myths or as goals to be attained" (Maffesoli 1996a, 2). Such values, although they likely maintain more influence than Maffesoli allows, are no longer sacrosanct; instead, "the imaginary that modernity could consider as being of the order of the superfluous or of frivolity tends to find once again a place of honor in social life" (19). In sum, one finds increasingly valued "a form of being-togetherness . . . that is no longer oriented to the faraway, toward the realization of a perfect society in the future, but rather is engaged in managing the present" (Maffesoli 1996a, xiii). These changing discursive or symbolic conditions evince the enhanced ethos of new rhetorical practices and social relations.

The social premium placed on "being-togetherness" marks, neither a dialectical sublimation of the "different constitutive elements of modernity" nor their sudden termination, but a subtler metamorphosis of existing values into "another configuration" (Maffesoli 1996a, 21–22). One cannot explain this arrangement with notions of a social contract or the logic of economic supply and demand. Rather than a consensual agenda or utilitarian rationale, the emerging animus of society is most evocatively described as a sentiment, passion, or collective effervescence. In a word, the current epoch appears to be informed, at least in its nascent stages, by an unprecedented investment in the *aesthetic*. Most notably, the present ubiquity of public spectacle has become a sustaining element of diverse social pursuits, from consumer culture and civic events to humanitarian causes and political programs. At such a historical moment, the category of *style* offers renewed explanatory force.

Style in this frame does not simply refer to abstract judgments about taste. Maffesoli proposes a broadening and diversifying of this category beyond its conventional domain: "Without denying the importance of style in 'great' culture, and without neglecting its metaphoric use for market studies, it is suitable to give it a much wider acceptation, which would be of a measure with the social stakes it represents" (7–8). Nevertheless, one can, according to Maffesoli, speak of style in terms of genius—not individual artistic genius, but in "its widest meaning: for example, the genius of a place, or the genius of a people" (1). Collective genius refers to the distinctive ethos of a cultural moment, "the style of an epoch: I mean to say that which writes or orients the epoch" (Maffesoli 1996a, 4). In the language of my previous chapter, one might equally describe what Maffesoli calls "the style of an epoch" as its ethos. So conceived, one should take Maffesoli's allusion to writing in the most robust sense of that term. Like Hayden White's (1992) description of the middle voice, in which the writer exists only in the process of writing, "an epoch" exists only in the symbolic enactment of its definitive style.

How is the current epoch written or oriented? In Maffesoli's estimation, by "tribalization, a culture of sentiment, the aesthetisization of life" (4). The growing cultural importance of these phenomena warrants an enlargement of the category of style to account for the ways in which they influence contemporary social relationships. "Hence there is nothing frivolous about attention to style, defined in this way," Maffesoli maintains. "On the contrary, it is what may make all the microevents stand out, all the imperceptible mutations, the apparently anecdotal situations that back-to-back make up culture; that is, they serve as substrate, compost, for that creation which is a whole social life" (4). The consumption of images, the public expression of shared emotions, and the iteration of aesthetic forms, in other words, animates contemporary social relations in a manner irreducible to principles of reason, economy, or utility.

The style of an epoch, therefore, brings its various social, economic, political, and institutional elements, not into objective identity or consensual harmony, but into some sort of characteristic configuration suffused by a cultural aesthetic. Such is the characteristic configuration to which Foucault referred, in *The Archaeology of Knowledge,* as the defining feature of a discursive formation. Maffesoli accordingly redefines style as the "specific mark" of a "collective sentiment": "In the strict meaning of the term, it becomes an all-encompassing form, a 'forming form' that gives birth to whole manners of being, to customs, representations, and the various fashions by which life in society is expressed" (1996a, 5). For Maffesoli, style does not refer to an antiquated distinction between form and substance but to the manner in which the representative aesthetic forms of a cultural epoch constitute its defining and substantive features, its ethos. In this connection, the style of an epoch manifests the middle voice of rhetoric. Style so conceived articulates the self-enacting symbolic practices that constitute the very ethos of a given era, the spectrum of discursive conditions according to which groups and individuals in that era can think, know, and speak of self and other, individual and community, past and present, or good and evil.

One must not conclude that style, by this definition, encompasses a uniform hegemony or a fundamental unity. Maffesoli himself periodically suggests as much. Drawing an analogy with "German thought" (presumably German Idealism), he posits that "style, as a force of aggregation, would be the property of culture in its founding inception. It is what at a determined moment assures the synthesis of values and thereby imposes a recognizable order and form" (11). In assessing the relevance of style to "postmodern societies" characterized by "fragmentation and heterogenization," Maffesoli proposes that "style can be understood as the 'principle of unity,' that which unites, deep down, the diversity of things" (9). Unfortunately, the Hegelian overtones of descriptors such as "founding inception," "synthesis," or "unity" threaten to invest the category of style once again with the kind of objectivity and uniformity for which Maffesoli critiques "modernist" explanations of social arrangements. Despite the sense of homogeneity invoked by these terms, Maffesoli elsewhere stipulates, "The very property of a particular style is to be heterogeneous, even to rest on contradictory tendencies" (6). Style "might mean," for instance, "the body that is constructed, the individual appearance that is groomed, the effort spent at presenting the production of ideas as well, the industrial product about to be aestheticized, the business whose public image is nursed, or even the political program to be presented with all the exterior attractiveness possible" (Maffesoli 1996a, 11). Whatever "unity" Maffesoli ascribes to the style of an epoch must be taken in its most metaphorical sense; style, he explains, "is the postmodern form of the social link—a social link 'in dotted outline,' shaken by violent, chaotic, and unforeseen jolts" (34). The style of an epoch thus encompasses a unity engendered by (sometimes profound) disunity. Or, instead of unity, however qualified, one might refer to style as the cultural expression of an aesthetic *vibration*. This vibration may be harmonious or violently discordant, it may produce cohesion or dispersion, but collective style invokes a meaningful resonance among disparate, even "contradictory," social interests.

Redefined in this manner, the category of style makes two initial contributions to the study of contemporary social and political relations. First, it provides a more incisive account of the nature of social transformation at a time of apparent fragmentation in previous values, relations, and institutions. Maffesoli's conception of style encompasses the heterogeneity of cultural forms irreducible to discrete analytic categories such as gender, race, or class. In his words, "It cuts across the boundary between different classes, social strata, or socio-professional categories" (37). More specifically, style as an analytic category is uniquely suited to account for the postmodern aesthetic, which is largely distinguished by, on the one hand, "the overlapping of styles" and, on the other hand, "the cyclical return of the events and 'types' of past history" (Maffesoli 1996a, 6). The "melange of genres" (6) so formative of current social relations naturally requires examination according to an aesthetic category. As our culture assigns increasing value and significance to a diversity of forms, appearances, and collective rituals—to the aesthetic dimensions of social relations—the category of style accounts for the nature of their value and significance in a way that established interpretive hierarchies cannot.

Second, rather than amounting to an apolitical intellectual diversion, the study of style in this frame underscores the animating aesthetic qualities of changing political relations. What Maffesoli calls "the saturation of the values of modernity" (xii) has been described often, and by many different commentators, as a postmodern political indifference, or even cynicism, crippling the democratic process. Based on traditional democratic ideals, the political efficacy of this fatigue with democratic participation, with the legislative pursuit of a better future, seems socially irresponsible at best, morally corrosive at worst. Such ideals, however, are ill-equipped to recognize the changing scene and quality of the political, which is no longer confined to civic forums but "best expressed in the numerous contradictory situations and attitudes that punctuate everyday life," no longer defined solely by "the framework of the social contract or the democratic ideal" but by a politics of "[p]olitical disengagement"(Maffesoli 1996a, 23; 29, 48).

Whether we like it or not, Maffesoli insists, the growing popular disenchantment with Enlightenment democratic ideals is reconfiguring political investments: "[T]he world is no longer to be transformed, or perfected; society and history are no longer to be made" (29). Instead, political values are increasingly expressed according to what he calls a "communitarian" (rather than a democratic) ideal: "[N]atural and social environments are accepted for what they are; it suffices to accommodate oneself to them, and to try, in an ecological manner, to draw the most possible benefits from them" (Maffesoli 1996a, 29). Thus, social practices that one would call politically wasteful and selfish according to traditional democratic ideals reflect a politics nonetheless in which "one intends less to 'act' on the social, to affect society, than to take from it all the well being one can and to best enjoy this well-being" (Maffesoli 1996a, 48). Consequently, aesthetic practices sustain this transfiguration of the political, which implements the tropes, forms, and rituals of "the quotidian, domestic, nearby—all things on the basis of which one can make of existence a veritable work of art" (Maffesoli 1996a, 49).[3] Without endorsing or refuting their political efficacy, Maffesoli contends, postmodern political dynamics "make themselves felt as much in juvenile effervescences as in the multiplication of aggregations developed on the basis of sexual, cultural, religious, or even political tastes. These aggregations no longer owe anything to rational programming, but rather rely on the desire to be with similar-minded people, even if it means excluding those who are different" (33). The politics of this "being-togetherness" is engendered by elements of collective style: "common emotions and sentiments" rather than social contracts (Maffesoli 1996a, 33). One might say that, in order to account for postmodern political relations, one must apprehend their contemporary rhetorical function instead of evaluating them according to traditional, universal frameworks of liberal democracy.

Unfortunately, Maffesoli flirts with an idealization of these transformed political values; the larger virtues of his account would be compromised, however, if one understood him to argue that the democratic ideal is essentially harmful and the communitarian ideal is completely liberating. Even if a "being-togetherness" currently reigns, there are factions whose shared passions, for a variety of reasons, one would not want to be shared. From western militia and white supremacist groups to religious fundamentalists and cultural demagogues throughout the world, shared hatreds rather than coherent and egalitarian political visions unite a broad spectrum of individuals around a common purpose. Maffesoli does not advocate a given politics but argues instead for the unrecognized political significance of a growing refusal of official politics and devises analytic tools to account for its increasing social and political value. In order to appreciate the acuity of his account, one should emphasize Maffesoli's recognition that the communitarian ideal, the political bonds of shared sentiment and emotion, establish a broad spectrum of social and political configurations, including "violence, and different racisms, fanaticisms, and urban uprisings are there to prove it, but it may equally be expressed in tolerance, and many are the groups that work in this direction; one finds it too, finally, in indifference, which is perhaps the most widespread case" (34). One must reckon with the nature of postmodern politics, then, by first acknowledging their formidable fluidity and symbolic expression rather than presupposing their rational uniformity and rhetorical transparency.

While granting this point, one might also suggest that others have well noted the aesthetic and emotive dimensions of Western politics. Monarchies and democracies alike have long feared the passions of the unruly mob. The majority of the rhetorical tradition demonstrates (although Hariman's account suggests that modern rhetoricians have lost sight of the fact) that the practical exercise of politics seldom has been conducted without attention to ceremony, performance, and popular taste; even a cultural aversion to sentiment is still a kind of cultural sentiment. A host of modern commentators have also warned that a politics reduced to aesthetic displays of power and appeals to popular sentiment represents a hallmark of fascism. In light of these facts, is Maffesoli claiming that society and politics are acquiring aesthetic dimensions they lacked until now, or that such dimensions have suddenly been liberated from their repression under the modernist reign of reason? "What one should retain from this analysis," Maffesoli urges, "is that quotidian style may, in certain epochs, give form and figure to the whole of society" (52). Yet he also suggests that something about the notion of style itself is uniquely transformed in its application to the current era. Do postmodern social and political formations exhibit truly new aesthetic forms, or simply an unprecedented popular awareness of them? Do those who act in the spirit of "being-togetherness" knowingly act on the communitarian ideal (in which case they would act much like the progressive coalitions of the so-called modern epoch), or is the crystallization of that ideal only an effect of Maffesoli's description? Simply put, does Maffesoli document an ontological or an epistemic shift?

Maffesoli provides ambiguous answers to these questions. His own rhetoric indicates that the defining social and political sentiment of the postmodern era entails both novelty and progress (thus, in critiquing an Enlightenment paradigm of democratic progress, Maffesoli unwittingly endorses it). But his appeal to a postmodern tribalism indicates a return to premodern social forms, even if they obtain an altered character in the postmodern era. Either affirmation—that of a new, better form of society and politics or of a nostalgia for traditional, supposedly uncorrupted, values and practices—is as characteristically modern as the democratic ideals that Maffesoli wishes to annul. More unfortunate still, these competing affirmations mute his comparatively sober recognition that the communitarian ideal, which he occasionally celebrates, results in disenfranchisement, indifference, or violence as much as in humanitarian causes and novel geopolitical alliances. Evidently, these themes require additional development. What further research does Maffesoli's redefinition of style warrant beyond highlighting the aesthetic character of postmodern social and political relations—beyond arguing merely that aesthetics are significant to contemporary Western culture and politics?

Eventually, I will argue that an attunement to rhetoric in the middle voice offers an invaluable means of tracing the sociopolitical functions of style, and thereby allows for a profitable refinement of Maffesoli's claims. One cannot apprehend the form and function of a particular style of politics without surveying the communicative or symbolic modes that engender and disseminate it. There is no politics without rhetoric, in other words—albeit a form of rhetoric in the middle voice that undermines its conventional reduction to Aristotelian principles and, as such, allows one to recognize the significance of style beyond its traditional equation with individual expression or artistic autonomy. In order to identify the benefit of rhetorical inquiry to Maffesoli's account, however, one must consider in further detail the curious nature of postmodern politics as he describes it.

POLITICS, ETHICS, AND ALTERITY

Evidently, contemporary political investments reflect a momentous change in political values. The cohesive sentiment of community now competes with the leadership of elected representatives; the collective fruits of the present trump the progressive vision of an improved future society; the *perception* of immediate needs and desires spurs collective action more than the promise of civic *representation*. Consequently, the style of current social and political formations, Maffesoli posits, supports an ethic of the aesthetic rather than a civic morality: "an ethic coming from below, in opposition to a morality imposed from above" (1996a, 52). Such a politics no longer adheres to a fixed hierarchy of commonly accepted values, transparently enunciated by the representatives of neatly demarcated constituencies, but is manifested in the aleatory interactions between social groups, motivated by any variety of either complementary or contradictory sentiments. In Maffesoli's words, this ethic "does not decree how one should behave and why it is necessary to do or not to do this or that, but is content to foster, or just to tolerate, the use of pleasures, whatever they are, from the most anodyne to the most perverse, as a condition of possibility of a being-togetherness" (52). Instead of a constitutional model, underwritten by the civic morality of a social contract, the postmodern era exhibits the increased value and significance of a revisable ethic in which groups and individuals relate to one another according to changing needs and desires, no matter how "anodyne" or "perverse."

These relations reveal the current social and political value of form, performance, or appearance. Maffesoli explains:

> Emotion cannot be reduced to the single sphere of the private, but is lived collectively, to an ever greater extent. One could even speak of an affective ambience in which pains and pleasures are experienced in common. It suffices to mention the role played by television during catastrophes, wars, or other bloody events in order to be convinced of this. It is the same with great national or international commemorations, royal weddings, or society events involving musical "stars" or celebrities of all kinds. Finally, one finds this ambience in the staging *(mis-en-scène)* of the crowds assembled for diverse sporting, musical, religious, or political events. (57)

The distinctive postmodern "melange of genres" is evident in these instances. We are incited, comforted, or affected in any number of ways by those with whom we would never interact were it not for the postmodern integration and reversibility of heterogeneous cultural forms and social rituals. The degree to which contemporary mass media proliferate and disseminate the horrific images of tragic events for consumption by diverse communities exemplifies such curious bonds.

The current social ethos therefore facilitates encounters between self and other, familiar and foreign, with unprecedented frequency. The symbolic communication of cultural forms acquires enhanced value and significance as our commitment to the pursuit of a universally transparent political idiom wavers. "This is how the transmutation of values engenders another social style," Maffesoli explains, "that is, another relation to alterity: the Other is no longer an abstraction, with which I must unite in order to construct a no less abstract, future society. The other is the one I touch and with whom I make something that touches me" (28). Recall that style in this conception is collective and heterogeneous, comprised of intersecting cultural forms, irreducible to the markers of a single class, gender, region, or ethnicity. As a result, style "allows and enables liaison among all the members of a society" according to the dissemination of certain cultural aesthetics, which have become, in many social situations, a more serviceable cultural "language" than democratic deliberation (Maffesoli 1996a, 38; 15). Style thus presupposes "an ethical aesthetic," which guides "how one manages relationships with alterity; how in all domains each and every one of us behaves in relation to the other" (28; 38). In such weird civic contexts, where we encounter, for whatever reason, those marked primarily by their difference from us, a static moral code may be less useful than a conditional ethical posture adaptable to the negotiation of multiple social interests and collective identities.

One could elaborate on these comments in order to comprehend the deeper significance of Maffesoli's contrast between the democratic and communitarian ideals. The democratic ideal, Maffesoli submits, is personified by the modernist principle of individual political action: individual rights and responsibilities are the atoms of an ordered, democratic society, to be employed productively for civic good. An ideal conception of the autonomous agent, whose identity and agency exist prior to his or her submersion in a cultural milieu, thus personifies the democratic ideal. Maffesoli's identification of an emerging communitarian ideal, however, underscores a transformation, not merely in conventional ideas about society and politics, but more profoundly in how societies understand the social character of the individual. In a postmodern *épistémé*, the self is not so much an autonomous agent who exists prior to the influence of social and political relations but an embodiment of certain capacities for agency formed at their intersection.

Even as he stresses the fundamental relationship of self to other in contemporary social and political relations, some of Maffesoli's phrasing suggests that self and other exist as two distinct, autonomous beings prior to their encounter. For example: "The other is the one I touch and with whom I make something that touches me"; the ethical aesthetic concerns how "each and every one of us behaves in relation to the other" (28; 38). Maffesoli's truly radical insight, however, is that "the individual, far from being an isolated atom, can only exist and grow by assuming a role in an ambience of communion" (60). The self, that is, acquires its nature and meaning within the heterogeneity, the "ambience," of a particular social milieu. "[I]n order to understand postmodern sociality," Maffesoli continues, "one must begin with the alterity that is at the core of the 'I' " (61)—namely, the collective consumption of socially and politically galvanizing forms, images, and symbols, participation in public rituals, and the bonds of common sentiment from which individuals derive their distinctive senses of belonging, of purpose and value.

The modernist ideal of an autonomous individual, endowed with an essential capacity for reason and agency prior to his or her passage through the gates of society, loses its former ethos in a cultural epoch shaped by unprecedented social heterogeneity and interdependence. One can explain the widespread contemporary experience of such heterogeneity and interdependence, not by principles of reason, utility, or citizenship, but by the function of a collective aesthetic, a shared sentiment. In Maffesoli's estimation, "one lives, along with other people, styles that constitute all of us in depth . . . the notion of style teaches us that a person is only such when he or she is rooted in a substratum that gives each its value, that he or she is only worth something within the framework of his or her social and natural environment" (16). As such, Maffesoli's conception of style accounts for a historic transformation in the political value of the individual. The autonomous agent is no longer recognized as the constitutive atom of society; instead, the social and political relations that shape the contours of a community establish the assortment of social and political roles without which an individual would not exist. Maffesoli contends that individuals are defined, not by the inhabitation of an authentic social role, but by "the passage from one role to another"—what he calls "a series of 'successive sincerities' " (60). These "successive sincerities" exemplify the dispersion of the subject to which Foucault refers, the many "positions and functions that the subject could occupy in the diversity of discourse" (1972, 200).

In sum, the postmodern *épistémé* values the notion that the self is a product of the changing needs and desires of the community. These changing needs and desires (the animus of collective style) establish social and political relations characterized, not by civic identity, but by multiple cultural differences. The self is a mode of social being formed by the relative poverties and fortunes of such attachments. In this frame, the social practices that create and maintain particular forms of subjectivity offer a crucial site of ethical inquiry: how are we shaped by displays of, and encounters with, cultural difference? Thus, the expression and maintenance of social identities, the ethical practices that enable forms of subjectivity, have emerged as the defining political investments of the postmodern era.

Under the rubric of politics so defined, Maffesoli locates, not the maintenance of a civic morality (how to create a better society conforming to ahistorical ideals), but an ethic engendered by the quality of symbolic interactions between various communities, and evaluated, even revised, according to changes therein. For whatever reason, those groups whose present needs and desires are not represented by presumably universal democratic representation satisfy them by sharing their motivating passions among others with similar motivations. The Seattle World Trade Organization protests in December 1999, for example, or the demonstrations against the G8 in Genoa during the summer of

2001, are remembered for a collective frenzy in which diverse groups, from anarchists to pacifists, were thrust together in a volatile climate of conflict and solidarity resulting from their common frustrations with representative politics. The politics of collective sentiment exhibited by such relations yield a variety of outcomes, from inclusion to exclusion, from tolerance to indifference, even violence. After defining the sociopolitical value and significance of these collective sentiments, how should one diagnose their ethical quality? How should one evaluate the social and political changes produced by the mercurialness of politics in this form without reverting to a moral interpretation of cultural phenomena—without reifying a set of ahistorical moral principles? In the next section, I provide answers to these pressing questions.

RHETORIC AND STYLE RECONFIGURED

The changing social and political conditions that Maffesoli identifies are not prescribed and organized by a transparent authority, in accord with a consensual civic morality, but are engendered by transitory modes of affective communication among diverse social groups. Collective sentiments and aesthetic rituals influence novel social alliances, affinities between markedly different groups, by virtue of the ways in which they are publicly expressed, performed, or symbolized. Such forms of communication establish, maintain, or transfigure contemporary social and political relations, no matter how harmonious or violently discordant. Inevitably, these processes of communication acquire a distinctive ethos that reflects their social and political currency: their perceived success or failure in cultivating desired social and political configurations. The iteration of related forms, symbols, or images manifests the rhetoric according to which those guided by similar sentiments or rituals participate, however momentarily, however effectively or not, in some social and political arrangement.

In this context, rhetoric encompasses something other than transparent or autonomous communication. It is an aesthetic, rather than a conceptual, rhetoric; an affective, not rational, communication; a collective, instead of individual, expression. Following Maffesoli's insights, the rhetoric of collective style involves "a communication" whose "sole objective [is] to 'touch' the other, to simply be in contact, to participate together in a form of gregariousness. This is the communication of sport, of music, of consumption, or else that banal communication of the daily or weekly stroll through the urban spaces designed for this effect. This 'tactile' communication is also a form of address: we speak to each other by touching" (1996a, 62). By this logic, we "touch" one another rhetorically—that is, we communicate affectively in the service of some pragmatic collective purpose—through sentiment, aesthetic, or performance instead of reason, ideals, or consensus.

One might propose that the meaning of rhetoric as such matters less than the social practices it enables. What Maffesoli calls the "interlocutive relation," the "form of 'we say' " invoked by this kind of rhetoric, retains greater significance than "a preestablished meaning" (64)—in other words, the essential, supposedly immutable, meaning of self, community, or society. The manner in which group identities cohere or disperse according to an aggregation of symbols, rituals, or other aesthetic phenomena (according to Maffesoli's "we say") constitutes the rhetoric of postmodern style. A conception of rhetoric in this frame recognizes that it engenders and disseminates the style of an epoch through multiple forms, in a manner irreducible to reasoned or transparent communication. Indeed, the dissemination of a particular style is manifested in the material relations, or the communal bonds of sentiment, that it either establishes or disrupts. Referring to Jean Baudrillard's famous adage, Maffesoli observes that "the profusion of communication" in this context "is the symptom of the absence of communication . . . a communication that, in all senses of the word, is used to touch the other, to favor contact with the other, either directly or indirectly" (66–67).

While recognizing the cogency of this distinction, one should avoid maintaining too rigid a boundary between meaningful and affective communication. Such a binary would reduce affective forms of rhetoric to one side of an artificial antithesis. Along with his allusion to Baudrillard, Maffesoli's proposal that "it matters little that the content of the communication [is] degree zero" (62) suggests that the communication of collective style occurs without recourse to any kind of meaning at all. For those groups compelled to establish emotive bonds in order to satisfy their mutual needs or desires, the public sharing of certain emotions can be quite meaningful. Maffesoli himself asserts that there is logic to the "nonlogical" (viii). One must recognize, however, that this logic of collective sentiment does not reflect conscious adherence to a universal civic morality but is derived from the fickle significance of common "passions, affects, and sentiments lived day to day" (Maffesoli 1996a, 64). In a sense, the very proliferation of meanings produced by the vectors of shared sentiment, rather than an absence thereof, accounts for the affective qualities of rhetoric in this mode. From this perspective, the very etymology of the term *discourse* explains the rhetorical function of collective style: "discurrere, meaning to run in several directions, and to do so in a disorganized, chaotic, and aleatory manner" (Maffesoli 1996a, 64). As in Foucault's notion of discourse, the very dispersion of an epoch's characteristic practices, symbols, and relations manifests its style or ethos.

Rhetorical inquiry is singularly equipped to account for the nature of the aesthetic dissemination—the character of the collective vibration or shared sentiment—through which a particular style is crystallized. Having recognized this affective dimension of rhetoric, one can pursue the study of style beyond Maffesoli's provisional recognition of its significance to social and political relations in order to account for the discursive means (the specific tropes, symbols, and rituals) that engender, maintain, or transfigure a given style. Rhetorical inquiry can evaluate the affective or aesthetic practices according to which a collective sentiment establishes communication between cultural groups rather than merely acknowledging the existence of such processes. If a collective style (as Maffesoli puts it), "enables liaison among all the members of a society"(38), then rhetorical inquiry crucially contributes to the ethical evaluation of social relations, to an understanding of their political function, in addition to simply classifying them as ethical phenomena.

Without an attunement to its rhetoric, any account of the social and political relations produced by a collective style is incomplete. The fragile bonds of collective sentiment and the interplay of cultural forms and appearances have acquired their recent social value by serving political ends more partial and immediate than those sought by democratic voluntarism; nevertheless, one would overlook the rhetoric of such sentiments, forms, and appearances if one concluded that they produced merely arbitrary social and political relations. There is logic to the illogical, a politics to the apolitical, even if they admit to inevitable mutation. As social and political currents, one should not define the shared and seemingly chaotic passions that Maffesoli describes as arbitrary excesses, thereby rendering any collective sentiment or aesthetic display as meaningful or meaningless as any other. "If merely 'feeling good' could decide," William James wrote, "drunkenness would be the supremely valid human experience" (1985, 16). A collective style generates certain imperatives: emotive and aesthetic rather than rational and universal.[4] Emotive and aesthetic practices that contribute to the formation of collective style, as James would likely put it, do not feel arbitrary when they are undertaken; their apparent necessity to those who undertake them may well explain their increasing value in postmodern social and political contexts. In this regard, the collective refusal of reasoned expression and democratic process invokes an implicit set of political assumptions and values: a rhetoric of the desired configuration among self, other, and community. Without diagnosing the nature of this rhetoric as it organizes social and political relations, one would risk ignoring the animating values and significance—the ethos—that sentiments, images, rituals, or forms acquire in their circulation throughout cultural institutions.

An account of rhetoric in this form amounts to an account of ethical judgment as it occurs, not in compliance to a universal morality, but according to specific sites of social, political, and communicative crisis. So-called postmodern encounters between communities and individuals marked primarily by their radical cultural difference from one another represent a site of ethical confusion. Having relinquished our faith in the harmonizing power of democratic ideals, how do we respond to those whose expressed values and rituals so explicitly contrast with ours? What mode of communication can we implement to manage our social and political needs and desires when communication as such has broken down? Responses to these ethical crises pocketing contemporary civic life each invoke a rhetoric of self, other, and community forged, not by artistic autonomy or humanistic reason, but by the ethical exigencies that influence the nature of our political investments.

The discursive or symbolic manifestations of these exigencies, and the rhetoric through which they are negotiated, comprise what one might call the text of postmodern society. Italian philosopher Maurizio Ferraris asserts that, "before describing an already given reality," a text "transmits and stylizes forms of life" (quoted in Maffesoli 1996a, 53).[5] In analogous fashion, the text of postmodern social life is shaped by the aesthetic patterns of cohesion and dispersion, of inclusion and exclusion, according to which groups and individuals participate in a common sentiment, a shared social or political style. Rhetorical inquiry can account for the aesthetic nature of a social text by interpreting the political functions of a common sentiment, of style in this form. It can investigate how the communication of style among certain groups, how the distribution and consumption of certain tropes, images, or rituals, engenders specific social and political practices. It can also scrutinize how these practices influence larger social arrangements by virtue of the patterns of aesthetic communication sustaining them. Finally, this form of rhetorical inquiry can evaluate the ethical quality of such relations, but not by deriving a moral lesson from them; instead, one must measure their ethical quality according to their capacity to maintain a robust aesthetic agon. The heterogeneous nature of collective style encompasses ongoing public competition between diverse aesthetic forms: "Images circulate and confront one another, competing mythologies are paraded, composite ideologies are patched together" (Maffesoli 1996a, 34). The agon of these competing "images," "mythologies," and "ideologies" manifests the rhetoric of a collective style. It denotes, not a normative civic ideal, but the preservation of social or discursive conditions suited to the affective expression of political needs and desires in equal measure to their rational representation. Ethical consideration of a communal style therefore amounts to asking if it either displays a capacity for producing a variety of responses to multiple social and political exigencies, or if it invokes a privileged sentiment merely to impose a dogmatic civic pathos on diverse cultural practices.

These recommendations comprise a rationale and methodology for research on the intersection of style and rhetoric that regards both categories as irreducible to the intentions or actions of a humanist agent. The foregoing demonstration of this methodology with respect to so-called postmodern style, moreover, illustrates how one might analyze an instance of rhetoric in the middle voice by evaluating the discursive or symbolic practices that constitute the ethos of a discursive formation and thereby engender a matrix of social, political, and ethical relations. I do not mean to suggest, by way of the analysis featured in this chapter, that something called individual rhetorical agency does not exist. Instead, I argue that such agency is fundamentally shaped by existing discursive and aesthetic conditions, which vary from one social context to another. If anything, I offer the possibility of a more comprehensive account of the contingent genesis and nature of rhetorical action: one that considers the broader social and political relations that enable a diversity of cultural expressions and ethical judgments. Nevertheless, I resist any attempt to account for a given rhetoric of collective style by identifying those individuals who partake of it as its exclusive principle of intelligibility. The politics of taste and decorum, aesthetic or performative conventions, and cultural sentiments each enjoy a rhetoric—a capacity to influence social arrangements and ethical deliberations—only partially explained by the imposition of a causal relationship between persuasive resources and subjective intentions. A wider interpretive lens demonstrates that the rhetoric of a given social and political style, by virtue of its discursive and aesthetic features rather than the intentions of a single speaker or author, organizes the formation of communities, stimulates relations between all manner of social agents, and publicly circulates conceptions of self, other, and community that define the social relations of a given epoch. In short, the rhetoric of collective style manifests, not the socially and politically unifying power of style per se, but the shifting currents of shared sentiment and the mutable value of cultural forms that influence how communities and individuals relate to one another through the expression of their changing needs and desires.

Part III

Rhetoric and the Politics
of Self and Other

Chapters 3 and 4 demonstrated that the ethos of social, political, and ethical relations manifests a rhetoric of subjectivity in which notions of self and other, individual and community, or good and evil acquire meaning and value from changing discursive conditions. The final pairing of chapters in this book provides a more sustained analysis of such developments. Chapters 5 and 6 examine, each in their own way, how the discursive formation of time, memory, and historical experience vitally constitutes the ethos of social, political, and ethical relations, principally in the form of their characteristic options for speech and judgment. Both chapters interrogate prevailing assumptions about the recovery and representation of marginalized historical experiences that symbolically integrate past and present, self and other. In doing so, they demonstrate that such recovery and representation presumes the possibility of an ideal and authentic communication between individuals in the present and traditionally objectified groups from the past.

Consequently, I interrogate the representational definitions of self and other, past and present, or speech and silence that authorize this notion of an ideal and authentic communication in order to assign a nonrepresentational sense and value to the political and ethical relations they sponsor. In both chapters, I examine how rhetoric in the middle voice—how the ethos of established discursive practices and social relations—engenders modes of thought, knowledge, speech, and judgment through the symbolic formation of time, memory, and historical experience. Analysis of these modes permits one to evaluate the nature of the discursive conditions that enable, as Maffesoli might say, the management of relations with alterity. Toward that end, I scrutinize in the following case studies the symbolic interplay of presence and absence that engenders notions of self and other and thereby establishes the rhetorical, political, and ethical conditions according to which they are negotiated.

Chapter 5

Jefferson's Other

In 1827, two male slaves named Madison and Eston Hemings were freed by the terms of Thomas Jefferson's will. Within five years of their emancipation, Madison and Eston both married women who, like them, were of racially mixed heritage. In 1835, the brothers moved to southern Ohio, where, no matter how light their skin color, law and social taboo enforced a radical gulf separating those known as white from those with even the subtlest "visible admixture" of "negro blood" (Stanton and Swann-Wright 1999, 164). Eventually, Eston moved with his family to Madison, Wisconsin, changed his name to Eston H. Jefferson, and, by virtue of his new-found anonymity, completed what Lucia Stanton and Dianne Swann-Wright describe as Eston's "northwestardly course, from slavery to freedom and, finally, to whiteness" (1999, 165). Madison and his family kept the Hemings name and remained in Ross County, Ohio, on what Stanton and Swann-Wright call "the black side of the color line" (165). Eston honored the name and memory of Thomas Jefferson, whose persona offered a valuable token of legitimacy in the white world he and his family inhabited. Madison preserved the name and memory of his mother Sally, almost never speaking of his family's rumored heritage as illegitimate descendants of Jefferson until late in life. Whereas Eston laid claim to the memory of the man he identified as his father in order to pass for white, Madison preserved the memory of his mother while living as a black man in a black community (Stanton and Swann-Wright 1999, 173).[1]

Memory and biology form a common alloy in this narrative, shaping the itinerary of Madison and Eston Hemings's lives. Indeed, the narrative suggests the workings of desire in the lived experience of memory: Eston's desire to pass as a white man and Madison's desire to preserve a heritage under threat of dissolution. Even today, a desire manifested in the confluence of memory and biology sustains the legend of an illicit affair between Thomas Jefferson and a slave named Sally Hemings. The homology of memory and biology informing this legend was no more evident than when, in November 1998, the scientific journal *Nature* published the results of DNA tests conducted in order to determine the likelihood of a sexual affair between Jefferson and Hemings (Foster et al. 1998). Instead of resolving controversy over enduring rumors of the affair, scientific evidence supporting its likelihood reinvigorated public debate over Jefferson (Lewis and Onuf 1999b; McMurray and McMurray 2002).

In this chapter, I explore a diverse array of texts in order to investigate the public memory of Thomas Jefferson. Together, such texts exemplify an especially provocative instance of rhetoric in the middle voice. Rhetoric in the form of this public memory does not represent individual memories or historical truth but manifests, rather, the discursive formation of multiple conditions for knowing, speaking of, and rendering judgments about the symbolic affinities between past and present. Curiously, the rhetoric of this memory represents a past for which no certain record exists. The depiction of Jefferson's alleged affair with Sally Hemings in novels, films, and other discourses demonstrates that the rhetoric of the past, which preserves its relevance and utility for audiences in the present, is often sustained, not by a transparent or even plausible understanding of former persons and events, but by profound and potentially irresolvable confusions over the relationship between what is commemorated and those doing the commemorating. Hence, the public memory of Thomas Jefferson is defined by what I refer to as Jefferson's other: a discursive haunting of his official reputation in which ghostly counterparts are said to represent what the official record can only suggest. Throughout this chapter, I view Jefferson's other as the characteristic trope of a discursive formation that vividly exemplifies contemporary relations between past and present, history and politics, self and other, good and evil.

The significance of such rhetoric exceeds the confines of academic debates. Thomas Jefferson's centrality to United States political philosophy and civic identity is well documented.[2] In 1874, Historian James Parton proclaimed, "If Jefferson was wrong, America is wrong. If America is right, Jefferson was right" (iii). More recently, Gordon Wood commented that Jefferson "remains a touchstone, a measure of what we Americans are or where we are going. No figure in our history has embodied so much of our heritage and so many of our hopes" (1999, 29). Symbolically, we have made Jefferson's character our own. Rhetorically speaking, Jefferson personifies contemporary anxieties over the legacy of race, slavery, and sex to our civic identity, to the symbolic meaning and value of current social, political, and ethical relations. In this connection, the discursive emergence, maintenance, and transformation of

Jefferson's public memory enables specific options for thought, speech, and judgment characteristic of contemporary subject positions as they are fashioned from ongoing civic debates over the meaning of the past to the present, of self to other, of civic virtue to social vice.

Given his famed personification of our civic identity, the likelihood that Jefferson pursued a lengthy sexual affair with one of his slaves lends new significance to a familiar chorus of questions. What twisted impulses would have driven the author of the Declaration of Independence to father several children with Sally Hemings only to keep them as slaves at Monticello? What sparked the affair and what sustained it—love, lust, or rape? What incestuous consequences did the suggestive complexion of Hemings and her children portend for the complexion of our nation as a whole?

The persistence of such questions in modern debates over Jefferson indicates that the defining features of his public memory are found less in a coherent set of facts about Jefferson and more in the perceived nature of his enigmatic psyche, in the blood and skin tone of his illegitimate children, and in the sexual acts that would have produced such offspring. Our contemporary memory of Jefferson is acutely voyeuristic, fixed upon the lurid qualities of Jefferson's unconscious and the nature of the sexual acts in which he and Hemings might have engaged: a memory that desires to be written on the very bodies it commemorates. The impossibility of satisfying this desire, however, only redoubles its intensity and multiplies its domain. If "public memory," in Stephen Browne's terms, "lives as it is given expressive form" (1995, 248), then desire so conceived stimulates the rhetorical forms that lend shape and coherence to memory's inherent fracture and obscurity. Far from effectively representing the ephemera of history, our public memory of Jefferson renders the impossibility of such representation productive. It gives expression to a host of collective desires that the record of the past cannot satisfy: the desire to understand Jefferson's psyche, to give Hemings the public voice she lacked during her lifetime, and to document their sexual passions. Rather than preserving or reflecting the past, the public memory of Jefferson belies our inability to communicate with the past's most ethereal and subjective phenomena.

In what follows, I examine the most provocative contemporary texts informing the public memory of Jefferson while attending to the collective desires that inspire them and the rhetorical functions they perform. Throughout, I scrutinize how differences between representations of Jefferson indicate changing discursive conditions for political and ethical judgment concerning the symbolic affinities between past and present, self and other, virtue and vice. I begin by exploring the rhetorical significance of recent attempts to deliver some form of judgment regarding two hundred years of rumor, speculation, and debate about the possibility of a sexual relationship between Thomas Jefferson and Sally Hemings. Next, I evaluate the modern tendency to represent the alleged affair according to the conventions of romance. Thereafter, I analyze a representation of Jefferson that offers an especially sober parable about the incestuous relationship between slavery and democracy. Together, these rhetorical forms illustrate the emergence and transformation of discursive conditions according to which we have conceived of the past as a means of responding to current social, political, and ethical dilemmas over our civic character. I conclude by considering the strange but common purpose uniting the diverse texts discussed in this chapter: that of representing historical phenomena for which no certain history exists, of commemorating that which lives on in official records as little more than hope, promise, or rumor.

MEMORY'S DESIRES

Widespread interest in the possibility of an affair between Jefferson and his slave was renewed fiercely in the late twentieth century, an era that experienced an unprecedented awareness of racial, sexual, and gender politics.[3] New audiences learned of this rumored affair with Winthrop Jordan's *White over Black: American Attitudes toward the Negro, 1550–1812* (1968). Although Jordan discussed the old rumors only briefly, he was the first modern historian to give the story credence. Fawn Brodie's *Thomas Jefferson: An Intimate History* (1974) treated tales of an affair between Jefferson and Hemings as factual and used Freudian interpretations of historical documents to prove its authenticity.[4] Other depictions followed in novels and films, suggesting that, if the rumors were true, fact in this case was stranger than any fictional account. To survey contemporary rhetoric about Jefferson and Hemings is to survey the emergence and proliferation of new symbolic relations between the past and the present, and with them new options for political and ethical judgment about the legacy of race, slavery, and sex to our civic identity.

In the modern era, the public memory of Jefferson acquired an increasingly alien quality in relation to a growing fascination with the figure of Sally Hemings. Public interest in the possibility of an affair between the sage of Monticello and his slave, once dismissed by historians as lascivious myth, became too significant to ignore. With varying degrees of objectivity and persuasiveness, historians began to consider the merits of the legend in greater detail. Nevertheless, the debate reached a point of stasis, often posing African American oral histories and popular fictional accounts, which accepted the rumors as fact, against the testimony of professional historians, many of whom deferred judgment by citing a lack of conclusive evidence. Referring to controversies over the Jefferson-Hemings rumors in the nineteenth century, Merrill Peterson wrote: "While there was not much evidence tending to prove the legend, neither was there positive disproof"; he concluded that the rumors "will probably never be proven. The legend survives, although no serious student of Jefferson has ever declared his [or her] belief in it" (1960, 184; 186). If the discourse of historians had failed to provide a satisfying judgment on this issue, what mode of discourse could?

The Desire for Judgment

In 1997, Annette Gordon-Reed's *Thomas Jefferson and Sally Hemings: An American Controversy* argued that the social, political, and institutional biases of Jefferson scholars had prevented "a serious and objective attempt to get at the truth of this matter" (224). Gordon-Reed, a professor at New York Law School, regarded historians' conventional arguments against the likelihood of an affair between Jefferson and his slave as suspiciously outmoded compared to the increasing sophistication of modern historiography. The nature of such denials, she asserted, "required the systematic dismissal of the words of black people who spoke on this matter" (xiv). Gordon-Reed subjected the arguments of Jefferson defenders to a legal cross-examination that exposed their inconsistencies.[5]

The rhetorical effect of Gordon-Reed's treatise was twofold. On the one hand, it signaled a political intervention, exposing the biases of Jefferson scholars as well as their investment in "restrict[ing] knowledge as a way of controlling allowable discourse on this subject" (Gordon-Reed 1997, 224). On the other hand, Gordon-Reed's forensic survey of the evidence transformed the criterion for judgment in this case. Contrary to the arguments of professional historians, she asserted that the absence of objective standards in historians' assessments of relevant circumstantial and, in her view, highly credible evidence had hindered judgment on this question.[6] Although professional historiography is an empirical study rooted in typically rigorous interpretive standards, Gordon-Reed argued that historians had failed to apply such standards consistently and fairly to the Jefferson-Hemings rumors. Her forensic discourse thus supplied what recurrent historical arguments dismissing the notion of an affair between Jefferson and Hemings had not: standards that could produce an equitable judgment. On the basis of these standards, Gordon-Reed's treatise functioned enthymematically. Her point-counterpoint rehearsal of cases for and against the likelihood of an affair allowed the credibility and reasonableness of that likelihood to emerge in self-evident fashion. Ultimately, then, the author produced a patently forensic judgment because the "plaintiff" in this case was able to meet an acceptable burden of proof—in Gordon-Reed's terms, "proof that makes the truth of an accusation more probable than not" (xvi).

Soon after the publication of Gordon-Reed's treatise, a second mode of inquiry decisively transformed the nature of this debate. In November 1998, pathologist Eugene A. Foster and his colleagues published the results of a study comparing DNA samples taken from descendants of Jefferson and Hemings. Foster and his colleagues identified a haplotype containing nineteen polymorphic markers taken from male-line descendants of Field Jefferson, Thomas Jefferson's paternal uncle.[7] Apparently, the haplotype is quite rare; "it has never been observed outside the Jefferson family," nor in a large genetic sample of "670 European men" and "more than 1,200 worldwide" (Foster et al. 1998, 27). Despite its rarity, the haplotype matched that of Eston Hemings's male-line descendant. According to the authors, the probability of this match occurring by chance is less than 1 percent. "We cannot completely rule out other explanations of our findings based on illegitimacy in various lines of descent," they concluded. "But in the absence of historical evidence to support such possibilities, we consider them to be unlikely" (27). Foster and colleagues' findings, while not irrefutable, represented the most compelling evidence yet presented in the Jefferson-Hemings debate.

Consequently, these findings dramatically transformed public deliberation on Jefferson and Hemings. Wood comments that "clearly the burden of proof has shifted" in the wake of Foster's findings: "[U]ntil otherwise disproved, Jefferson is now presumed to have fathered one or more of Sally Hemings's children. Indeed, what is remarkable is the alacrity and enthusiasm with which historians . . . have come to accept the truth of the Jefferson-Hemings relationship" (1999, 27). Little more than a year after the publication of Foster and his colleagues' results, the Thomas Jefferson Memorial Foundation, which owns Monticello, completed its review of Foster's findings, along with the reactions of prominent historians, and publicly agreed that Jefferson's affair with Sally Hemings was essentially a proven fact (Smith 2000).[8]

Despite the apparent self-evidence of the DNA findings, Foster and his colleagues' study functioned rhetorically. Prior to the appearance of Gordon-Reed and Foster's inquiries, the question of a sexual liaison between Jefferson and his slave was regarded as indeterminate owing to a lack of conclusive evidence. In 1997, Joseph Ellis opined, "[T]he available evidence on each side of the controversy is just sufficient to sustain the debate but wholly insufficient to resolve it one way or another. Anyone who claims to have a clear answer to the most titillating question about the historical Jefferson is engaging in massive self-deception or outright lying. This is one mystery destined to remain unsolved" (21).[9] Ellis, however, underestimated the power of what he called "the sphinxlike Jefferson" to demand a solution to its riddle.

In this case, the very lack of a satisfying resolution to the riddles of the past incited novel forms of knowledge, speech, and judgment. Jacques Derrida observes that the "undecidable opens the field of decision or of decidability. It calls for decision in the order of ethical-political responsibility" (1988, 116). According to Derrida, "There can be no moral or political responsibility without this trial and this passage by way of the undecidable" (116). Far from representing the mere lack of a factual determination, the "pathos of an indecision" (Derrida 1988, 116) actively *provokes* a response because it stimulates a crisis over standards and procedures. Gordon-Reed and Foster's work offered provocative rhetorical responses to the "trial" of the undecidable that shaped the Jefferson-Hemings debate at the end of the twentieth century. Gordon-Reed's application of forensic standards yielded both a political intervention and an ethical judgment that purported to weigh all forms of evidence equitably. The ethos of Foster and his colleagues' genetic tests, moreover, proved especially persuasive in response to the desire for judgment stimulated by the presumed "undecidability" of the Jefferson-Hemings debate.

Nonetheless, the public memory of Jefferson remains largely "undecided." Eric Lander and Joseph Ellis comment, "Nothing in Foster and colleagues' study, and nothing in the vast historical literature, sheds any light on the character of the relationship between Jefferson and Sally Hemings" (1998, 13). Far from entirely resolving this controversy, Gordon-Reed and Foster's responses have only identified further zones of "undecidability," and with them still deeper ethical and political desires: to imagine the lived burdens of Sally Hemings's existence in terms other than those of historical caricature, and to exhume the alleged psychological torments that Jefferson's marbled public persona has entombed for centuries. "The reassessment of Jefferson occasioned by the DNA evidence," Jan Ellen Lewis and Peter Onuf observe, "gives us the opportunity to write new stories, to hear different voices" (1999a, 7). In what follows, I consider how these "new stories" and "different voices" have helped define our memory of Jefferson, and thus our current ethical and political obligations as bearers of his civic legacy.

Romance and *Ressentiment*

For generations, Sally Hemings has haunted Jefferson's official reputation. Even during her lifetime, public discourse about Sally Hemings was marked by profound racial and sexual anxieties. In 1802, a journalist named James Callender slandered Jefferson in the *Richmond Recorder,* announcing: "It is well known that the man, *whom it delighteth the people to honor,* keeps, and for many years past has kept, as his concubine, one of his own slaves. Her name is SALLY" (quoted in Gordon-Reed 1997, 61). Callender's subsequent articles exhibited his own racial pathologies: he described Hemings as a "wench," "a slut as common as the pavement" who had "fifteen, or thirty" lovers "of *all colours,*" and referred to her children, supposedly fathered by Jefferson, as a "yellow litter" (Gordon-Reed 1997, 61). In Gordon-Reed's words, Callender "was accusing Thomas Jefferson of something on the order of bestiality" (1997, 62).

Of course, such depictions were fodder for political attacks. John Chester Miller writes of "Black Sally" and "Congo Harem" stories propagated by Federalists following Callender's reports (1977, 148–61). Joshua Rothman relates that, in Jefferson's time, "A public accusation of an interracial sexual affair frequently had its foundation in a larger set of calculations, part of a battle between conflicting white parties over other issues" (1999, 88). As such, the earliest descriptions of Hemings played upon eighteenth-century anxieties about miscegenation,[10] portraying her as a hypersexualized beast whose odious eroticism could arouse an unnatural lust even in Jefferson, an avatar of civic virtue.

Representations of skin color and sexuality are blatantly linked in such accounts. Other contemporaneous descriptions of Hemings, featuring a different skin tone and, hence, a less malignant sexuality, more closely resemble her portrayals in modern memory. Such accounts also conform better to historical evidence: Sally Hemings's mother, Betty, was the daughter of an English sea captain and an African slave; according to the racial classifications of Jefferson's time, Sally was a quadroon. Testimony from slaves at Monticello as well as Jefferson's own grandson describe Hemings as nearly white with straight hair, leading many at the time to refer to her as "Dashing Sally." This rendering of Hemings has proved more sympathetic to popular sensibilities.

Wood predicts that, in the wake of Foster's DNA tests, "[t]he historical arguments are now likely to be not over the existence of the relationship but over whether there was any affection involved in it" (1999, 27). Sally Hemings thus remains Jefferson's elusive yet intensely provocative other. At the same time, Jefferson himself becomes something other by virtue of his association with the mystery of Hemings, as if he must have succumbed to his own tortured alter ego in order to father several of her children. Hence, Jefferson's other is always double: both the enigma of his racial, economic, and sexual other (Hemings) and the silhouette of a Jefferson nowhere present in official history. Such symbolic otherness manifests the characteristic ethos of contemporary discourse about Jefferson's meaning and value to current social and political relations. It represents a crucial discursive condition shaping what can be thought, known, and said about Jefferson and Hemings in the current era.

Although we may never know the nature of whatever feelings existed between Jefferson and Hemings, contemporary discourse about their relationship is driven by a persistent desire to explore the possibility of mutual affection. If Jefferson and Hemings are imagined to have borne a deep fondness for one another, especially over a period of thirty-eight years, the memory of their relationship acquires the mystique of romance. This mystique has the effect of redeeming Jefferson, despite his own paranoia about miscegenation and regardless of the fact that Hemings was, according to the law of the day, Jefferson's property. Fetishizing the image of Hemings as nearly white with long, straight hair (as beautiful, according to Eurocentric standards) neutralizes, on the one hand, persisting anxieties over the notion of a sexual affair between Jefferson and a black woman while deflecting attention, on the other hand, from the fact that Hemings was Jefferson's slave.

The ubiquity of the romantic genre in contemporary portrayals of the Jefferson-Hemings affair is symptomatic of a desire to humanize and redeem Jefferson: to remember him neither by his racist attributes nor as a man who would force himself upon Sally Hemings when she was a mere teenager. Fawn Brodie's much-maligned psychobiography of Jefferson features such a cleansing aspiration. "Jefferson," she claims, "had been responsible for miscegenation—but innocently—with love and without debauchery of the slave woman" (1974, 433). The feature film *Jefferson in Paris* (1995) follows a similar logic, portraying the inception of Jefferson and Hemings's relationship as a Parisian romance. In 1787, while serving as Ambassador to France, Jefferson sent for his nine-year-old daughter, Mary (also called Polly), with instructions that a slave named Isabel should accompany her. Because Isabel was about to give birth, fourteen-year-old Sally Hemings was sent instead. Sally stayed on as one of Jefferson's servants in Paris; although little documentation of her stay exists, her time there is often recounted as a period when she blossomed into womanhood, thus catching Jefferson's eye.[11] Brodie writes that, at this time, Hemings was "supremely ready for the first great love of her life" (1974, 228). Legend has it that Hemings was pregnant when she and Jefferson returned to Monticello in December 1789 (Gordon-Reed 1997, 195). Although we may never know whether or not sexual encounters between Jefferson and Hemings began in Paris, contemporary writers have found the idea of a Parisian romance between the stately Jefferson and a young, exotic beauty intensely appealing. Modern accounts of Jefferson and Hemings, from Fawn Brodie's book to *Jefferson in Paris,* depict their relationship as a passionate romance induced by the fairy tale context in which it supposedly began. These accounts naturally invoke the pathos of romance, which, Hubert McDermott notes, historically has been used to portray the courtly love of an idealized "closed caste" (1989, 100).

If the vision of Jefferson and Hemings as tragic lovers satisfies a contemporary desire to humanize and so cleanse the memory of Jefferson, then this same romantic discourse also facilitates a reciprocal desire to rescue Hemings from historical caricature and racist stereotype. Romantic iterations of the Jefferson-Hemings affair transform Hemings into a passionate heroine, endowed with an enhanced agency because she had won Jefferson's heart. By portraying the alleged affair from a new perspective, that of Hemings herself, Barbara Chase-Riboud's novel entitled *Sally Hemings* (1979) represented a pivotal effort to render Hemings with a fuller palette. In the words of Scot

French and Edward Ayers, Chase-Riboud used fiction "to supply what document-based history could not" (1993, 437). Fiction gave her license to narrate, through long inner monologues, the unique psychology and emotions of Sally Hemings. Romantic fiction is defined, according to Ben Edwin Perry, by its narration of "the adventures or experiences of one or more individuals in their private capacities and from the viewpoint of their private interests and emotions" (1967, 44). Its conventions, therefore, are perfectly suited to represent Hemings's thoughts and desires. "Over three decades their passionate, complex love affair endured and flowered," reads a description of *Sally Hemings* in the 1979 Viking Press catalog: "While most documents related to that passion were carefully destroyed by Jefferson's white family after his death, enough remained to substantiate the basic facts of the case. Using this historical premise and data, Barbara Chase-Riboud has fashioned a dramatic—and unashamedly romantic—novel" (quoted in French and Ayers 1993, 437). Despite the melodrama of this synopsis, the trope of a romantic affair between Jefferson and his slave allowed Chase-Riboud to portray Hemings, for the first time, with a multidimensional persona.

Of course, political implications attended this more fulsome portrait. Jefferson scholars were upset by the initial publication of *Sally Hemings;* proposals to adapt the novel into a CBS miniseries proved too blasphemous for such historians to tolerate. Although *Sally Hemings* was a popular best-seller and an award-winning novel, Jefferson defenders Virginius Dabney and Dumas Malone successfully badgered CBS executives into scrapping the project (French and Ayers 1993, 436–43; Gordon-Reed 1997, 182–84).[12] Gordon-Reed offers an explanation for why Jefferson defenders might have found the visual portrayal of an affair between Jefferson and Hemings acutely repellent: "A film adaptation with real people playing these two roles, would tend to bring Jefferson down from the status of god to mortal, and if it was true to the novel, would lift Sally Hemings from the status of mere chattel to that of a human being" (1997, 184). Fifteen years later, the film *Jefferson in Paris* defied this prohibition; yet it did so by portraying this legendary instance of interracial passion in a reserved, antiseptic manner. In Gordon-Reed's description, "The film treats the relationship as true, but its makers could barely bring themselves to allow the two characters to touch one another on screen" (1999, 247–48).

The alleged passions of Jefferson and Hemings finally enjoyed an un-bridled portrayal in the CBS miniseries *Sally Hemings: An American Scandal* (2000).[13] With a license granted by the results of Foster's DNA tests, the miniseries explored the possibility of a robust and abiding romance between Jefferson and his slave, depicting the narrative from the perspective of a spirited Sally Hemings much like the one featured in Chase-Riboud's novel. The production's final frame informed viewers through superimposed text that genetic tests conducted in 1998 proved the affair between Jefferson and Hemings was historical fact. The ethos of the DNA tests thus lent a factual status to the entire miniseries, including the lush and tragic romance between Jefferson and Hemings. Ostensibly certified by the authority of science, *Sally Hemings: An American Scandal* represents the boldest articulation yet of a desire to create a sympathetic portrait of Hemings in public memory.

The miniseries adheres to the romantic formula of Jefferson-Hemings lore. Almost immediately upon her arrival in Paris, Sally is informed by her brother James (Jefferson's head chef)[14] that on French soil she is no longer a slave and that she will learn to read and write. Surprised at dinner that night by Sally's womanly beauty, it is Jefferson, not James, who takes an interest in refining Sally's speech and manners. Jefferson brings her along during an outing to a bookstore and even suggests that she read Thomas Paine's *Common Sense*.[15] The chemistry between Jefferson and Sally deepens in concert with Sally's social and intellectual maturation. Jefferson's attraction to her intensifies after she questions the integrity of his famous appeals to equality in the Declaration of Independence and when she charms Thomas Paine himself during a party at the Palace of Versailles. Jefferson and Sally's scenes of passion are interspersed with images of Jefferson reading to her or of the two lovers strolling through a garden, identifying different flora and fauna. The portrait of Hemings fashioned in this miniseries is not one of a mere teenager whose status as Jefferson's concubine was a simple extension of her enslavement, but of a vibrant, even cosmopolitan, woman whose intellect proved every bit as desirable as her physical beauty to one of our history's most celebrated intellectuals. The genre of romance elevates the persona of Sally Hemings to the status of Jefferson's equal by lending her a stature worthy of aristocratic love.

Jefferson's attention to the improvement of Hemings's education allows her to achieve a nascent political consciousness. Sally is intrigued by French revolutionaries agitating in the streets, one of whom advises her, "Remember—you stand for something!" (*American Scandal*, 2000). Sally's love for Jefferson and her fledgling libertarian ideals are brought into conflict when Jefferson decides to leave Paris on the eve of revolution—a momentous incident in Jefferson-Hemings lore. An account of this episode first appeared in Madison Hemings's memoir, published in the *Pike County (Ohio) Republican* in 1873: "He [Jefferson] desired to bring my mother back to Virginia with him but she demurred. She was just beginning to understand the French language well, and in France she was free, while if she returned to Virginia she would be re-enslaved. So she refused to return with him. To induce her to do so he promised her extraordinary privileges, and made a solemn pledge that her children should be freed at the age of twenty-one years" (quoted in Gordon-Reed 1997, 246). That Jefferson freed all of

Hemings's children when they came of age, and that the only female slave he ever freed was the daughter of Sally Hemings, is among the strongest circumstantial evidence that the relationship between Jefferson and Hemings was sanctioned by an agreement like the one in Madison Hemings's account. The notion that Jefferson made the contract for love, and not simply to retain a concubine, humanizes and even ennobles his character. Despite the obvious selfishness of this contract, the tale conjures a sympathetic vision of Jefferson struggling against the institution of slavery for the sake of love. The scenario also heightens the perception of Sally Hemings as a tragic heroine: in order to assent to this alleged contract, she would have had to relinquish her freedom in exchange for that of her unborn children.

Yet there is evidence that Hemings's "choice" may have been more complicated than these accounts would suggest. Philip Morgan raises doubts about the nature of her supposed dilemma in Paris:

> From 1787 to 1789, when Sally was in Paris, the issue of freedom was still contested, racism was mounting, and master-initiated manumissions outnumbered petitions for freedom. Sally would have had to find a lawyer, go to court, have her case successfully argued, and find a new employer—all this in a foreign tongue and without access to a local support network. Further, by challenging her freedom in court after 1777, when the *Police des Noirs* was in effect, Sally risked being confiscated and transported to the living hell of Saint Dominique, not back to her family and friends in Virginia. (1999, 84, n45)

Morgan's skepticism suggests that Hemings faced no dilemma at all as Jefferson fled Paris. Debating this historical point, however, is less important than observing the rhetorical functions of such a romantic narrative. The fuller rendering of Hemings invoked by this legend establishes the memory of a heroic figure sacrificing her freedom for that of her children. True to the discourse of romance, Hemings's agency in this account is derived from her ability to challenge Jefferson as only a lover could, as his equal in intellect and affection if not in law.

The remainder of *Sally Hemings: An American Scandal* develops this tragically heroic depiction of its title character. The drama is propelled by Sally's courageous struggles against the injustices of slavery, Jefferson all the while representing both her savior and master. Throughout these struggles, Sally's political consciousness, which she owes to Jefferson's tutelage, drives her actions and strains their relationship. One motif combines images of Sally and Jefferson reading each other's love letters with scenes of Sally teaching another slave to read, reminding us that Jefferson taught her how to perform such transgressions. As the horrors of slavery punctuate Sally's life with greater frequency, her indictments of Jefferson's hypocrisy grow more vitriolic. Sally mocks Jefferson's celebrated words in the Declaration of Independence: " 'We hold these truths to be self evident'? What truths? To whom?" (*American Scandal*, 2000). She becomes enraged at Jefferson after discovering his notorious statements on "blacks" in a copy of his *Notes on the State of Virginia*.[16] "You disgust me," she fumes. "I was wrong," he replies (*American Scandal*, 2000). The dialectical tension between Sally's political consciousness and her affection for Jefferson indicates a modern desire to imagine their affair, not as a protracted form of concubinage, but as a passionate drama of the mind as well as the body. At one point, Jefferson delights in the idea to build a room for Sally in Monticello, his beloved mansion: "Spirited discourse requires privacy," he beams, "and so do you and I" (*American Scandal*, 2000).

Despite constant upheavals, love always triumphs over the burdens placed upon Sally and Jefferson's relationship by intervening forces. The production's closing scenes show an aging and sickly Jefferson during his last years, strolling arm in arm around his estate with a graying Sally Hemings: the perfect portrait of an elderly husband and wife. Romantic conventions elevate Hemings to the status of an idealistic political agent and pardon Jefferson's hypocrisy, for if she forgave him—indeed, continued to love and honor him for the rest of his life—then why can't we? Perhaps no more poignant testimony exists regarding the persuasive power of romance in this case than the oral history of the Hemings family. Rhys Isaac writes, "Sally and Thomas's descendents believed that these two loved each other but understood that disparity of status made a marriage impossible, as indeed it did. The Hemings descendents have asserted that since blood is thicker than water, the great ancestor made due provision for his children. They have honored Jefferson as a white man who—unlike most white men in their bitter collective experience—kept his word to a black woman, and kept his promise for the children that she bore him" (1999, 123). Even for those with reason to malign his memory, the genre of romance preserves Jefferson, with bittersweet affection, as "the great ancestor."

The romantic rhetoric of the Jefferson-Hemings legend, whose form reached its zenith with the broadcast of *Sally Hemings: An American Scandal,* supplies a convenient resolution to the ethical conundrums that Jefferson symbolizes. The elixir of this alleged romance conjures an agreeable explanation for the nature of Jefferson and Hemings's relationship where none exists in the historical record. Lewis and Onuf posit that, "perhaps, in wanting to see in the complex history of slavery simply the story of a man and a woman, we hope to discover some measure of love that might redeem—or deny—the brutal exercise of power" (1999a, 12).

My analysis of romantic rhetoric about Jefferson and Hemings's relationship provides a framework for evaluating the symbolic relations between past and present that they sanction. One cannot help but sympathize with the desire to fashion a more accurate portrait of Sally Hemings in modern memory and understand better the nature of her unique burdens. Doing so draws attention to the politics of memory, lighting up the historical voids whose darkness privileges the already privileged. In the miniseries, Jefferson's daughter Martha burns her father's love letters to Sally, declaring, "I will not allow these shameful letters to make their way into history" (*American Scandal,* 2000). Philip Morgan nevertheless argues, "Modern notions of romance— seeing Hemings and Jefferson as America's premier biracial couple—should not be projected onto unions born of trauma, dependence, and constraint" (1999, 75). Indeed, Jay Fliegelman writes that the power of sentiment was both feared and revered in Jefferson's age; for him, "[t]he protection of the private self was a drama analogous to the protection of the colonies from prying Customs officers, appointed officials, and occupying armies" (1993, 108). A Jefferson overcome by his passion for Sally Hemings and bent on protecting his romance with her, the gossip of others be damned, is a patently modern Jefferson, inexplicable according to the cultural sentiments and anxieties of which he was a consummate personification. Romantic portrayals of Sally Hemings—Jefferson's most famous other—therefore produce a certain doubling of Jefferson as well.

Relinquishing this Byronic conception of Jefferson obliges one to relinquish the heroic image of Hemings. The romantic rendering of Hemings is defined by what we desire her to have done or to have been rather than what she actually did or who she actually was. As such, this romantic discourse deadens consideration of the profound sexual and racial inequities that would have existed between Jefferson and his slave, especially if one remembers that Hemings was only fifteen or sixteen years old at the time of their alleged Parisian romance.[17] Far from ennobling the memory of Hemings by having her study *Common Sense* and *Notes on the State of Virginia,* the conventions of modern romance merely facilitate the latest perversion of her existence.[18]

In effect, the romantic depiction of Hemings satisfies a modern desire to indict Jefferson for the hypocrisy of thoughts and actions not generally considered hypocritical until our time. The articulation of this desire in Hemings's fictional voice reverberates against a profound collective anxiety: any pleasure we may take in making these accusations by proxy is a pleasure easily won. The questions that the heroic Sally Hemings asks of Jefferson do not oblige us to rethink our contemporary ethics and politics concerning the unsettling history of race, gender, and slavery in the United States. Even if Jefferson never had a sexual affair with Hemings, the fact nonetheless remains that Hemings was the half-sister of Jefferson's late wife, a product of the so-called dalliances between Martha Jefferson's father and Sally Hemings's mother.[19] Any interpretation of Jefferson's relationship with Hemings necessarily relies on undisputed evidence that, despite their pathological fears about miscegenation, social and political elites such as Jefferson, including members of his own extended family, condoned and participated in that practice as a matter of course. The slavery in which our nation's founding icons held generations of their fellow human beings was far more carnal and complex than economic bondage alone. Have we yet to achieve a mode of public discourse that allows us to reckon, ethically and politically, with all that these largely unacknowledged facts about race, power, and sex portend for our past and present? Romance fails at this task. The notion of a romantic love affair between Jefferson and Hemings allows audiences to dress the past in period costumes while ignoring the largely unspoken histories of slavery and the apparent inability of our current ethics and politics to fully acknowledge them.

Consequently, one should interrogate these romantic narratives for their influence on the ethos of the present as well as the past. Nietzsche (1989a) asserts that a spirit of "imaginary revenge" produces what he calls *ressentiment*. The desire for revenge weakens us, Nietzsche contends, because it can never be satiated, because it rewards us for assigning blame; its only purpose is that it "says No to what is 'outside,' what is 'different,' what is 'not itself' " (I 10, 36). Nietzsche thus posits that *ressentiment,* this insatiable desire for revenge, is actually a form of self-loathing in disguise, a mask obscuring our belief that we are inadequate. Our modern attraction to the melodrama of Jefferson and Hemings's alleged romance is a symptom of such *ressentiment.* The spirited figure of Sally Hemings fashioned by this romance acts as a ventriloquist for our own feelings of betrayal toward Jefferson, channeling a desire for revenge that cannot be answered by Jefferson himself, regardless of however much we might like to hold him accountable. In Nietzsche's terminology, the romantic rendering of Jefferson and Hemings turns them into ourselves, into personifications of our own values, and thus "says No" to the ways in which they were irreducibly different from us. The transformation of Hemings into a tragic heroine and the redemption of Jefferson accomplished by this discourse suggests a hidden self-resentment: insofar as Jefferson is said to have embodied our national character, the unsettling truth about his relationship with Hemings may be a truth about ourselves. "This inversion of the value-positing eye," Nietzsche warns, "this *need* to direct one's view outward instead of back to oneself—is of the essence of *ressentiment*" (I 10, 36–37). The repeated depiction of Jefferson's alleged romance with a strong-willed, exotic beauty in the annals of our public memory suggests how pleasing this explanation for his enigmatic past may be. I now turn to a more sober account of Jefferson and Hemings's rumored affair that exhibits a strong aversion for the convenient remedies of romance. As such, it provides radically different conditions for contemporary judgments about Jefferson's symbolic influence on our modern civic ethos.

"At Once Both King and Slave"

In 1868, Jefferson biographer Henry S. Randall described, in a letter to historian James Parton, an alleged conversation with Jeff Randolph, Jefferson's oldest grandson. According to Randall, he and Randolph discussed Jefferson's affair with Sally Hemings at length, including the curiosities it spawned at Monticello. Apparently, Randolph told Randall that one of Hemings's children so closely resembled his grandfather "that at some distance or in the dusk the slave, dressed in the same way, might be mistaken for Mr. Jefferson." "He said in one instance," Randall added, "a gentleman dining with Mr. Jefferson, looked so startled as he raised his eyes from the latter to the servant behind him, that his discovery of the resemblance was perfectly obvious to all" (quoted in Gordon-Reed 1997, 254). Gordon-Reed has cast doubt on crucial portions of Randall's letter that were used in the past to provide an alibi for Jefferson (1997, 80–82); nevertheless, the life of Eston Hemings indicates that at least some children born of a union between Jefferson and Hemings would have been able to pass for white after being freed from slavery when they reached adulthood.[20] The peculiar spectacle of white slaves with red hair may have been a common sight at Jefferson's estate.[21] Such an image forms a striking contrast to traditional visions of life at Monticello, which remains a stately and bucolic setting in the national imaginary.

When Gordon-Reed speculated that filmed images of a romance between Jefferson and Hemings would give pause to a largely white viewing audience, she may have underestimated the inevitable shock of other images associated with this story. Indeed, the portrayal in *Sally Hemings: An American Scandal* of Jefferson and Hemings's pale, red-haired children, whom Jefferson would have kept as slaves at Monticello, presents a disturbing spectacle. Despite the conventions of romance with which it is often decorated, the Jefferson-Hemings folklore contains many elements disquieting to conventional sensibilities. Not the least of these are Hemings's youth at the alleged inception of their sexual relationship, the possibility that for nearly four decades Jefferson availed himself of Hemings as he did the labor of any other slave, and the notion that Jefferson could have coexisted, quite happily and for a number of years, with his own children as slaves at Monticello, some of whom were said to be his double in likeness and manner.[22] In many ways, the legend of a sexual affair between Jefferson and Hemings is comprised of visions that, particularly to modern sensibilities, can only be described as horrible.

Thus, the breach between romance and horror in the modern memory of Jefferson may be slight indeed. Whereas much contemporary discourse about Jefferson and Hemings employs romantic themes in order to neutralize the most chilling prospects of their relationship, Steve Erickson's novel *Arc d'X* (1993) displays a sober willingness, unmatched in the annals of Jefferson's public memory, to linger over such prospects.[23] In contrast to romantic accounts of Jefferson and Hemings's relationship, *Arc d'X* dwells voyeuristically within the unconscious of another Thomas Jefferson: a Jefferson lusting after a mere teenager, who was both his slave and his late wife's half-sister, and whom he would only enslave again by molesting her. Whereas Jefferson's public principles form the scaffold of his canonical memory, Erickson conjures a vision of Jefferson's private and unconscious drives, which can only be represented fictionally. In sum, he produces an unadulterated encounter with Jefferson's other: the private demon that may have dwelled within the civic saint.

Erickson's appropriation of pivotal scenes from the Jefferson-Hemings legend inverts the romantic interpretation of their relationship. He portrays Jefferson and Hemings's first sexual encounter as a rape, narrated from Jefferson's perspective as he is overcome with lust, maddened by the furor of revolution swelling in the streets below his hotel: "It thrilled him, not to be a saint for once, not to be a champion. Not to bear, for once, the responsibility of something noble or good. Didn't he believe that one must pursue his happiness? Such a pursuit is as ruthless as any other" (25). Intoxicated by the mounting insurrection, Jefferson's pursuit of happiness becomes, like that of the French revolutionaries, an especially dreadful enterprise. "Thomas" realizes that the pursuit of happiness "is as ruthless as any other" (25). Rather than suggesting that Jefferson's molestation of Sally amounts to a failure of his character, *Arc d'X* portrays the expenditure of his fevered lust as the means by which Jefferson replenishes his democratic convictions. Thomas's inner monologue continues: "In the nights that have passed since, I accepted such moments not as the crimes that contradicted what I believed in but as the passionate chaos that justified and liberated the god of reason living within me. . . . Surrendering to passion, I came to believe my convictions not less, but more" (46). In this allegorical account, the right to self-determination and the republican optimism that attends it are validated by the disenfranchisement of others.

Thomas represents a synecdoche of America.[24] He calls it "a flawed thing, and I know the flaw is of me" (46). By associating his rape of Sally with the pursuit of happiness, Jefferson allegorizes the rape committed by America in the name of liberty. Erickson's exploration of this other Jefferson's unconscious unveils the sinister politics cloaked by America's most pristine ideals. Thomas's hidden motivations reveal that the celebrated rights enumerated in the Declaration of Independence are anything but inalienable. The impious imagery of *Arc d'X* suggests that the pursuit of happiness for one political body is conducted through the sacrifice of another's self-determination, that some form of slavery is not anomalous to liberty but a necessary complement to the articulation of its "self-evident" nature. Democracy is not an antidote to tyranny, only another form of despotism.

Arc d'X invokes an image of Jefferson much like that proposed by Edmund S. Morgan, who argued that those in Jefferson's position were able to pursue a democratic agenda precisely because slavery had neutralized the threat of an unstable working class (1975). "Morgan's Jefferson," according to French and Ayers, "did not appear tormented or contradictory, but ruthlessly consistent. His was the most harrowing vision of all" (1993, 436). Such a vision is suggested by Jefferson's own words. In *Notes on the State of Virginia* Jefferson presented a despotic account of slavery, calling it a system that permits "one half the citizens thus to trample on the rights of the other, transforms these into despots, and these into enemies, destroys the morals of one part, and the amor patriae of the other" (1982, 162–63). Thus in *Arc d'X,* as Thomas rapes Sally, he feels "like a master, a king" (23).

Arc d'X also alludes to the alleged contract between Jefferson and Hemings. In Erickson's retelling, the contract is made, not for love, but because Sally is the dark secret in which the goodness of America is rooted. Sally agrees to the contract on certain conditions: "First, I will be the mistress of your house. Second, you will never sell me to another. Third, you will free all our children when they come of age" (44). After Thomas and Sally return to Virginia, she somehow slips outside the time and place of Jefferson's America, waking up in a postapocalyptic city of the future; like the real Sally Hemings, she exists as a ghost of history, absent from the official record of any known era. Eventually, after several nomadic journeys through time, Sally finds herself again facing Thomas in a Parisian alley, bargaining for her freedom as the revolution begins. This time, Sally chooses to remain in Paris.

Her decision spurs a series of events that rewrite history in bizarre fashion. Thomas returns to Virginia and, stricken with debilitating grief over the loss of Sally, sells himself to his slaves. President John Adams visits Jefferson and discovers that Monticello has been turned into a training ground for a black guerrilla army as it prepares a massive campaign against the new republic. Thomas, naked and chained by his former slaves, confesses to Adams, "It's the final resolution of the dilemma of power . . . to be at once both king and slave" (289). *Arc d'X* thus remakes the pastoral world of Monticello into a burlesque theater and inverts the aristocratic bearing of its master, effectively aping the historical Jefferson by transforming him into the sort of base, unnatural creature he would have abhorred. The novel lays bare the nature of Jefferson's (and, hence, the nation's) investment in the mechanisms of slavery. The institution is presented as an omnipresent temptation, offering a constant allure of power even for apparently rational and idealistic men such as Jefferson. Such a philosophy mirrors Jefferson's own views on the subject. "There must doubtless be an unhappy influence," he lamented, "on the manners of our people produced by the existence of slavery among us. The whole commerce between master and slave is a perpetual exercise of the most boisterous passions, the most unremitting despotism on the one part, and degrading submission on the other" (1982, 162). For Jefferson, a man whose Epicurean ethic fed a nearly pathological concern over the competition between reason and emotion, slavery was abominable because it effectively made unreasoned slaves of its masters, shackling them by means of "the most boisterous passions."[25] One's addiction to such passions, Jefferson wrote, and the form of tyranny they sanction, was passed on from parent to child: "The parent storms, the child looks on, catches the lineaments of wrath, puts on the same airs in the circle of smaller slaves, gives a loose to his worst of passions, and thus nursed, educated, and daily exercised in tyranny, cannot but be stamped by it with odious peculiarities. The man must be a prodigy who can retain his manners and morals undepraved in such circumstances" (162). *Arc d'X*'s aping of Jefferson dramatizes this political lesson: the slave master's economic sovereignty is the instrument of his bondage.

In this respect, the novel dramatizes the paradoxical personae of the sovereign as described in Hegel's famous master/slave dialectic. According to Hegel, the sovereign's freedom and liberty are secured only through the servitude of another, such that "the object in which the lord has achieved his lordship has in reality turned out to be something quite different from an independent consciousness. What now really confronts him is not an independent consciousness, but a dependent one" (1977, 117). In this manner, Hegel concludes, "lordship showed that its essential nature is the reverse of what it wants to be" (117).[26] By dramatizing the repressed unconscious of the sovereign, Erickson's caricature of Jefferson produces yet another allegory about America, which, in its infancy, fed on the tainted milk of slavery in order to declare itself the cradle of liberty. In composing this allegory, Erickson exhumes those hypnotic desires that sustained the system of slavery and lingers over the image of a sovereign confronted with his own fragile dependency, thereby reminding us that the question of slavery, especially for Jefferson, was less a matter of cavalierly enforcing one's principles than of sheltering them from the overwhelming passions of the institution.

Erickson's novel is motivated by a desire to bring Jefferson's unconscious into the stark light of the late twentieth century. *Arc d'X* pursues to its logical extreme the contemporary desire to expose Jefferson's libidinous other, the demon that we imagine must have dwelled within one of our civic saints. The lewd voyeurism of Erickson's novel, however, serves a rhetorical function aside from simply shaming the memory of Jefferson. The ends that ultimately follow from Erickson's means distinguish him from Jefferson's contemporary detractors. Conor Cruise O'Brien, for instance, calls Jefferson the "prophet and patron of the fanatical racist far right in America" and applies modern standards of morality to his conduct in an effort to excise him from the pantheon of American idols (1996b, 325).[27] Erickson's aping of Jefferson exhausts this patently modern desire to mock and seek revenge on him, making way for a sobering judgment delivered by Jefferson's fictional surrogate as he addresses a French mob on the eve of revolution: " 'I'm a poor champion. . . . You should remember . . . that when a poor champion fails a great idea, it's not the failure of the idea itself. The idea is as great as it ever was. It survives its poor champion and goes on and on' " (1993, 35). Erickson produces a burlesque of Jefferson's human imperfections while elevating the ideals he articulated above reproach. *Arc d'X* depletes the vengeful desire to impeach Jefferson for his alleged crimes in order to arrive at the unimpeachable quality of the principles he cherished. Unlike so much contemporary discourse about Jefferson, Erickson's narrative disassociates the man from the ideals he authored, suggesting, in the logic of the novel, that they need not share the same alloy, because the man will always fail the ideals but the ideals will never fail the man. Ultimately, *Arc d'X* debases the public memory of Jefferson, perverts his puritan ethos, in order to renew the ideals to which he lent his voice.

Ironically, then, this literary renewal proves that our hallowed ideals, as standards of collective belief, speech, and judgment, do not exist independent of our discursive practices. Instead, they must be continually forged and transfigured as features of those practices themselves. Such ideals, that is, do not reflect the untarnished morality of their political and rhetorical champions but the continual symbolic formation and transformation of those ideals in response to changing civic needs and desires.

MEMORY'S MEMORY

The public memory of Thomas Jefferson, as I have analyzed it in this chapter, exemplifies an especially vivid form of rhetoric in the middle voice. The discursive formation of this memory occurs, not in conformity with subjective intentions or proclamations, but through the emergence, maintenance, and transformation of multiple discursive practices. In this context, contemporary rhetoric concerning the public memory of Thomas Jefferson provokes a series of insights regarding the nature of so-called public memory in general. To begin with, collective memory often arises over a crisis of representation. In such cases, commemoration is not the product of a deep and coherent knowledge of the past. To the contrary, the rhetoric of public memory indicates that it comes into being as the manifestation of a desire to regard our frequently shallow and elliptical knowledge of the past otherwise. The memory of Jefferson retains its peculiar magnetism so long as his secret past, whatever its nature, continues to pose a problem of knowledge, truth, and desire in the present.

Our modern memory of Jefferson commemorates a figure we scarcely recognize. Rather than retaining some intrinsic essence of Jefferson and his time, we have remade our memory of Jefferson in accord with the culture and politics of the day. French and Ayers write, "In the nineteenth century, abolitionists used Jefferson's words as swords; slaveholders used his example as a shield. Deep into the twentieth century, white segregationists summoned Jefferson as the defender of local rights and limited government; advocates of black equality even more effectively summoned Jefferson as the author of the Declaration of Independence" (1993, 418). Even today, radical conservatives and liberal multiculturalists do battle for the prize of Jefferson's ethos.[28] Jefferson's ethos thus forms a site of civic engagement according to which we establish, sustain, or transform social, political, and ethical relations. In the mercurial context of memory, Jefferson exists as a historical ghost who dwells among us, continually haunting us in equal measure with his promises and his shortcomings. Jefferson has acquired such an alien quality in our recollections that we now tend to remember him by his other: by the ghost of Sally Hemings or the ghosts of his own passions. But how is it possible for us to remember such historical ephemera, to remember what we may never have known in the first place?

According to conventional wisdom, public memory represents an original object or event. It comes into being, by this logic, when artifice or synthetic performance is modeled on an original essence. Public memory so conceived acquires the shape of a lineage, the source of which begets a vertical line of imperfect descendants. In this formulation, public memory functions platonically: as the representation of an ideal form.

Such a conception of memory assumes distinctive clarity in the case of Thomas Jefferson. For nearly two centuries, Jefferson has been regarded as the ideal form, the embodiment, of our civic essence and subsequent generations have been regarded as its imperfect representation. Anxiety attends the imperfect nature of this representation, a fear that Jefferson's essence will be lost, and so will we. Even modern fictional accounts that attempt to portray unknowable elements of Jefferson and Hemings's character depend on this logic. Despite the remarkable transformations they have wrought in our public memories of both Jefferson and Hemings, such narratives ostensibly employ a fictional license in order to recover the ethereal yet authentic *sentiment* of their relationship. Fiction here functions, not as the antithesis of historical fact, but as a means by which to approximate its essence and guard against its decay.

Does the definition suggested by this representational logic, however, fully account for the rhetorical dynamics of public memory? In contrast to a *vertical* conception of memory (formed by a line of imperfect descendants), one might consider a *lateral* conception. According to this alternate rendering, public memory is elaborated by a *horizontal series,* a lateral sequence of iterations with no objective beginning or end, in which memory is not the echo of an origin, only the memory of another memory. Public memory in this frame is engendered, not by its fidelity to an original form, but by its iteration, each instance of which introduces inevitable mutations into its nature.[29]

Such a phenomenon also informs the public memory of Jefferson. As such, it illustrates vividly a form of rhetoric in this middle voice. The sheer repetition of this memory across changing contexts, in response to new exigencies, transforms its character and brings about new iterations, new desires: the desire for judgment, the desire to recover the true persona of Sally Hemings, the desire to redeem Jefferson, and the desire to indict him. Despite their ostensible purposes, these desires do not confirm the accuracy of memory but redouble its intensity and multiply its domain. They lend memory new sites of application, new discursive figures, and new capacities: the "daunting multiplicity" of public memory, as Browne would have it (1995, 237). Such multiplicity is manifested in the trope of Jefferson's other, which personifies the ghost of Sally Hemings in some texts and the specter of Jefferson's unconscious in others. Ironically, then, the image of Jefferson in modern memory has acquired its disquieting otherness precisely because of our fierce desire to remember the authentic Jefferson. The more we labor to recover the original, the more alien he becomes.

Does this lateral conception of public memory risk ignoring the importance of commemorative authenticity? Is the notion of memory explicable without a principle of fidelity to some original object or event? Certainly, the ethos of authenticity plays a vital role in the production of public memory; yet it matters much whether we accept this authenticity on its own terms or as a feature of the discourse through which memory is enacted. I propose that the platonic conception of public memory (as a diminishing series of representations) is engendered by the lateral model of memory, which reveals that a public memory's ethos of authenticity derives from its rhetorical ability to demonstrate fidelity to an original form. Charles Scott summarizes this line of thought with particular economy: "Memory's 'truth,' " he posits, "appears to be its manifestation, not its object or an aspect of its object" (1999, 7). Far from constituting the model on which all likenesses are based, the authentic memory is, instead, the consummate symbolic artifice: the one whose ethos of authenticity is most convincing. An apparently accurate, unmediated representation of an original form is itself a discursive form of remembrance. Scott argues, "[M]emory in all of its appearances and determinations does not happen according to the criteria of some primal and original reality. Memory is ungrounded if 'grounded' means that kind of reality" (211). Based on this account, the authenticity of a given memory is not proof of its fidelity to the past, but one of its semblances. In Scott's terms, "The 'facts' of memory are themselves memorial" (211). The connective tissue of remembrance is not an essence preserved by the vessel of memory, but memory's discursive, ephemeral, and imperfect memory of itself. In this way, such forms of remembrance evince the function of rhetoric in the middle voice.

The public memory of Jefferson teaches us that, in the rhetoric of such memory, change is more significant than constancy. What is produced, not what is preserved, encompasses the criterion by which we must judge the ethical and political implications of public memory. In *Arc d'X*, the character called Thomas muses about his masterpiece: America. If Thomas Jefferson is said to have been the source of America, to have embodied its character, then the fictional Thomas's description of America might, inversely, be used to describe our nation's invention of Jefferson: "I've invented something. . . . I've set it loose gyrating across the world. It spins through villages, hamlets, towns, grand cities. It's a thing to be confronted every moment of every day by everyone who hears its rumor: it will test most of those who presume too glibly to believe in it" (S. Erickson 1993, 46). The modern era's unceasing fascination with Jefferson has dramatically and irrevocably transformed his image. It is not the original, authentic Jefferson—the Jefferson of "those who presume too glibly to believe in it"—that houses the essence of a nation. Indeed, modern transformations in our memory of Jefferson have produced reciprocal transformations in the flesh and blood of that imperfect lineage known as America, in the categories commonly referred to as "black" and "white," whose ethos of authenticity has masked the politics of memory for far too long. The refraction of Jefferson's original likeness, the phantom of his rumor, the portrait of Jefferson's other, remains the faithful reflection of ourselves.

Chapter 6

The Rest Is Silence

In the previous chapter, I showed how the ethos of the past, embodied in symbolic personae such as Thomas Jefferson and Sally Hemings, provides the discursive conditions according to which we define our relationship to such historical figures in defining ourselves as inheritors of their troubled social, political, and ethical legacy. The present chapter provides further analysis of the ways in which our symbolic relations with figures from the past engender the political and ethical practices through which we conceive of ourselves. In what follows, I expand on the discursive interplay of past and present featured in the previous chapter by examining the interplay of speech and silence that discloses in greater detail the symbolic formation and transformation of time, memory, and historical experience constitutive of different subject positions and institutional relations.

Since antiquity, the topic of silence has posed a dubious significance for the arts of discourse. In her study of women's rhetoric in Pharaonic Egypt, Barbara Lesko outlines the fundamental principles of Egyptian rhetoric, which contemporary scholars might describe as its "five canons." The first "canon" of Egyptian rhetoric, she reports, was silence: "When one finds oneself attacked, one holds back and lets the opponent have his say, in the likelihood the opponent or accuser will make a fool of himself, becoming enraged while you exhibit cool, detached self-possession, which in itself should win you points" (1997, 90). Instead of regarding silence as an obstacle or hindrance to rhetorical practice, such pedagogy recommended it as a guiding artistic principle. But what was the symbolic nature of silence in this context? Lesko's description suggests that silence was defined in Egyptian rhetoric much like it would be defined by the Greco-Roman tradition and Western ontology more generally: in dialectical contrast to the voice, as the contrasting negative phenomenon that merely amplified the rhetorical impact of one's speech.

Can one apprehend the rhetorical sense and value of this silence, its utility as a basis for rhetorical practice, according to the dominant logic of metaphysics, with its incessant valorization of speech over silence or presence over absence? Foucault once remarked that "silence is one of those things that has unfortunately been dropped from our culture. We don't have a culture of silence" (1988b, 4). If Foucault's assessment is correct, then one may attribute such an omission to the predominant metaphysical orientation of Western values and ideals, which have been defined, for centuries, by the demand that one provide a logos of thought, knowledge, and experience—a demand that Foucault characterizes as "the obligation of speaking" (4). Simply put, the founding distinction between sensible and intelligible phenomena in Western philosophy has prevented silence from attaining little more than a negative value in our heritage.

For a culture in which the transcendent ethos of speech and presence retain considerable organizing value, encounters with the ineffable, the mystical, or the inexplicable are among the strangest experiences of alterity. The silences of the past characterize perhaps the most ghostly of former persons and events. In his classic essay "Theses on the Philosophy of History" (1968), Walter Benjamin observes that selective elements of the past remain symbolically lodged in the present, as much a part of an epoch's defining substance and character, its ethos, as any contemporary phenomena. The present is not simply isolated by the immediate past on one side and the proximate future on the other; styles, values, and experiences of bygone eras may share a profoundly deeper symbolic relevance to the present than its most recent yesterday. The social, political, or ethical sense and value of our symbolic relations with even the most foreign and mysterious elements of the past crucially engender the seemingly transparent and familiar ethos of contemporary subject positions.

In this chapter, I interrogate traditional notions of silence in order to explore further how the rhetoric of self and other, present and past, or good and evil discursively produces conditions for political and ethical judgment. The enigmatic status of silence in Western inquiry serves as a lens through which one may scrutinize common assumptions about the relationship between present and past, history and politics, immanence and transcendence. Contemporary scholarship habitually defines the rhetorical properties of silence according to a metaphysical logic that relegates silence to the status of a negative, absence, or lack. Although scholars throughout the humanities and social sciences have exhibited an increasing fascination with the phenomenon of silence, they have been able to countenance this phenomenon only by transforming it into its ontological opposite: a voice that has been lost or an essence that must be recovered.

The "logocentrism" of this tendency, as Derrida would surely call it, is acute in rhetorical studies. According to its traditional representational definitions, rhetoric begins and ends with logos. Robert Scott, for instance, describes silence as one of "the borders of rhetoric" (2000, 110)—a non-rhetorical domain whose contrasting absence lends definition to the full presence of rhetoric. Presumably, silence must be countered or even eradicated by practitioners of the art. It represents the mark of negative value, absence, or lack that must be replaced with the transparent expression of intended and essential meaning.

To speak of silence, according to conventional wisdom, is at once impossible and necessary. Georges Bataille proclaims, "The idea of silence (that is the inaccessible) is disarming! I cannot speak of an absence of meaning, except to give it a meaning it does not have. The silence is broken, since I have spoken" (1998a, 144). One cannot speak of silence qua silence because doing so renders it "broken," interrupting and enveloping it with some form of verbalization, conceptualization, or representation—with "a meaning it does not have." However, Western inquiry, beginning in the late twentieth century, exhibited a growing attention to the political mechanisms by which social groups historically have been silenced. Such mechanisms resulted in either explicit or implicit prohibitions that comprise a regrettable, though recurrent, feature of the humanist tradition and continue to exclude particular subjects from fulsome participation or representation therein. The investigation of silence thus remains necessary to the extent that modern liberal thought remains committed to uncovering and transforming the structural conditions that enforce the silence of particular subjects.

How might one reconcile the simultaneous impossibility and necessity of silence? How might one acknowledge the impossibility of silence qua silence while nevertheless recognizing the very real existence of silence in the lived experience of those muted by certain social, political, or historical injunctions? Foucault posits that there are "many forms of silence" (1988b, 3). Based on his conception of discourse, Foucault maintains that silence is not the categorical opposite to speech. Instead, silences acquire distinctive forms in that they are discursively engendered; they comprise a defining symbolic element of discursive practices and attain a characteristic sense and value in social, political, and ethical relations. Elsewhere, Foucault maintains that "[s]ilence itself—the things one declines to say, or is forbidden to name . . . is less the absolute limit of discourse, the other side from which it is separated by a strict boundary, than an element that functions alongside the things said, with them and in relation to them within over-all strategies" (1990, 27). Silence is not the opposite or negative of speech but a constitutive element of discourse. In order to evaluate its rhetorical function, then, one must analyze the characteristic form of a given silence, attending to the discursive means that engender, maintain, or transform it. "[W]e must try to determine," in Foucault's logic, "the different ways of not saying such things, how those who can and those who cannot speak of them are distributed, which type of discourse is authorized, or which form of discretion is required in either case" (27). Such is the method I employ in order to determine how the discursive production of silences engenders notions of self and other, history and politics, past and present.

In the following analysis, I argue that silences, even in their appearance as categorical absences, are discursively engendered, and thereby acquire rhetorical sense and value in the articulation of social, political, and ethical relations. An attunement to rhetoric in the middle voice allows one to delineate the accepted sense and value, the very ethos, of silence and to consequently analyze its rhetorical function in discursive practices and social relations. In offering this argument, I refuse to concede, as Robert Scott does, that speech and silence are joined in a purely dialectical relationship—that the question of silence is relevant to rhetoric only when we "test its borders," only as that which "mark[s] the borders of rhetoric" (Scott 2000, 110). Mirroring Benjamin's vision of history, in which times and places far removed from one another become deeply affiliated, the discursive sense and value of certain silences authorizes contemporary notions of self and other by engendering symbolic relations between individuals in the past and present.

I pursue this argument through an analysis of Malek Alloula's *The Colonial Harem* (1986). Alloula's text demonstrates vividly the intertwined political and intellectual desires that motivate most contemporary studies of silence. As such, I use it to identify the often conflicted institutional sense and value of silence in current academic discourse. But Alloula's study offers more than a simple extended example; its ambiguity regarding the topic of silence offers competing yet instructive conceptions, however implicit, of the manner in which the discursive production of silence engenders modes of thought, knowledge, speech, and judgment concerning the symbolic value and utility of the past to the present. Ultimately, *The Colonial Harem* illustrates how silence forms a discursive limit simultaneously dividing but also distributing what one can see and what one can say in a given social and historical context while remaining irreducible to either category. In this way, my interpretation of Alloula's text evaluates conditions for knowing, speaking of, and establishing relations with others no longer mediated by representation but conditioned by discursive practices.

SILENCE AS REPRESENTATION

During the early decades of the twentieth century, photographers in the French colony of Algeria manufactured postcards allegedly featuring Muslim women lounging in the forbidden space of the harem, caught in various states of unveiling. These postcards became a popular form of correspondence for French colonists writing to friends, family, or business associates in France, especially from 1900 to 1930 (Alloula 1986, 5). Without question, the images on these postcards carried an erotic charge. Contact between Westerners and covered Muslim women was rare and taboo even in public, but acutely prohibited, of course, in Muslim women's private quarters. In truth, the bare-breasted women featured in these images were actually "paid models" hired by photographers and the interior scenes of the harems were mere studio backdrops. Despite their fictitious and libidinous nature, the ubiquity of these photographs in imperial French society indicates that their eroticism and exoticism acquired the status of ethnographic documentation, offering what were taken to be commonplace representations of Muslim women in Algeria.[1] Such representational artifacts provide traces of a discursive formation in which certain ways of imagining, knowing, and speaking of Algerian women acquired authoritative sense and value, or the status of truth.

Alloula's *The Colonial Harem* offers an annotated collection of these postcards. Alloula describes such images as "the deployment of phantasms": "There is no phantasm," he writes, "without sex, and in this Orientalism, a confection of the best and the worst—mostly the worst—a central figure emerges, the very embodiment of the obsession: the harem" (3). The "obsession" to which Alloula refers is reflected in the European gaze and its incessant desire to pierce the "unfathomable mysteries" (3) of the Orient and thereby behold the sensual delights imagined therein. The fantasy of the harem, and the seductive pleasures beckoning from deep within its recesses, is reproduced on the surface of every postcard, every "deployment" of such phantasms. Alloula, himself an Algerian, explains his motivation behind his reading of these postcards—"this vast operation of systematic distortion," as he describes them; he intends "[t]o map out, from under the plethora of images, the obsessive scheme that regulates the totality of the output of this enterprise and endows it with meaning . . . to force the postcard to reveal what it holds back (the ideology of colonialism) and to expose what is repressed in it (the sexual phantasm)" (4–5). By re-contextualizing these images, and thereby exposing their illusory nature, Alloula intends to present a "symptomatic" reading (4) that reveals the role these seemingly innocuous postcards played in the maintenance of imperial ideology and sexual fantasy. To reproduce "colonial representations of Algerian women—the figures of a phantasm" in this context, Alloula explains, "is to attempt a double operation: first, to uncover the nature and the meaning of the colonialist gaze; then, to subvert the stereotype that is so tenaciously attached to the bodies of [these] women" (5). *The Colonial Harem*'s chapters are grouped according to particular photographic tropes in order to impugn this stereotype in its dominant forms: women's prisons, women's quarters, couples, dress and jewelry, song and dance, suberoticism. In each chapter, Alloula's commentary on these photographs consists largely of a narrative that exposes the psyche of "the photographer" so as to discern within his gaze the sexual and colonial fantasy, the *"scopic desire"* (7), that gives rise to the phantasms captured through his lens.

The Colonial Harem offers a particularly vivid example of social criticism intended to uncover the institutional conditions that oppress certain historical or cultural groups. This form of critique operates by unmasking the allegedly natural or self-evident appearance of representations that in fact function through distortion and exclusion, principally according to the interests of those privileged enough to control or manipulate them. The efficacy of such representations naturally depends upon the silence of specific groups who, lacking a "voice" of their own, are now lent one by the contemporary work of critique. "A reading of the sort that I propose to undertake," Alloula writes, "would be entirely superfluous if there existed photographic traces of the gaze of the colonized upon the colonizer" (5). Presumably, the hypothetical "photographic traces of the gaze of the colonized" function metaphorically here, suggesting that Alloula's text is an imperfect substitute for a more ideal political critique of the postcards articulated by the very women objectified and silenced therein.

What is the nature of the relationship between the postcards collected in Alloula's text and the silence of the subjects pictured therein? And if any correspondence exists between silence and these images, what does it suggest about the discursive relationship between silence and images in general? By way of response, I argue that the silence of the women pictured in these postcards is engendered by the images themselves. If one is to say that these women "lacked a voice," that they had no recourse to a form of critique concerning their representation in colonial discourse, then the very images in which they are captured invoke the lack of this voice. Indeed, our only access to the experience of these women in the present is through the scopic fantasy of the postcards, which nevertheless remain an unremitting photographic distortion of and prohibition to any certain knowledge of that experience. Such images stimulate one's desire to hear the testimony of these women across the historical breach that divides their time and culture from our own. Rather than existing prior to the designs of the photographer, the silence of these women is invoked by the postcards he produces. They are silent precisely to the extent that they have been captured in this pictorial fantasy. "The perfection and the credibility of the illusion," Alloula concludes, "are ensured by the fact that the absent other is, by definition, unavailable and cannot issue a challenge" (17). The pathos of the image thus depends upon the muteness of its subjects.

Alloula's re-contextualization of the colonial postcards evokes a symbolic experience of silence especially meaningful for those conversant with the contemporary politics of voice, agency, and subjectivity. The identifiable *forms* that this silence assumes are acutely significant. I cite Alloula's text in order to document the first such form of silence that I interrogate in this chapter: *silence as representation*. One could describe a conception of silence in this form, specifically in relation to *The Colonial Harem,* as follows: The silence of the women in these postcards must serve as their historical and political testimony, despite the absence of any literal discourse of their own. Their silence becomes significant insofar as it *communicates* a moral lesson to us across time, urging us to prevent similar prohibitions in the future. In turn, the silence of these women becomes *meaningful,* becomes so much more than mere silence, because it *represents* a particular form of exclusion and struggle as well as its *truth*. Let the silence of these women thus serve as the most eloquent counterdiscourse to the colonial mechanisms that have, throughout history, deprived them of a voice.

This representational form of silence is characteristic of much contemporary scholarship on the subject of voice and agency, particularly in the fields of women's studies, minority studies, social history, and critical pedagogy. Silence so conceived exemplifies the predominant approach to the study of silence throughout the humanities and social sciences. Anthropological linguist Adam Jaworski, for instance, argues that we should regard *"silence as a metaphor for communication"* precisely in order "to go beyond the simple view of silence as 'absence of sound' " (1997, 3). In communication studies, Robin Patric Clair likewise argues for a conception of silence as "an expressive activity" (1998, xiv),[2] while philosopher Dennis Kurzon claims that "[s]ilence is meaningful" and posits that "[t]he central problem of silence in discourse is to discover that meaning" (1998, 5). Despite the disciplinary diversity reflected in this collection of scholarship, the formulations of silence featured here are nonetheless unified by their tendency to transform silence into "communication," "expression," or "meaning."

Alloula promotes a reading of the Algerian postcards according to this very conception of silence. He argues that, despite the paradoxical manner in which these mass-produced, entirely fabricated representations of Arab life once functioned as a transparent form of visual truth, clues regarding the deception on which they were founded escape through the images themselves—in particular, through the silence of the subjects pictured therein. The subjects of these portraits, Alloula claims, "express more than they are capable of saying"—that is, they become expressive precisely through not saying anything (1986, 40). The women pictured in these images express "a meaning of which their bodies," Alloula writes, "are the silent yet eloquent signs" (40). The image's inability to efface all traces of its theatrical fabrication, Alloula argues, ultimately allows one to discern the original thoughts and intentions of the women pictured in these postcards, despite the absence of their own voices. Behind every seductive smile they have been paid to wear, and behind every exterior pose in which they have been placed, Alloula intuits the reticent consciousness of these women, held silent until now, and discloses its contents in striking detail: "When a model smiles in these cards, one is not sure whether it is on command . . . or at the ridiculous salacity of the shot in which she is posing. . . . As if the models themselves had no illusion about the effect they would produce. Or as if they understood that only their breasts could find favor with the photographer and his clients. Reduced to what is enticing about them, these young women can only efface themselves behind their own breasts, which they push forward to earn better payment" (98). In the very silence of these women, in the visual simulacrum that invokes it, Alloula discovers the meaningfulness of that silence. Evidently, a political critique of these images is possible only if the silence of the subjects pictured therein can be made to represent the critique that they *would* have articulated—indeed, that they *must* have articulated, even if nowhere else than in their own thoughts—had they not lacked the voice to do so. Curiously, silence has value in this economy only if one can turn it into speech or meaning, only if one can indenture it to representation.

What are the implications of interpreting silence according to a representational economy and of treating it as a tacit form of logos? Naturally, silence acquires the characteristic functions and effects of speech. Deborah Tannen and Muriel Saville-Troike's claim that "[s]ilence can be used to fulfill the functions of most speech acts" (1985, xii) relies upon this functional conflation of speech and silence. When one assigns to silence the function of representation, one devotes it, like speech, to the disclosure of subjective consciousness, perhaps according to a medium more pure than even speech itself. It somehow becomes possible to rationally apprehend the meaning of a silence based upon that very silence without risking a detour by way of the sensible. By this logic, a purity and continuity of intuition and intention governs the rhetorical sense and value of silence. One observes the sovereignty of intuition and intention at work in *The Colonial Harem,* for Alloula performs a *hermeneutic* interpretation of the Algerian women's silence. His presumption that this interpretation will objectively summon their consciousness, and thereby retain a transcendent identity between present and past, never wavers. Alloula's method thus exemplifies Derrida's description of "interpretation" in its most intuitive sense—as the effort "to decipher . . . a truth or an origin which is free from freeplay and from the order of the sign, and lives like an exile the necessity of interpretation" (1972, 264).

SILENCE AS AN ORIGIN

Contemporary desires to regard silence as a form of representation indicate the fundamental and enduring allergy to disruptions of essential meaning or presence characteristic of Western ontological values and ideals. Yet another form of silence provides an even deeper indication of the extent to which ideal and original notions of speech, meaning, and subjective experience retain a commanding ethos in the current *épistémé*. This second form defines *silence as an origin*.

One may also observe this form of silence operating in *The Colonial Harem*. The text posits that one should regard the silence of the women pictured in French colonial photographs as communicative or meaningful precisely to the degree that their "experience," symbolized by that silence, is taken to represent the experience of all such women at that time. In Alloula's study, one cannot know or describe *these women* as anything other than a general category comprised by a principle of identity—namely, their shared silence, which is effected by the images in which their likenesses continue to circulate throughout time and space. The logic of Alloula's analysis, as I have noted, endeavors to counteract the colonial fantasy staged in these photographic representations. Alloula's professed agenda of forcing the postcard "to expose what is repressed in it" (1986, 5) suggests that another story is waiting to be told—one that has been "repressed," kept silent until now. In making it speak, one commands such silence to explain the ways in which the distorted, salacious representations emblazoned on the surface of the postcard originally acquired the status and authority of photographic truth.

Silence conserves the ideal and original truth of historical events to the extent that it represents, however elusively, the meaning of a cultural oppression. Absent a critique offered by the very women pictured in the postcards, Alloula proclaims, "I attempt here, lagging far behind History, to return this immense postcard to its sender" (5). The silence of these women represents a principle of transcendent unity and coherence to historical narrative, for the word "History" as Alloula uses it suggests a transparent and therefore reversible phenomenon. Despite his "lagging far behind" it, Alloula intends "to return this postcard to its sender," to reverse the flow of time and undo the narrative told until now by exposing the truth that had been withheld in silence—indeed, that can be communicated or represented through that very silence. In this discourse, silence provides a condition of essential similitude and equilibrium: the postcard that ensured the silence of those arrested in its gaze can be now returned to its sender, the prohibitions enforced in the past can be reversed in the present.

This desire for an ideal and original knowledge of former subjects and events endows silence with metonymic status. James Young explains that the modern impulse to equate a fragmented artifact with the whole of an event informs the nature of contemporary public memory, especially as it is given form in the space of the museum:

> The fragment presents itself not only as natural knowledge, but as a piece of the event itself. At least part of our veneration of ruins and artifacts stems

from the nineteenth-century belief that such objects embody the spirit of the people who made and used them. In this view, museum objects are not only remnants of the people they once belonged to, but also traces of the values, ideas, and character of the time. In the subsequent fetishization of artifacts by curators, and of ruins by the "memory-tourist," however, we risk mistaking the piece for the whole, the implied whole for unmediated history. (1993, 127)

Analogously, silence in Alloula's critique acquires the ethos of a fragment. It attains its rhetorical sense and value through discursive practices that define it as the metonymic representation of a complete and uniform historical experience. Silence retains its ideal and original ethos because it is taken to represent the essence of a subject's experience, which represents, in turn, the ideal and original nature, "the implied whole," of a given political and ideological formation. The silent part comes to stand for the whole and render it fully present.

Silence as such restores a complete portrait of the individual subject and his or her world by acquiring transcendent meaning. Such a transformation is analogous to those traditional methods of historiography that transform monuments into documents. "[H]istory, in its traditional form," Foucault explains, "undertook to 'memorize' the *monuments* of the past, transform them into *documents,* and lend speech to those traces which, in themselves, are often not verbal, or which say in silence something other than what they actually say" (1972, 7). Whether the "document" in this formulation is an artifact, voice, or silence makes little difference. One's fetishization of the fragment, or metonymic definition of silence, bespeaks one's desire to achieve an ideal knowledge of historical subjects or events. This preservation naturally follows from the desire for an unmediated origin. To render past events wholly known and contained in "monuments of the past" or to endow silence with an essential meaning is, ultimately, to impress a fundamental identity upon historical subjects and events by dressing the inherent lacunae of a discursive formation in the appearance of full presence. Whether through material fragments or meaningful silences, historical narrative thus remains undisturbed and whole—"unmediated," in Young's terms. Based on this logic, the discourse of contemporary social critique not only posits the fundamental identity of former persons and events but thereby presumes a cognitive identity between past and present subjects. The discursive ethos of a common humanity thus allows one to transform historical discontinuities into representations of a transcendent experience.

Silence, Voice, and Authentic Subjectivity

The Colonial Harem illustrates the principal forms that silence assumes in contemporary critical discourse. Such forms constitute convincing evidence that ideal notions of speech, meaning, and subjective experience retain a controlling ethos in modern inquiry. In the current *épistémé*, silence functions as a substitute for speech by sequestering the elusive yet essential meaning in virtue of which one may narrate the truth of human experiences and historical events: *silence as representation, silence as an origin.*

Why should one seek to undermine the dialectical logic of speech and silence, self and other, or present and past to which Western inquiry traditionally has adhered? Alloula's study confirms that the tendency to regard silence as an evanescent vessel of communication invariably suggests that silence faintly but faithfully conserves the transcendent truth of historical subjects or events within its void. Consequently, these discursive conditions ensure that whatever meaning is communicated or represented by silence acquires a mystique of *authenticity,* for such meaning appears to transcend the inherent limitations of speech and historical context.

James Scott's *Domination and the Arts of Resistance* (1990) offers a fitting demonstration of this logic. Scott argues that one can identify the nature of asymmetrical power relations, which structure the lived conditions of oppressor and oppressed, by examining modes of discourse that he labels "the public transcript and the hidden transcript" (x). Scott defines the "*public transcript* as a shorthand way of describing the open interaction between subordinates and those who dominate" while he uses "the term *hidden transcript*" in referring to "discourse that takes place 'offstage,' beyond direct observation of powerholders" (4). To all but its subordinate authors, then, the hidden transcript is defined by its silence. Presumably, if one could somehow replace the public silence of the hidden transcript with the voices of its fugitive authors, "in principle, a shared critique of domination may develop" (Scott 1990, xi). This structural opposition between the public and hidden transcripts, between speech and silence or presence and absence so conceived, induces a deep ambivalence in Scott's analysis. He concedes that the public and hidden transcripts are not divided by "a solid wall," recognizing that the hidden transcript may be opaque and thus hostile to decoding by outsiders (14). Despite these qualifications, however, Scott's goal undoubtedly is to lend speech to the vouchsafed presence of a silent and uniform consciousness.

The logic of Scott's analysis thereby endows the hidden transcript with a mystique of authenticity. In this discourse, silence constitutes an indispensable hermeneutic principle in that it presumably withholds both the truth of domination and the subjective consciousness of an oppressed subject within its void. To transform silence into voice, therefore, is to equate that voice with the essence of the person allegedly speaking through his or her silence—a remarkable feat of ventriloquism.

James Scott's analysis resembles a diverse array of scholarship motivated by what one might call consciousness raising. The politics of such work seeks to engender an awareness of asymmetrical power relations by lending speech to the silences they produce. Barbara Biesecker explains that " 'consciousness raising' signifies the project of bringing to the surface something that is hidden, the task of making manifest something that is concealed or covered over" (1992a, 145). According to the rules of such a discourse, the political project of lending speech to silence is facilitated by what Biesecker calls "a depth hermeneutics that posits an irreducible essence inhabiting the subject" (146). One's presumption that every silence always already represents a concealed voice equates that voice with the essence of the subject made to speak it.

Such discursive conditions produce and maintain an essential notion of the subject, a reduction of human being to the representation of a transcendent subjectivity. The politics engendered by this conception of the subject originate, not in what a subject once said, thought, or felt, but in what we today might like to say or feel concerning his or her station in life. The silence of the past thus constitutes the ground of political critique only when it is metamorphosed into the din of characteristically contemporary historical interpretations. One thus expunges the defining and irreducible differences of former subjects when one transforms their silence into an ideal and original speech, positing an essential humanity and transparent communication uniting self and other. "The representation of supposedly unvarnished truth," John Durham Peters reckons, "can be just as reckless as outright deception" (1999, 266). A political critique guided by this sort of "consciousness-raising" or "depth hermeneutics" proceeds unaware that, in Peters's terms, "the hope of doubling the self always misses the autonomy of the other. Authenticity can be a profoundly selfish ideal" (266).

The interpretation of silence according to a discourse of representation is fundamental to such a politics. Without the logic of representation, silence would not serve as a surrogate for speech and correspond to the "irreducible essence" of the individual subject. If one is to undermine the supposed transparency between silence and representation, then, one must begin to do so by questioning definitions of silence based on the academically fashionable but intellectually vague category of voice. By treating silence as a suppressed voice, one allows subjective intentions to speak ideally and originally, to speak in the very transcendence of speech.

But how might one apprehend the discursive sense and value of silence without recourse to the intentions or essence of a subject as its principle of intelligibility? Biesecker's critique of feminist efforts to recuperate the so-called voices of women once excluded from the rhetorical canon offers an initial answer to this question. According to Biesecker, this process of recovery is well exemplified by feminist rhetoricians' project of recognizing the hitherto neglected speeches of women in order to justify their canonization in the rhetorical tradition. Not coincidentally, this project also exemplifies many critical feminist approaches to silence in other disciplines. Elaine Hedges and Shelly Fisher Fishkin, for instance, approach silence in terms of women's "unnatural silences" and the struggle of women "coming to voice" (1994, 3; 5). Similarly, the seminal feminist volume *Women's Ways of Knowing* describes silence as "a position in which women experience themselves as mindless and voiceless and subject to the whims of external authority" (Belenky et al. 1986, 15). Biesecker contends that this reduction of a subject to her voice, or of silence to speech, preserves the same criteria of inclusion and exclusion according which women originally were silenced. "To each of these proper names," allowed into the rhetorical canon for whatever reason, there "corresponds a text or a set of texts," she writes, "and between them is marked a certain kind of originating function that wins the individual membership in a distinguished ensemble of individuals" (1992a, 143–44). Hence, Biesecker argues that "even as the list of 'great works' expands over time," and comes to include the once silenced voices of women orators, "the criteria for determining that list need not change. Indeed, for the most part the criteria have remained firmly in place" (143).

Biesecker proposes that, in light of these facts, one must ask unconventional questions concerning women's marginalized voices. One must no longer ask simply, "[W]ho is speaking?" but "[W]hat play of forces made it possible for a particular speaking subject to emerge?" (148). Said differently, one must no longer attempt to preserve the ideal and original thoughts and experiences of a given subject; instead, one must identify those discursive conditions that enabled the speech of some and hindered, even foreclosed, the speech of others. Such a project relinquishes the desire for an apprehension of essential meaning or transcendental subjectivity in order to evaluate the social, political, and ethical relations that engender multiple forms of agency and subject positions.

Biesecker's critique warrants an analogous methodological change in the rhetorical study of silence. I have noted that contemporary scholarship (feminist or otherwise) habitually regards silence as a transparent medium of subjective consciousness. In short, one must no longer ask, What does this silence mean?, but rather, What discursive conditions produced the sense and value—the ethos—of this silence, and what social, political, or ethical relations did it produce in turn? Such an approach refrains from regarding silence as a medium of transcendent meaning or subjectivity in order to contend that the ethos of particular silences informs the character of a given discursive formation. In comprising a constitutive feature of discursive formations, the institutional sense and value of a given silence engenders social relations as well as the symbolic conditions for their management and negotiation.

SILENCE AS A RHETORICAL CONDITION

Having interrogated the previous forms of silence, I investigate yet a third form thereof. I scrutinize this third form in order to assign alternate sense and value to the aforementioned conceptions of silence. On the basis of this alternate sense and value, I evaluate further the social, political, and ethical relations engendered by these forms of silence in the production of symbolic relations between self and other, past and present, or history and politics. Accordingly, I argue that silence also acquires the form of *a rhetorical condition* in that it discursively produces conditions for thinking, knowing, speaking, and rendering judgment about the relationship between historical and contemporary experiences.

In order to resist the conventional reduction of silence to a voice or origin, and thereby better account for its rhetorical sense and value, one must adopt a more incisive critical terminology than that of simple oppositions between presence and absence or speech and silence. Based on conventional metaphysical oppositions, one logically concludes that contemporary readers *lack* both the voices of the Algerian women pictured in *The Colonial Harem* and an unmediated history of the French colonial fantasy manifested in its collection of imperial-era postcards, regardless of the fact that they never possessed these voices or this history in the first place. In Alloula's text, silence marks the irreducibility of one's own finitude: the limit of one's thought, knowledge, and speech—indeed, one's subjectivity itself—in relation to the past. The absences symbolically invoked by these silences, however, are discursive phenomena rather than categorical voids. They constitute the discursive conditions that define how subjects in the present can imagine, know, and speak of subjects and social relations characteristic of a previous *épistémé*. The discursive production of absence as such, and not the supposedly transcendent meaning or subjectivity that a given silence represents, evinces the characteristically rhetorical sense and value of silence as a condition of thinking, knowing, and speaking. One must therefore employ a suppler critical terminology than that of simple metaphysical antitheses in order to analyze the ways in which this mercurial rhetoric of silence disrupts conventional distinctions between the categories of presence and absence or speech and silence, as well as the positive and negative values with which they are invested.

Not coincidentally, the question of silence is often linked to notions of embodiment and disembodiment. Every "voice" (and, by implication, every silence) carries with it the trace of some speaker (or lack thereof). In those circumstances where silence disrupts the transparency of speech to consciousness, representation facilitates the seemingly transparent restoration of a subject's intentions, of that subject's very essence. The especially vivid relation between body, voice, and silence in *The Colonial Harem,* as I have already argued, is discursively invoked by the images themselves; the symbolic interpolation of these women's bodies into the colonial fantasy of the harem produces their silence. Alloula, however, remains convinced that the voices of these women are somewhere, somehow, to be found behind such images in an ideal and original state, that these images offer merely the false traces of their corporeal experience, the truth of which must still be accessible beneath the surfaces of the postcards themselves in the form of a withdrawn presence. In sum, the reader is symbolically haunted by the specters of these women, and their silence constitutes a crucial discursive condition of this haunting.

The act of viewing these postcards, of meeting the hollow gazes of the women pictured therein, is a ghostly experience. It somehow makes the past intensely present, sustains the imprimatur of their bodies even at a deathly remove, and renders palpable the silence with which they greet us. To meet the gazes of these women across the temporal breach that separates their age from our own is to feel caught in a gaze we cannot return, to feel that we are being seen while the seer remains hidden. In *Specters of Marx,* Derrida refers to this experience as "the visor effect" (1994, 7). He discerns this visor effect in Shakespeare's *Hamlet;* the young prince, arrested in the gaze of his father's spirit, cannot return that gaze because the apparition wears body armor from head to foot, including a helmet whose lowered visor shrouds the "face" of the ghost in darkness. The ghost's visor and body armor, "[t]his protection," Derrida writes, "is rigorously *problematic* (*problema* is also a shield) for it prevents perception from deciding on the identity that it wraps so solidly in its carapace" (8). To be seen without being able to gaze back, in other words, disrupts the alleged identity of the other in whose gaze one is caught, rendering that identity *"problematic,"* inaccessible to our "perception." The visor effect invokes the symbolic experience of a haunting because the specter, the ghostly figure, "is watching, observing, staring at the spectators and the blind seers, but you do not see it seeing, it remains invulnerable beneath its visored armor" (Derrida 1994, 100). Hence the effect engenders a crisis of knowledge and judgment. Derrida explains, "We do not know whether [the armor] is or is not part of the spectral apparition. . . . The armor may be but the body of a real artifact, a kind of technical prosthesis, a body foreign to the spectral body that it dresses, dissimulates, and protects, masking even its identity" (8).

The disquieting ethos of this visor effect motivates Alloula's desire to unmask the colonial phantasms in which the bodies of the pictured Algerian women have been costumed for generations. By virtue of this ethos, the postcards compiled in Alloula's study appear to encase their pictured subjects in a kind of photographic armor—a phantasm that holds us in its gaze while preventing us from gazing back, while masking the "true identity" of these historical subjects and thus rendering that identity "problematic," to use Derrida's term. The presumed silence of these photographic apparitions engenders the characteristic sense and value of the visor effect in this instance. The ethos of this symbolic relation thereby provokes a desire to hear these women speak, to receive their testimony about the truth of their experience. Such a desire, however, remains unfulfilled because they can never speak to us in their own voice. One's knowledge of and statements about the past cannot circumvent this silence; it forms, rather, the very condition of possibility for knowing and speaking of former persons and events. The rhetorical sense and value of this silence (its function as a defining condition of knowledge and speech) and the symbolic experience of the visor effect are thus joined in a reciprocal relationship. The visor remains lowered, the lurid and "distorted" images of the postcards endure throughout time, yet those images persistently invoke one's desire to hear these subjects speak, to replace the image with speech. Such is a desire fundamentally, if not paradoxically, conditioned by silence, by the irreducible differences that define one's relations with historical subjects, by the fact that we are seen but cannot see back or, reciprocally, that we can speak but cannot be addressed. The affinities between the discursive production of silence and the symbolic experience of the visor effect in *The Colonial Harem* suggest that forms of seeing, saying, and silence mutually inform one another in constituting the ethos of a discursive formation.

Seeing, Saying, and Silence

In previous chapters, my commentary on Foucault's historical researches implied that knowledge is constituted in every age by what can be seen and what can be said—not only by what *was* seen and said but, more fundamentally, by the discursive *conditions* or *rules* that enabled certain ways of seeing and speaking within a discursive formation. On the one hand, Foucault speaks of "visibilities," the "seeable," or the "visible," by which he does not mean pictures or photographs (discrete images) but historically characteristic *ways* of seeing, *forms* of visibility, such as observation, surveillance, or perception. To see the world as an arrangement of divinely inspired monarchical order is a radically different way of seeing phenomena, and thus of knowing them, than that of, say, modern scientific observation. Discursive conditions or rules enable the act of seeing, the ways in which objects acquire meaning and value in perception. Seeing is never a transparent, unmediated event. On the other hand, Foucault refers to the order of "statements," the "sayable," or the "articulable," which he describes, not as the actual content of a statement or a set of statements, but as the discursive rules (the conditions of enunciation, the forms of meaning and truth) that suffuse the sense and value of statements in a given *épistémé*. Specific discursive conditions, for example, engendered modern discourses of "madness," "delinquency," or "sexuality." In defining modes of perception and expression, of seeing and speaking, discursive practices engender social relations and therefore subject positions.[3]

According to Derrida, the appearance of the specter and one's effort to gain knowledge of it raises the question of visibility, of the conditions according to which one's knowledge of the past is informed by the ways in which its symbols remain strangely and elliptically visible to us. To understand the nature of this visibility, Derrida suggests, one must distinguish between the *spirit* and the *specter*: "[T]he specter," he writes, "is a paradoxical incorporation, the becoming-body, a certain phenomenal and carnal form of the spirit" (1994, 6). One may describe the specter as a kind of symbolic embodiment, as if the spirit could not appear to us, could not haunt the mortal plane, without a spectral form or some ghostly frame. "As soon as one no longer distinguishes spirit from specter," Derrida writes, "the former assumes a body, it incarnates itself, as spirit, in the specter" (6). Although the spirit "assumes a body" and "incarnates itself" in the form of a specter, the spirit and specter are never isomorphic. Indeed, Derrida warns that the figure created by this self-embodiment becomes "some 'thing' that remains difficult to name: neither soul nor body, and both one and the other" (6). Like the bodies captured in the postcards of *The Colonial Harem*, the specter appears before one as *the symbolic embodiment of an absence*. "For it is flesh and phenomenality," Derrida insists, "that give to the spirit its spectral apparition, but which disappear right away in the apparition" (6). Because the specter's embodiment is constituted by the very disappearance or withdrawal of its corporeality, the body of the specter only comes into being by virtue of the *appearance* of its disappearing, by the *visibility* of its irreversible withdrawal. Consequently, Derrida comments, "[t]he specter, as its name indicates, is the *frequency* of a certain visibility. But the visibility of the invisible" (100). "For there is no ghost," he continues, "there is never any becoming-specter of the spirit without at least an appearance of flesh, in a space of invisible visibility, like the disappearing of an apparition" (126). The discursive condition upon which the specter is given to perception thus derives from its *liminal* status, in the full sense of that word: as both a threshold between realities and a phenomenon perceptible only in obscurity. "For there to be a ghost," Derrida asserts, "there must be a return to the body, but to a body that is more abstract than ever"—a body that is "sensuous-non-sensuous, visible-invisible" (126; 101). This "sensuous-non-sensuous, visible-invisible" quality defines the ethos of these photographs as a condition for the discursive production of subjectivities rather than the representation thereof.

I employ the distinction between spirit and specter in order to analyze the peculiar visibility of the women featured in the postcards of *The Colonial Harem*. Alloula's desire to somehow liberate these women from the perverse dressings in which they have been held for generations suggests a desire to pierce the spectral body, the unyielding photographic armor, in which their bodies now appear so as to apprehend their intrinsic spirit, meaning the truth of their subjectivity or the essence of their being. Does this spirit actually lie in wait for us within the spectral body? Does this spirit, the essential and unchanging truth of these women's subjectivity, represent the repressed underside of what was seen, of what *could* be seen, at the time these photographs were taken, as if the photographs themselves, these acetate armaments, actively prevented one's otherwise ideal access to or knowledge of such women? In truth, one's desire to view the spirit embodied in the form of the specter, to gain an intuitive knowledge of it, is merely a discursive condition engendered by the "sensuous-non-sensuous, visible-invisible" nature of the specter, by the haunting ethos of this absence, by the symbolic invitation to behold something visible only in its withdrawal—in its having already and irrevocably been withdrawn.

Even in one's desire to behold it, one senses that this spirit was never ideally and originally preserved. As such, one can neither lose nor lack it. The spectral embodiment of this spirit's absence is not a means by which to gain an unmediated knowledge of these subjects but, rather, the symbolic figure, the semblance, assumed by the very impossibility of knowledge as such. W. J. T. Mitchell's description of his experience upon viewing *The Colonial Harem* is informed by the sensation of this impossibility; he describes "a feeling of *impotence* in the face of these women, whose beauty is now mixed with danger, whose nakedness now becomes a veil that has always excluded me from the labyrinth of their world. I feel exiled from what I want to know, to understand, or (more precisely) what I want to acknowledge and be acknowledged by" (1994, 310–11). Hamlet, haunted by his father's specter (by the ghostly ethos of his father's absence) knew well the dread of this "visor effect," this feeling of exile from that which he wanted "to acknowledge and be acknowledged by."

Because one can neither apprehend the spirit embodied by this specter nor "identify it in all certainty," Derrida writes, "we must fall back on its voice" (1994, 7). The identity of the King's ghost in Shakespeare's play is so unnatural, so unthinkable, that "[t]he one who says 'I am thy Fathers Spirit' can only be taken at his word" (7). Taking the ghost of Hamlet's father at his word constitutes, in Derrida's estimation, "[a]n essentially blind submission to his secret, to the secret of his origin" (7). Unfortunately, no voice issues from the Algerian postcards; the specters of these women remain silent. One's symbolic haunting by such liminal figures produces a corollary desire to hear them speak; yet one cannot take these specters at their word because they remain silent, without voice. Ostensibly deprived of this voice, one can only proceed as Alloula does, and as so many have done when confronted by the silence of particular subjects; one can only give this silence, in Bataille's words, "a meaning it does not have," endowing it with the essence of what we would have liked such subjects to have said or with what we today would say about their station in life.

But do we effectively *lack* their voices? Have we lost them? Do their voices remain repressed deep within or beneath the density of their intervening silence? To the contrary, Foucault teaches us that the perdurance of these voices across time was never possible, that it was never "sayable" or "articulable" in the first place. In his interpretation of Foucault's historical method, Deleuze surmises that "[e]ach age says everything it can according to the conditions laid down for its statements. . . . That everything is always said in every age is perhaps Foucault's greatest historical principle" (1988, 54). Like the romantic depictions of Sally Hemings featured in chapter 5, one's discovery of the meaning represented by these women's silence is not the recovery of a truth omitted from the archive of history but one's contemporary *interpretation* of the past, a symptom of what one can think, know, and say about a previous era, about historical subjects characterized by their irreducible difference from us instead of the essential humanity we supposedly hold in common.

Suppose that one could intuit the voices of those women whose apparitions haunt the pages of *The Colonial Harem*. Suppose their "hidden transcript," to invoke James Scott's phrase, somehow survived. Could we trust this testimony? Could we "fall back on" these voices, as Derrida might say? Could we rest assured that they persisted intact across the turbulence of time and space, immune to the vicissitudes of history and chance? Even Hamlet could not trust the authenticity of his ghostly father's testimony, or at least could only believe it by virtue of an "essentially blind submission to his secret" (Derrida 1994, 7). The ethos of the specter (the symbolic character of historical subjects made visible despite their absence or withdrawal) is never isomorphic with its voice, much less with the voice that one lends to it, because practices of seeing and speaking are not equivalent. In presuming such an equivalence, one would assume that an essential meaning transcends the historical context of changing discursive practices so as to unify word and image.

Foucault explicitly addresses the fundamental disunity between words and images throughout his early writings. In his remarkable description of Velasquez's *Las Meninas,* Foucault declares: "[I]t is in vain that we say what we see; what we see never resides in what we say. And it is in vain that we attempt to show, by the use of images, metaphors, or similes, what we are saying" (1994b, 9). Foucault's work on Magritte's surrealist paintings (1981) further illustrates this postulate. In it, he shows that the *statement* "this is a pipe" is forever irreducible to, divided from, Magritte's *image* of the pipe. The painting can neither contain nor represent the essence of the statement. Consequently, in referring to Magritte's image, the statement "this is not a pipe" is as truthful as the statement "this is a pipe." Nevertheless, Foucault continues, "between the figure and the text we must admit a whole series of crisscrossings . . . images falling into the midst of words, verbal flashes crisscrossing drawings . . . discourse cutting into the form of things" (30, 48, 50). A fundamental non-relation, therefore, irrevocably separates what one can see from what one can say, the visible from the articulable. For Foucault, this non-relation constitutes a meaningful relation nonetheless, albeit one that invalidates the conception of knowledge as a mediation of ideal truth or objective presence.[4] According to his description, the characteristic finitude of images causes them to gravitate toward the realm of statements while the inherent fallibility of words propels them toward the domain of images, thus constituting an ongoing series of "crisscrossings" between one discursive form and the other—a perpetual (if not dynamically flawed) series of attempts, at least, to pass with continuity from words to images.

What discursive conditions produce these "crisscrossings?" What discursive conditions engender the vigorous traffic of this non-relation that both distinguishes and distributes what one can see and what one can say? In the case of *The Colonial Harem,* and in scholarship equally committed to the recovery of historical experiences, this non-relation assumes the form of a silence. Silence in this context marks a *limit* or fault line, the place of this non-relation, that at once distinguishes and distributes what can be seen and what can be said. Naturally, Alloula's text responds to a dehiscence that simultaneously separates and affiliates images and text, specters and their imagined voices, much like the suspicion that attends the voice of the King's ghost in *Hamlet* or the irreducible caesura that Foucault locates between the image and text of Magritte's painting.[5]

Confronted with the images of the French colonial postcards, haunted by the specters of the women pictured therein, one is provoked by the invisibility of what has been made visible. One longs to view the absent spirit at once embodied in and deflected by the colonial fantasy in which these women are costumed. Yet the appearance of this spirit, this truth or essence, remains fundamentally withdrawn, always already beyond one's perception. Like Horatio in Shakespeare's play, one entreats the specter to speak; unlike the apparition of Hamlet's father, the specters of these women remain silent, without voice. In the discursive economy of these photographs, one has thus passed from what can one can see toward what one can say—from the visual order of the specter to that of statements. In doing so, one discovers merely the limit of what one can say about the past and its representative subject positions.

Is this limit, the enduring silence of these specters, the mark of a categorical negative, absence, or lack? Or is it, rather, merely a symptom of our finitude in relation to the past, a finitude immanent to every historical moment but which acquires unique symbolic features according to different epochs? In truth, this silence does not embody a categorical lack or absence that marks our knowledge as insufficient until it is made whole, but offers, rather, a relation of non-relation, as Foucault might say—a tangible limit, a discursive absence characterized by rhetorical sense and value—on the basis of which other forms of speech become possible. Alloula's attempt to endow the women of the colonial postcards with a voice confirms that silence in the form of this limit actually engenders new voices and statements without being reducible to such expressions. Rather than mediating the subjective consciousness of these women, or representing their testimony across time through the very lack of their speech, silence as this limit comprises the discursive condition that enables new statements.

Perhaps one's desire to achieve an unmediated relation with former persons and events, shaped as it is by the metaphysical ideals of the current *épistémé*, remains unsatisfied by these new statements. Perhaps one remains haunted by the irreducible cleft between speech and image, sensing that one can never speak, or render present, the truth lying beyond the specters of these postcards. Despite his efforts to the contrary, Horatio's attempt to vanquish the ghost of Hamlet's father by provoking it to speech ultimately fails: "By charging or conjuring him to speak," Derrida writes, "Horatio wants to inspect, stabilize, *arrest* the specter in its speech" (1994, 12). Yet the specter of Hamlet's father remains essentially uninspected, threatening, and free to appear or disappear at whim. Perhaps, then, one passes back again from the realm of statements to that of images when one realizes that one can never literally speak the truth of the spirit embodied by these specters, and so the new forms of expression stimulated by an encounter with silence must be personified by new phenomenal appearances. This return to the visible is necessary, in other words, because the specter continues to haunt us despite these new forms of speech, these new explanations of its being. "[A] ghost never dies," Derrida warns: "it remains always to come and to come-back" (99).

Silence, in the form of a non-relation between what one can see and what one can say, therefore produces a double event. It engenders, on the one hand, new conditions of enunciation while provoking, on the other hand, a return to the image, to new forms of visibility, all of which Derrida describes as "a theatricalization of speech" (101). Indeed, "The specter is also, among other things," Derrida muses, "what one imagines, what one thinks one sees and which one projects—on an imaginary screen where there is nothing to see" (100–101). One's imparting of speech to the specter, to the reimagined phenomenal form, constitutes a crucial element of this "theatricalization." Alloula's study illustrates such "theatricalization of speech" in that Alloula labors to show how one can literally see the postcards compiled in his text otherwise, with how his written critique might "force the postcard to reveal what it holds back" or to "expose what is repressed in it" (1986, 4–5). Alloula's word choice is telling: he intends, not to abolish, but to "subvert the stereotype" (5) maintained by these postcards—in other words, to see these same images differently, to imagine them anew and so produce new forms of visibility to accompany the representation of their (silent) thoughts and desires, these new forms of enunciation. He intends to produce, as Mitchell puts it, a "counter-magic, a contrary incantation" (1994, 308)—a rival quickening of images and apparitions. In this regard, Alloula's description of his project as "*my* exorcism" (1986, 5) is particularly evocative. Hence the value, in his terms, of "return[ing] this immense postcard to its sender" (5), of causing these images to function otherwise so as to produce new symbolic hauntings once one has produced a new set of statements about them.

Throughout these "crisscrossings" back and forth between the visibility of the specter and what could be said by or about it, silence constitutes the non-relation that both divides and distributes such modes of knowledge. Silence in this form functions as both a limit and a discursive condition of possibility: at once the boundary of what former persons could think, know, and say as well as what one can think, know, and say today about those persons and the time in which they lived. A repressed yet intuitively available plentitude of voices that we now lack does not lie in wait beyond this boundary; regardless of our desires to the contrary, we never possessed this ideal plentitude nor could we ever hope to do so. Instead, silence in the form of this limit marks a place that we cross and yet tarry along time and again, that stimulates the desire for new forms of speaking or new images that condition our knowledge of the past and our relation to its representative subjects. This limit is governed, not by representation, but by the symbolic immanence of the present to the past, of self to other, of the strange to the familiar.

If silence in the form of representation appears to mediate the lost voices of Algerian women forever objectified by the perverse theatre of French imperial fantasies, then silence as a discursive condition characterizes the finitude of what such women could say, or what one can say about them now. If silence in the form of an origin provides an ethos of unity and transcendence to the alleged truth of historical events and subjectivities, then silence as a discursive condition characterizes the inherently contingent meaning and value of such truth. If notions of essence, transcendence, and identity (in short, a metaphysics of presence) define silence in the form of representation, or as an origin, then immanence, finitude, and the disruption of presence distinguish silence in the form of a limit. In sum, the ethos of silence in the form of representation or as an origin is engendered by the rhetorical function of silences, by their affective capacity to produce new forms of knowledge and speech.

By inscribing the finitude of what can be said in a given age, the discursive production of silence gives rise to the desire for new conditions of enunciation along with new forms of visibility in which they might be embodied or personified. The question of silence as such is no longer, What does a given silence represent, what truth does it withhold?, but rather, What discursive conditions produced this silence—how did it acquire its characteristic ethos, its defining sense and value—and what quality of social, political, or ethical relations did it thereby produce? By attending to the discursive production of silence as such, one may at least venture beyond the familiar metaphysical opposition between the presence of speech and the absence of silence, beyond the wearied resignation of silence to the transcendent realm of the ineffable so often justified by Wittgenstein's famous concession that "[w]hereof one cannot speak, thereof one must be silent" (1990, 189). Such a venture compels one to evaluate how the very ethos of particular silences engenders social relations and subjects positions by establishing symbolic affinities between the past and the present.

Derrida finds much significance in Marcellus's plea to Horatio when the two encounter the ghost of Hamlet's father: "Thou art a scholar," Marcellus says, "speak to it, Horatio" (1994, 175).[6] Like Alloula, we today find ourselves in Horatio's—the scholar's—position, haunted by silent specters, by the ghostly apparitions of historical subjects whose very silence entreats us to know them better, to apprehend the truth or essence of their lives—their spirit. Perhaps we are so haunted because, like Hamlet as well as Horatio, we find ourselves in the position of the so-called "man of right" (Derrida 1994, 21), of the one who discovers that the crimes of the past have gone unanswered and that "[t]he time is out of joint" (*Hamlet* 1.5.18). Like the ghost of Hamlet's father, who beseeched his son to "[r]evenge his foul and most unnatural murder" (1.5.25), we find ourselves sworn to make right, not necessarily by our own choosing, but because we, like Hamlet, are "necessarily" part of what Derrida calls a "second generation, originally late and therefore destined to *inherit*"—to inherit, as a condition of knowledge, speech, and judgment, the silent specters of the past, which rise before us "impatient and nostalgic waiting for a redemption" (Derrida 1994, 136). But our knowledge of the past, our relation to it, and our ability to redeem or exorcise it, are always already finite, conditioned by our images of former persons and events, which Maffesoli evocatively describes as "a vector of communion" (1996a, 75). There is, on the one hand, what the specters of the past can say—or better, what they have always already said—and what we might say in return. There are, on the other hand, the images and re-animations that arise from what could not be said. And the rest, the empty fulcrum that both rends and relates these competing forms, is silence.

Conclusion

Rhetoric in a Nonmoral Sense

The very idea of rhetoric, its institutional meaning and value, is based on universal notions of human being. *By definition,* rhetoric originally was conceived as a pedagogical, cultural, and political practice uniquely suited to the expression of essential human truths, values, and virtues. Even contemporary rhetoricians who define the art in seemingly neutral terms, as persuasion or argumentation, inherit definitions of rhetoric first made possible by its codification, in the fifth and fourth centuries B.C.E., according to intellectually narrow and socially prejudiced ideals of reason, truth, knowledge, and morality.

Rhetoricians seldom have questioned, much less relinquished, the doubly representational logic long used to define and legitimate their domain of inquiry. Throughout the rhetorical tradition, rhetoricians have claimed that, in representing (or lending speech) to transcendent phenomena such as truth or virtue, the rhetor represents (or personifies) the defining truth and virtue of human being. Consequently, this representational logic facilitated a definition of the art (and, by implication, the human subject) in moral terms. Sound rhetoric manifested the rhetor's wise and virtuous intentions, the integrity of his or her reason and truthfulness, and thus the rectitude of his or her person. Specious rhetoric manifested the rhetor's unlearned and dissolute intentions, the faultiness of his or her reason, and thus the errancy of his or her person. Since its inception, the discipline of rhetoric has measured not merely "the way one speaks" but "the way one lives" (Baumlin 1994, xv). To paraphrase Quintilian, a good orator is, by definition, a good person speaking well.

To develop a conception of rhetoric beyond representation is to develop a nonmoral definition of rhetoric. Toward that end, the focal point of my inquiry throughout this book has been the category of ethos. I take Aristotle's description of this proof as the "controlling factor" of rhetoric in its literal sense: traditionally defined, one's appeals to character should confer favor on whatever other proofs one employs by manifesting an ethos indicative of the ideal reason and good conduct to which all of humanity should aspire (Corbett 1989, 204). Even in modern public speaking textbooks, which offer the most elementary treatments of ethos, the proof is said to undermine one's combined efforts at persuasion precisely when one's ethos appears to violate accepted standards of character and credibility. Significantly, then, the discipline of rhetoric has, for centuries, constituted a principal intellectual and cultural practice according to which universal notions of human being have been refined into commonly accepted standards of reason, truth, knowledge, and virtue. Conceiving of rhetoric beyond representation, contrary to universal notions of human being, thus offers the prospect of refuting the seemingly categorical, but actually privileged and partial, moral imperatives that have pervasively informed social identities and civic affairs throughout much of our heritage.

Developing a conception of ethos no longer defined by the rhetorical expression of a universal human nature is integral to developing a conception of rhetoric beyond representation. Because ethos, the controlling factor of rhetoric, represents categorical notions of "practical wisdom *[phronēsis]* and virtue *[aretē]* and good will *[eunoia]*" (*On Rhetoric*, 2.1.5), one must question such supposedly categorical attributes of human being in order to forge a nonrepresentational conception of ethos. More daunting still, one must do so by questioning the basic ontology that endows the category of being, human or otherwise, with its conventionally ideal and original meaning or value.

I have sought to do so, not by advocating an alternate ontology with starkly contrasting definitions of truth, meaning, and human being, but by assigning an alternate sense and value to such fundamental metaphysical categories. Attempting to either reveal the inherent falsity of such categories or transcend them altogether would simply emulate the metaphysical pretensions to an ideal truth that first produced the universal notions of human wisdom and virtue according to which rhetoric, throughout its history, has been defined. Instead, I have demonstrated (in Parts 1 and 2 of this book especially) that differences and transformations in orders of discourse, rather than an intrinsic and transparent sameness, produce the apparent identity between sensible and intelligible phenomena.

In this context, I have assigned a discursive, or nonrepresentational, sense and value to the very category of representation. By implication, assigning this altered significance to the category of representation bestows a discursive sense and value to the category of human being. Its putative representation of an ideal and original being no longer functions as a categorical truth but as a discursive phenomenon subject to change. With such a gesture, I do not oppose all forms of representation and identity; I do not propose an antirepresentational or antimetaphysical stance, in other words. Rather, by emphasizing the discursive or nonrepresentational elements of representation, by emphasizing the discursive differences that engender appeals to identity, I question the dialectical logic that originally opposed sensible to intelligible phenomena, reason to speech, identity to difference, truth to error, and virtue to vice. The effect of this questioning is not to assert the authority of a more ideal and original truth or form of subjectivity but to prove that supposedly universal standards of truth and subjectivity are based on intellectually narrow and socially prejudiced notions of reason, knowledge, and virtue.

Readers will grossly misinterpret my intentions in this book if they presume that I reject altogether appeals to representational principles—to identity, intention, the transparency of speech, or fundamental human virtues. I admit that such *topoi* retain a crucial organizing value in our conventional thought, discourse, conduct, and values. By offering such an admission, however, I am in no way obligated to conclude that rhetoric can and should be reduced to the representation of essential human reason and virtue. As I noted in chapter 2, such a reduction actually negates the worth of human experience by rendering it subservient to transcendent truth. The moral imperative upon which rhetoric was conceived—to speak with the intention of expressing truth as ideally as possible—reveals a deceptively nihilistic impulse. In order to counter such nihilism, I recognize the rhetorical function of categories such as representation, identity, intention, speech in its ideal form, and the transcendental subject while nevertheless rejecting their commonly accepted categorical status.

These initial gestures made possible a definition of rhetoric in the middle voice. Rather than amounting to a radical departure from the history and theory of rhetoric, this definition is warranted by the rich connotations of *peithō* prevalent during the early history of public address, yet essentially unexplored by modern rhetoricians. Instead of regarding *peithō* as a more ideal and original form of rhetoric, I maintain that Foucault's treatment of discourse offers the most suitable modern analogue to this classical form of persuasion in the middle voice. My conception of rhetoric in the middle voice stems from Foucault's insights because they establish a middle-voiced conception of discourse that undermines the very categories of truth, knowledge, speech, and human being upon which rhetoric is based. Rhetoric in the middle voice refers to the ethos of a discursive formation, to the established symbolic character of social, political, and ethical relations, as well as the beliefs, values, and ideals in affirmation of which they are forged. Ethos so conceived refers to the discursive production of social relations and, consequently, subject positions. The ethos of multiple subjectivities, including the sense and value of the institutional relations that sponsor them, manifests rhetoric in the middle voice. Through its formulation of rhetoric in the middle voice, of rhetoric beyond representation, this book offers at least three scholarly contributions to the humanistic and social scientific study of subjectivity.

The first is *rhetorical.* An attunement to rhetoric in the middle voice allows one to improve upon Foucault's conception of discourse, which provides initial verification that discourse produces subject positions. Consideration of rhetoric in the middle voice enables one to investigate how and why changing discursive practices engender, maintain, or transform social, political, and ethical relations. It allows one to account for and thereby evaluate the affective rhetoric—the symbolic sense and value, the conditions for thought, knowledge, speech, and judgment—that social, political, and ethical relations produce in response to historical exigencies. On the whole, rhetoric in the middle voice manifests the rhetoric of subjectivity—the ethos of multiple subject positions engendered by changing social, political, and ethical relations—characteristic of a discursive formation. Simply stated, one's investigation of rhetoric in the middle voice, instead of merely confirming *that* discourse produces subject positions and institutional relations, enables one to reveal *how,* through discursive practices, a discursive formation engenders the truths and ideals, beliefs and commitments, desires and motivations, or laws and transgressions that constitute its ethos of self and other, past and present, good and evil.

More generally, an attunement to rhetoric in the middle voice facilitates a definition of rhetoric no longer based on representational principles or dialectical logic. In this conception, rhetoric is defined, not as a civic practice uniquely devoted to representing the supposed truth of human reason and virtue (much less of humanity itself), but as the discursive production of multiple subject positions and institutional relations, of *an entire distribution* of capacities for thought, knowledge, speech, and judgment. Rhetoric in the middle voice engenders and disseminates such capacities through discursive differences and transformations. It does so, moreover, without faith in an ideal, transcendental subject.

With these claims, I do not deny the rhetorical sense and value exhibited by appeals to a universal humanity or ideal subject. I nevertheless insist that such appeals enact specific social, political, and ethical functions instead of representing categorical, and implicitly exclusionary, truths and moral standards. Such is the purpose of defining rhetoric beyond representation: not to oppose traditional definitions of rhetoric but to question the representational values and ideals long used to legitimate its theory and practice. This questioning is advantageous because it authorizes one to formulate new criteria with which to evaluate the capacities for speech and judgment characteristic of existing subject positions and social relations.

The second contribution of the book is therefore *ethical* in nature. It offers an account of the discursive formation, maintenance, and transformation of subject positions and social relations in nonmoral terms. Here I do not suggest that an attunement to rhetoric in the middle voice, to the ethos of multiple subject positions, devolves upon a moral relativism in which the speech and judgment of any subject position, or the quality of any institutional relation, is presumed to be as moral or immoral as any other. I do not oppose binding moral conceptions of human virtues and actions to a complete dearth of criteria for judgment. To the contrary, I submit that one must replace the categorically *moral* standards of truth, reason, and virtue that have defined the nature and purpose of rhetoric since its classical inception with a nimble yet principled *ethical* posture in order to lend priority to the very differences in options for thought, knowledge, speech, and judgment characteristic of different subject positions as well as the institutional relations that engender them. The implied distinction here between moral and ethical standards is subtle but profound, and therefore requires further elaboration.

One may clarify this distinction by considering an especially prominent form of contemporary progressive politics. Although scholars committed to critical projects colloquially described as *identity politics* aim to remove the historical and institutional prejudices that have led to the exclusion and even persecution of cultural or ethnic groups, their assessments of subject positions and institutional relations typically preserve the priority of identity as an analytic category. The goal of their critique is to achieve formal recognition and informal validation of a cultural or ethnic group (based on gender, race, class, or other criteria) whose identity traditionally has been used to justify social and political discrimination, or even persecution. In this manner, forms of identity politics hold as their telos the social and political representation of an ideal subject predicated on a common identity.

These efforts admittedly have produced improvements in the social and political status of some groups and individuals; yet the theoretical virtues of identity politics obscure its practical liabilities. In liberal democratic forums, the political and cultural representation of a group depends upon public consensus as to the meaning and value of its identity. The logical result of such representation, therefore, would be to sublimate cultural or ethnic differences in order to achieve an intersubjective political agenda. By virtue of this Habermasian logic, one must base one's evaluations of present institutional relations on simultaneously ideal and universal standards: *ideal* because they aspire to a civic arrangement characterized by liberal consensus and *universal* because the validation of presently excluded groups is attained by uniform political and rhetorical criteria. Unfortunately, as Nancy Fraser (1992) concludes, presumptions of consensus predicated on mutual recognition create merely the appearance of parity among unequal social groups while leaving intact the causes of that inequity. In Jeffrey Nealon's frank assessment, this desired "intersubjective community is a community of lack in which each person or group is compelled to give up the hopeless project of totalization for the attainable mini-totality of social recognition. Such a political community of the 'we' finds its commonality in difference defined as sameness" (1998, 5). Consequently, the crucial liability of this critical project is its retention of an ideal social and political standard against which one must measure present circumstances, and to which existing differences eventually must conform.[1]

Based on this description, one might describe the prohibitive political short-coming of identity politics as its moral calculus. Such a politics evaluates the status of groups and individuals, or the quality of social relations, according to a transhistorical identity or an ideal subject position. The singular pursuit of this ideal insufficiently prepares one to value and negotiate cultural differences because it renders consideration of such differences secondary to the represen-tation of a common identity. In a political parallel to the ontological negation of difference I have underscored throughout this book, Jonah Goldstein and Jeremy Rayer observe that "[i]dentity-claims depend on others for their viabil-ity but this fact is rarely acknowledged by the claimants, for to do so would be to acknowledge dependency, *and this is precisely what the claimants want to deny.* This helps explain why the politics of identity fosters grievances that are so difficult to resolve" (1994, 371). Politics of this sort, in other words, seeks recognition of a cultural or ethnic identity, not through an affirmation and management of irreducible differences, but in transcendence thereof. The pref-erable alternative, in Nealon's terms, is a politics "beholden and responsive first and foremost to the other" (1998, 2).[2]

Here, then, is the critical distinction between moral and ethical standards of judgment: moral standards commit one to the priority of transcendent identities while ethical standards enable one to evaluate and respond to irre-ducible differences. Ethics so defined, as what Nealon calls "a politics of the other" (2), obliges one to neither condemn nor celebrate, according to univer-sal and ideal standards, existing conditions for thought, knowledge, speech, and judgment, but to diagnose the quality of the social relations manifested therein. One must ask: Do such capacities exhibit the potential to produce social relations in which differences are valued, in which groups and individu-als could foster different conditions for thinking, knowing, speaking, and judg-ing? Or are they symptoms of institutional arrangements in which orthodox standards conserve the value of prejudices against otherness? In either case, one's ethical judgments are warranted by one's assessment of the ways in which social, political, and ethical relations engender accepted notions of sameness and otherness, or difference and identity.

Such judgments therefore depend, not on the unquestioned piety of universal standards or the moral obligations they confer, but on one's ability to continually question the very sense and value of one's criteria for judgment. In rudimentary terms, morality supplies answers whereas ethics provokes questions. According to Charles Scott, such questioning, which "does not arise outside of ethics, but from within it," consists of a necessarily agile yet meticulous methodology: "Learning to name things anew, to become alert to exclusions and to forgotten aspects in a people's history, to overhear what is usually drowned out by the predominant values, to rethink what is ordinarily taken for granted, to find out how to hold itself in question: these are aspects of the thought of the question of ethics" (1990, 7–8). Maintaining what Scott calls "the question of ethics" enables one to render ethical judgments by relentlessly interrogating the standards in affirmation of which one has rendered them. The goal of this continual interrogation is to persistently cultivate discursive conditions and institutional relations suitable to the valuation of difference over claims to essential identity.

In this spirit, I have produced an ethical evaluation of the very concept of rhetoric. I have endeavored to "name things anew," to assign alternate sense and value to the canonical ideals and values in deference to which rhetoric originally was codified into an educational and cultural discipline. I have endeavored "to rethink what is ordinarily taken for granted" in rhetorical studies through my critique of the supposedly universal, but actually privileged and partial, notions of humanity to which rhetoricians historically have appealed in order to legitimate their theory and practice. The principal result of this endeavor is to inaugurate a nonrepresentational, nonmoral sense of rhetoric better suited to the affirmation of social, political, and ethical differences, better attuned to the multiple ways in which discourses establish, maintain, and transform modes of thought, knowledge, speech, and judgment. An attunement to rhetoric in this sense facilitates resolute ethical evaluation of the ethos that characterizes specific social, political, and ethical relations. It yields an evaluation of the ways in which their defining sense and value engenders symbolic relations between self and other, individual and community, past and present, or good and evil. Such an attunement thereby permits one to identify discursive conditions from which different relations, more conducive to a politics of the other, might emerge.

This ethical contribution bears profound significance for studies of subjectivity throughout the humanities and social sciences. In emphasizing the social identity of historically underrepresented groups and individuals, primarily for the purposes of political solidarity, forms of identity politics typically have formulated, however innocently, a conception of the subject as a reflection of some intrinsic sameness. According to this logic, the intrinsic commonality of cultural or ethnic identities determines the significance of differences among them. An attunement to rhetoric in the middle voice, however, enables one to analyze how discursive conditions endow social relations with their characteristic capacity to establish truths and ideals, beliefs and commitments, desires and motivations, or laws and transgressions. The revised conception of ethos formulated in this book thereby provides a preferable heuristic principle with which to render critical judgments about forms of subjectivity and institutional relations because it authorizes one to account for the contingent, rhetorical sense and value of those relations instead of measuring them against an ideal subjectivity or institutional arrangement. It permits one to challenge the ethos, or governing authority, of established social and political relations, not by establishing an ideal counterpoint to their present state, but by evaluating the quality of the capacities for thought, knowledge, speech, and judgment they produce. In brief, an attunement to rhetoric in the middle voice promotes an ethical inquiry into the status of the subject by continually questioning the sometimes explicit, sometimes implicit, moral standards that continue to shape common assumptions, both cultural and academic, about the meaning and value of our being.

The foregoing observations warrant the final contribution of this book, which is *political* in nature. The more incisive, ethical evaluation of subjectivity and social relations enabled by an attunement to rhetoric in the middle voice allows one to affirm difference, rather than identity, as a vital condition of civic and political affairs. Such valuation, despite currently fashionable academic commitments to the promotion of difference, runs counter to the civic values and ideals that epitomize much of the Western tradition. The word *community* in English is descended from the Latin *communitas,* which is derived from *communis,* meaning "common." Not surprisingly, the word is related to *communion* and *communication.* Connotations of an indelible sameness therefore pervade the very meaning of community in our heritage (*Wesbster's Ninth New Collegiate Dictionary,* s. v., "community").

As a conspicuous cultural and intellectual feature of that heritage, the discipline of rhetoric historically has been valued for its capacity to secure assent to common civic ideals, values, and agendas. Throughout the early history of the United States in particular, one may observe repeated appeals, in all manner of public address, to the supposed common sentiment or bonds of affection by which members of the new nation allegedly were joined, regardless of their different cultural, racial, and economic backgrounds. Kendall Phillips adroitly observes that, even today, "Rhetorical theory continues to be dominated by the centrality of consensus," evincing little inclination to question its ostensible *raison d'être:* the search for a "discursive framework that might once again establish a sense of commonality" (1996, 231). Indeed, the intellectual and cultural value retained by the discipline of rhetoric throughout the Western heritage likely corresponds to its utility in facilitating deliberative consensus or civic identity as bases for social and political orders, however democratic or authoritarian they might have been.

In the context of the Western heritage generally, and the rhetorical tradition in particular, the prospect of basing community on irreducible cultural differences rather than an intrinsic sameness thus amounts to a radical political possibility. Even today, appeals to individual moral and political judgment, perhaps the most enduring and pernicious form of identity in the Western tradition, powerfully influence the quality of our communal commitments. Such appeals are most evident in various forms of contemporary conservative polemics. Deriding what she calls "the trap of groupthink" indicative of liberal feminism, Laura Ingraham declares that "being a truly liberated woman means being your own person—not a victim whining for special privileges or a mindless soldier of anyone's political agenda, liberal or conservative" (2000, 13). Naturally, her language resonates deeply with the romantic individualism that both typifies traditional North American cultural ideals and retains considerable appeal for many social constituencies. In using such an appeal to invalidate the "identity politics" (13) of modern feminism, Ingraham merely counters such politics with an even narrower form of social and political identity: the reasoned and autonomous individual. In doing so, she implicitly revives a well-worn social dialectic observable throughout the history of Western political theory that pits the virtuous individual against the impassioned mob.

On the other end of the conservative spectrum, Andrew Sullivan baldly appeals to individualism in basing his agenda for "homosexual politics" on "a simple and limited principle" (1995, 171). In the best tradition of laissez-faire social and economic policies, he advocates a stringent effort to "enshrine formal public equality" for homosexuals while ignoring questions of so-called private discrimination (171). In Sullivan's estimation, the virtue of such a politics is that "[i]t allows homosexuals to define their own future and their own identity and does not place it in the hands of the other" (186). As in Ingraham's proposal, Sullivan seeks to remedy current political ills by reducing politics as such to simultaneously individual and universal rights while severing substantive connections with "the other." Together, Ingraham and Sullivan's arguments, instead of providing a meaningful "politics of the other," paradoxically challenge the social influence of identity politics by advocating a narrower and more conservative form of identity.

Yet a politics based on the inherent identity of an autonomous agent is superficially political at best. Sullivan himself comes dangerously close to justifying this very claim. "It is, of course, not the least of the ironies of this politics," he observes, "that, in the last resort, its objectives are in some sense not political at all. . . . Our battle, after all, is not for political victory but for personal integrity" (187). By this reasoning, one's valorization of the private or autonomous individual as a community's representative political agent amounts to a retreat from politics, from civic engagement, from community itself. James Darsey argues that political proposals such as Sullivan's endorse "a passive conception of liberty" in which it "is no longer a right endowed by nature, but a permission" (1997, 184; 178). "Liberty conceived as 'freedom from,'" Darsey maintains, "operates to loosen the bonds that obligate us to the welfare of the community. . . . Its appeal is not to *de cive* but to each person as the maker of his or her own destiny. It is a rhetoric of disengagement. In all this, the rhetoric of gay rights establishes itself, not as a rhetoric of judgment, but as a rhetoric of nonjudgment" (184). Although I ultimately question Darsey's advocacy of rights based on "nature" and binding moral standards as preferable elements of "liberty," his critique here of "gay rights rhetoric" is equally applicable to any form of politics based on a romantic notion of individual judgment or personal identity. Such is a dubiously apolitical sponsor of community politics. Entrusting a community's political vitality to consensus among apolitical individuals may well create a more harmonious polis, but only because, in order to achieve that consensus, its constituents exchange all forms of difference for identity, of agon for stability, of judgment for tolerance, and of politics for privacy. One does not doubt that, with the end of politics, such consensus would herald the end of rhetoric. Combined with the problematic entailments of liberal identity politics, this politically conservative faith in the autonomous individual demonstrates that, despite the ostensible differences between current liberal and conservative politics, forms of identity retain a controlling authority over our communal values and ideals.

Given these deep affinities between the ideals of individual and community in our tradition, one might, by developing a conception of the subject based on difference rather than identity, inaugurate a model of community based on difference, and thus resistant to the civic liabilities of intrinsic identity, universal humanity, or uniform consensus. Imagining a community organized by the affirmation of difference, Maurice Blanchot muses, "[I]f the relation of man with man ceases to be that of the Same with the Same, but rather introduces the Other as irreducible and—given the equality between them—always in a situation of dissymmetry in relation to the one looking at that Other, then a completely different relationship imposes itself and imposes another form of society which one would hardly dare call a 'community'" (1988, 3). One could not conceive of a political formation in which otherness attains priority over forms of sameness, Blanchot surmises, without a wholesale transformation in the nature and meaning of community itself. Naturally, such valuation of otherness compels one to advocate social, political, and ethical relations that posit the meaning of community, not as a confirmation of perpetual bonds and sacrosanct ideals, but as a robust civic engagement in which groups and individuals scrupulously question the ethos of those very bonds and ideals.

The obligations of membership in such a community originate in one's commitment to the question of ethics rather than a consensual civic morality. Thus faced with the prospect of a social and political order that "one would hardly dare call a 'community,'" Blanchot writes, "one accepts the idea of naming it thus, while asking oneself what is at stake in the concept of a community and whether the community, no matter if it has existed or not, does not in the end always posit the *absence* of community" (3). In this way, an attunement to rhetoric in the middle voice allows one to identify the discursive conditions according to which one might assign an alternate sense and value to the putative sameness constitutive of community in our culture. The effect of this transmutation in our inherited conceptions of sameness would be to affirm the merit of otherness as a condition of political and ethical engagement. Affirmation of community so defined, Blanchot suggests, entails an affirmation of the *absence* of community, meaning an affirmation of irreducible differences, rather than an intrinsic commonality, as the basis of social, political, and ethical orders. Such an affirmation can be had, I argue, only by interrogating the rhetorical sense and value of our current ideals, beliefs, and commitments concerning the status of the subject and the political orders founded in the name of its allegedly universal virtues and abilities. In this book, I have provided a rationale and methodology for doing so.

The implementation of this methodology likely will confirm that one's commitment to such a radical sense of community, which marks the very absence of community as we know it, obligates one to a conditional ethical practice rather than an ideal civic arrangement. The adoption of this practice commences when one seeks to dispel the ideal and original ethos of our identities in the discursive differences from which they emerged and to which they ineluctably return. A conception of rhetoric beyond representation, I contend, authorizes one to do so, not by transcending the universal notions of humanity that pervade Western culture even today, but by assigning an alternate, nonrepresentational, or nonmoral sense and value to the pedagogical and cultural organ devoted exclusively to their refinement and expression. Questioning our traditional rhetoric of subjectivity, to borrow Foucault's reasoning, "does not establish the fact of our identity by the play of distinctions. It establishes that we are difference, that our reason is the difference of discourses, our history the difference of times, our selves the difference of masks. That difference, far from being the forgotten and recovered origin, is this dispersion that we are and make" (1972, 131). One apprehends the ethos of this dispersion by orienting oneself to *the question of rhetoric:* to a persistent questioning of the discursive means by which our reason, our histories, and our identities acquire symbolic presence within, and governing authority over, our ideals, beliefs, and commitments—an inquiry, moreover, according to which one might disclose the *aporias,* forgotten pasts, and alter egos that occasion different conditions for thinking, knowing, speaking, and judging.

To pursue the question of rhetoric is to ask: *What does rhetoric want?* That is, what truths, histories, customs, subject positions, social relations, virtues, and ideals does one endorse when one endorses the very concept of rhetoric as it has been defined in our heritage? And how might one hold in suspension the ethos that rhetoric—the ideal of public address that we take for granted as an instrument of civic order—has attained in our heritage so as to cultivate different discursive practices, and with them different traditions, communities, values, and political relations? In attending to the question of rhetoric, one transfigures the institutional character of rhetoric itself into a valuable hermeneutic principle of civic culture. By scrutinizing existing forms of address and the social relations they sponsor, one can diagnose how the ethos, the accepted sense and value of common truths, ideals, and relations, determines who, quite literally, is allowed to speak in our culture and how one is authorized to do so.

I have attended to the question of rhetoric in this book by questioning the predominance of representation as an organizing principle of rhetorical theory and practice. In its simplest form, such a method amounts to revealing, as Nietzsche did, not what good and evil *are,* but how and why one comes to speak of oneself as *agathos* while speaking of another as *deilos* (1989a, I 5, 28–31). One does not conceive of rhetoric in a nonmoral sense by disregarding moral questions but by questioning the discursive means according to which moral claims gain sense and value as formative elements of subjectivity and political or ethical judgment. In order to sustain this sense of rhetoric, one must necessarily affirm the differences between discourses, times, and masks to which Foucault refers. Between identity and difference, between past and present, between self and other, our being— once so transparent and familiar—suddenly appears strange. In the interstices of this strangeness, of this "dispersion that we are," rhetoric acquires an ethos no longer identical with representation.

Notes

PREFACE

1. For more on the longstanding affiliation between wisdom and eloquence in Western education, see Kimball (1986).

2. See, for example, Benhabib (1986 and 1996); Blaug (1996); Bohman (1996); Fraser (1985, 1989, 1992); Landes (1998); McCarthy (1994); Phillips (1996); Iris Young (1987, 1990).

3. On the historical connections between rhetoric and colonialism, see Abbott (1996); Cheyfitz (1997); Greenblatt (1991); Gustafson (2000).

INTRODUCTION

1. For surveys of the origins of rhetoric in ancient Greece, consult Cole (1991); Enos (1993); Havelock and Hershbell (1978); Lemen (1957); Johnstone (1996); Kennedy (1963, 1994, 1999); Schiappa (1999).

2. For a succinct account of the cultural and intellectual influences that shaped the classical Greek veneration of "man's" elevated nature, see Freeman (1999, chapter 13).

3. For more on Isocrates, see Hubbell (1913); Takis Poulakos (1997); Too (1995).

4. Surveys of the sophists' influence on Greek culture and rhetoric include Guthrie ([1971] 1998); Kerferd (1981a, 1981b); John Poulakos (1983, 1984, 1987, 1994); Romilly (1998); Sprague (1972); Untersteiner (1953). For modern and contemporary interpretations or appropriations of the sophists, see Hegel (1995, chapter 2); Jarratt (1991); Mailloux (1981); Marback (1999); Vitanza (1997).

5. See, especially, Plato's *Gorgias* and *Phaedrus*.

6. For more on Aristotle and rhetoric, see Erickson (1974, 1975); Furley and Alexander (1994); Garver (1994); Gross and Walzer (2000); Rorty (1996).

7. Surveys of the ancient Roman influence on Western education and the discipline of rhetoric also include Anderson (1993); Bonner (1949, 1977); Clarke (1953); Dominik (1997); Kennedy (1972).

8. Aside from Christian eloquence, the most notable innovations in rhetoric during the medieval period were grammar and *dictamen* (instruction in letter writing). For more on medieval rhetoric generally, see Baldwin (1928); Copeland (1991); McKeon (1942); Miller, Prosser, and Benson (1973); Murphy (1971a, 1971b, 1974, 1978); Reynolds (1996).

9. On Christian eloquence, see Brown (1992); Cameron (1991); Jaeger (1961); Kinneavy (1987).

10. See Salutati (1951).

11. See Guazzo (1856, 14).

12. For a sampling of scholarship on rhetoric during the Renaissance, see Baldwin (1939); Clark (1992); Fumaroli (1980); Gray (1963); Mack (1993, 1994); Murphy (1981, 1983); Seigel (1968); Sonnino (1968); Weinberg (1961).

13. See Sheridan ([1796] 1991).

14. Further studies of eighteenth- and nineteenth-century rhetoric include Golden and Corbett (1990); Horner (1993); Howell (1971); Mill (1997); Warnick (1993).

15. Relevant reappraisals of the rhetorical tradition include Bitzer and Black (1971); Blair (1992); Conley ([1990] 1993); Fisher (1975); Horner (1990); Kastely (1997); John Poulakos (1993); Schildgen (1997); Vickers (1988, 1982); Vitanza (1994); and Eugene White (1980).

16. One of the very few exceptions is Baumlin and Baumlin (1994). Like my study, their project takes as its point of departure modern critiques of classical categories central to rhetorical theory and practice. Unlike my study, however, it presents a variety of historical and contemporary reappraisals of ethos rather than developing an integrated contemporary theory thereof. Doxtader (2000) also explores the decidedly unconventional notion of ethos in the middle voice but does so by way of Hegelian philosophy, which is theoretically incompatible with my project. My central conviction in this book is to develop an account of the affinity between rhetoric and the subject that gives priority to difference rather than identity, which seems impossible under the aegis of Hegelian ontology.

17. Works that establish precedents for such a project, or that offer more philosophically inflected approaches to rhetoric, include Angus and Langsdorf (1993); Backman (1991); Biesecker (1997); Cherwitz (1990); Corbin (1998); Fogarty (1959); Grassi (1980); Gray-Rosendale and Gruber (2001); Heidlebaugh (2001); Hyde (2001); Kastely (1997); Mailloux (1981); Meyer (1994); Rosteck (1999); Simons (1989); Smith (1998); Swartz (1998); Thomas (1999); Valesio (1980); Vitanza (1997); Yarborough (1999).

CHAPTER 1. THE SUBJECT AND OBJECT OF REPRESENTATION

1. Gaonkar (1997) refers to this phenomenon in rhetorical scholarship as "coarticulation"; Robbins (1990) terms it "the rhetoric of rhetoric."

2. Aristotle (1966, B998a20-B999a20; Γ159a20-Γ1061b15).

3. Deleuze highlights Nietzsche's aversion to a literal understanding of termination (1983, 47).

4. See especially Nietzsche (1968, 1974, 1982, 1990).

5. Despite the insufficiencies to which Sallis alludes, *Aufhebung* is commonly translated in English as "sublation."

6. See also Hegel (1977).

7. See especially Heidegger (1973, 1993, 1996, 1999).

8. See Sallis (1995, 139–51) for his commentary on the connections between Heidegger and Derrida.

9. In his treatise on the sophistic origins of rhetoric, Schiappa (1999) notes the emerging value of intuition evident in early conceptions being and logos.

10. Vickers may overstate the case here; occasional comparisons between rhetoric and painting or architecture exist in classical texts. Nonetheless, these perceived parallels were novel to and most systematically explored during the Renaissance.

11. Derrida (1978) in fact offers this sort of objection to Foucault's earlier work, *Madness and Civilization* (1988), which first appeared in 1961. Foucault's later work became less susceptible to such objections; for his response to Derrida, see Foucault (1998).

CHAPTER 2. THE IDEAL OF RHETORIC

1. Nietzsche's (1989a) delineation of the ascetic ideal naturally provides a broader frame of reference for his insights concerning the metaphysical primacy of truth and the debasement of life. Not coincidentally, the language of credit and debt figures prominently in his account.

2. See Gadamer (1984, 345–447; 491–98) for more on his views about the relationship between language and understanding.

3. For more on Nietzsche's commentaries on rhetoric, see Gilman, Blair, and Parent (1989). Other treatments of Nietzsche and rhetoric include Behler (1995, 1996); Crawford (1988).

4. For further commentaries on the middle voice, see Barthes (1972b); Benjamin (1996); Jay (1993). The middle voice is often explained by way of examples from Sanskrit; consult Goldman (1980). On the challenges that the middle voice poses to metaphysical thought, see Derrida (1982, 9–10); Heidegger (1996, sections 7, 74, 75, 78, 80); Charles Scott, (1990, 19–25).

5. For further background on Saussure or semiotics, see Badir (2001); Culler (1974, 1986); Hawkes (1977); Holdcroft (1991); Sebeok (2001); Silverman (1983).

6. Claude Lévi-Strauss's (1994) use of Saussure offers a prominent example of how structuralism preserved the implicit totality and closure of language in this rendering. Lévi-Strauss endorses the view that language forms a necessarily complete symbolic system, no matter how arbitrary its atomic structure. Consequently, the inherent arbitrariness (and thus instability) of language is subordinated in such inquiry to its apparent completeness.

7. These comments suggest the common Western narrative of an even progression from orality to literacy, from speech to writing (as a formulation of language); see Eisenstein (1979); Goody (1986, 1987); McLuhan (1962); Ong (1967, 1982).

8. Ricoeur defines Saussure's emphasis of linguistic difference as a conceptualization of form rather than substance: "As Saussure said, in a system of signs there are only differences, but no substantial existence. This postulate defines the formal properties of linguistic entities, formal here being opposed to the substantial in the sense of an autonomous positive existence of the entities at stake in linguistics and, in general, in semiotics" (1976, 5).

9. For more on the connections between structuralism and deconstruction, see Culler (1981); Derrida (1972); Spivak (1974); Strozier (1988).

10. In his translation of Saussure's *Course in General Linguistics* (1972), Roy Harris questions whether Saussure was stringently committed to this valorization of speech. Harris includes "*language* rendered as 'speech' " as one of many previous "mistranslations" of Saussure's teachings, "from the trivial to the grossly misleading" (xiii). He therefore substitutes "language" where previous translations used "speech," as in the following example: "In the lives of individuals and societies, language is a factor of greater importance than any other" (7). Clearly a certain inflection is lost here; does Harris's translation consequently nullify Derrida's critique of Saussure's alleged phonocentrism? Even if Harris were proved correct in his consistent preference for "language" rather than "speech," language as such is vividly differentiated from the corrosions of writing in Saussure's text. In Harris's translation, Saussure still worries that "the written word is so intimately connected with the spoken word it represents that it manages to usurp the principal role"; that "[i]n certain circumstances, writing may well retard changes in a language"; and that "[a] language, then, has an oral tradition independent of writing, and much more stable" (25). Regardless of Harris's "corrections" in translation, "language" in Saussure's thinking remains ideal and original in contrast to writing, and thus undeniably encompasses speech by default.

11. See Derrida (1981a) for perhaps the most currently fashionable reading of Plato's *Phaedrus,* specifically concerning the significance of writing. Other notable treatments include Benardete (1991); DuBois (1985); Ferrari (1987); Griswold (1986); Heath (1987); Kastely (2002); Mackenzie (1982); Rowe (1986); Svenbro (1988); Vries (1969); Weaver (1953, 3–26). Plato's interest in writing is also evident in his *Seventh Letter.*

12. Of course, Heidegger's full discussion of logos (1996, 28–30) is extremely helpful in drawing out the larger complexity of that term's classical connotations. He admittedly derives his analysis of the concept, however, from Aristotle's definition of logos; see Aristotle (1966).

13. One may profitably read Saussure's text, as Derrida does, for its resonance with Enlightenment treatises on the question of natural language. See Condillac (1974); Hume (1975); Locke (1979); Rousseau (1999).

14. On speech act theory, see also Searle (1969, 1979).

CHAPTER 3. RHETORIC IN THE MIDDLE VOICE

1. Muckelbauer's (2001) reading of the *Sophist* deftly explores the trope of the hunt as the dialogue's organizing principle.

2. One can observe Deleuze's investment in the reversal of Platonism throughout his corpus; for perhaps his most concise treatment of it, however, see Deleuze (1990, 253–66). Other notable readings of Plato's *Sophist* include Heidegger (1997); Kostman (1989); Marback (1999); Rosen (1983); Thomas (1999, chapter 2).

3. For introductory commentary on the origins of the term *rhetoric,* see Bennett and Tyrrell (1990); John Poulakos (1990); Schiappa (1990a, 1990b, 1992).

4. This formulation employs Spivak's delineation of Derrida's derivation of the concept of writing under erasure from Heidegger: "What is this question of Being that is necessarily precomprehended in order that thinking itself occur? Since it is always anterior to thinking, it can never be formulated as an answer to the question, "what is . . . :" (1974, xiv).

5. In order to avoid confusion, one should note that Foucault's neologism here carries a different (though not incompatible) meaning from Derrida's "logocentrism." Foucault uses "logophobia" to refer to Western thought's habitual fear of discourse not domesticated under the aegis of reason, whereas Derrida's "logocentrism" refers to the same tradition's drive to apprehend a truth located prior to the order of discourse.

6. To be sure, followers as well as critics of Foucault (not to mention Foucault himself) raised concerns about *The Archaeology of Knowledge.* Foucault later extended his philosophy beyond archaeological notions of discourse and knowledge into genealogies of power principally because the metaphor of archaeology, despite his intentions, implied a quasi-structural understanding of discourse. Regardless, I utilize Foucault's *The Archaeology of Knowledge* here for its attempts to consider the status of the subject, not as an essential identity, but as a dispersion of difference; despite the subsequent evolution of Foucault's thought, this preoccupation remained constant throughout his corpus.

CHAPTER 4. STYLE WITHOUT IDENTITY

1. Obviously, modern rhetorical scholarship features much consideration of genre; while genre studies acknowledge the formal elements of texts and modes of address, they fail to offer an explicit rhetorical theory of style as such.

2. In addition to Hariman, Steve Whitson and John Poulakos (1993) argue for an aesthetic rather than epistemic conception of rhetoric, although they do not offer a systematic treatment of rhetoric and style per se.

3. Maffesoli's description here recalls Foucault's later work on ethics and subjectivity; he cites Foucault's research on the uses of pleasure and the care of the self as one of several inspirations for his definition of social life as an aesthetic creation. Biesecker (1992b) offers the best treatment of the later Foucault's insights on style in the context of rhetorical studies.

4. For a treatment of emotional and other nonrational imperatives, see Lingis (1994, 1998).

5. See Ferraris (1987).

CHAPTER 5. JEFFERSON'S OTHER

1. See also Lewis (1999).

2. See Ellis (1997); Lewis and Onuf (1998); Onuf (1993); Peterson (1960, 1970); Schwarz (1997).

3. I focus on the memory of Jefferson from 1968 forward, not to excise the oral histories of African Americans, but to underscore the changes by which such oral histories, as well as other new ways of understanding the past, have attained unprecedented significance. See, for example, Woodson (2001).

4. See also Ledgin (2000).

5. The Association of the Bar of the City of New York conducted a mock trial of Jefferson in 1994, with Charles Ogletree and William Rehnquist participating (Gordon-Reed 1997, 105).

6. Those who believe that Jefferson and Hemings had a sexual affair point to four pieces of circumstantial evidence: accounts of a resemblance between Jefferson and at least some of the Hemings children; the testimony of Madison Hemings that Jefferson was his father; the fact that Jefferson was in residence at Monticello when each of Hemings's children were conceived; and that Hemings never conceived a child when Jefferson was away.

7. Jefferson had no surviving sons by Martha Jefferson. Because sons inherit the Y chromosome from their father unchanged, Jefferson is presumed to have shared the haplotype identified in the descendants of his uncle; see Foster et al. (1998).

8. A group of scholars has refuted vociferously the findings of Foster's DNA tests in Coates (2001).

9. See also Halliday (2001).

10. Jefferson, of course, shared these anxieties.

11. Brodie finds significant Jefferson's use of the word "mulatto" to describe features of the European landscape, a term he apparently disliked prior to Hemings's arrival in Paris (1974, 228–45).

12. See also Coates (2001); Dabney (1981); Malone (1948–1981).

13. The miniseries began as a play based on Fawn Brodie's work. See Andrews (2001); Williams (2000).

14. James Hemings was freed by Jefferson in 1796, another indication of Jefferson's benevolence toward the Hemings family.

15. A French tutor was hired shortly after Sally's arrival, but for whom we cannot be certain.

16. In this text, Jefferson documented his beliefs regarding the inferiority of African Americans and the dangers of miscegenation (1982, 137–43; 162–63).

17. For more on Jefferson, race, and slavery, see Finkelman (1993); French and Ayers (1993, 418–56); Jefferson (1982, 137–43; 162–63); Miller (1977); Edmund Morgan (1975); Onuf (1988); Stanton (1993). Prominent research on the asymmetrical power relations that shaped the lives of female slaves includes Fox-Genovese (1988); Genovese (1972); Deborah Gray White (1985).

18. Girls of Hemings's age were thought to be eligible for romantic relationships with men; nevertheless, the idea of Jefferson courting a fifteen- or sixteen-year-old girl is disturbing to modern sensibilities.

19. John Wayles, Martha Jefferson's father, owned the Hemings family prior to Martha and Thomas Jefferson's marriage. Sally Hemings was the child of an affair between John Wayles and Betty Hemings. Martha Jefferson and Sally Hemings, therefore, were half-sisters. Rumors that Hemings closely resembled Jefferson's late wife survive in historical documents and have been cited as one explanation for Jefferson's alleged attraction to Hemings.

20. According to Jefferson's own formula, any children by Sally Hemings would have been legally white. Jefferson once "wrote out an algebraic equation demonstrating that after 'three crossings' with whites, the black person was legally white. By this definition, Sally Hemings's children were, in fact, Caucasian. Their father, whoever he was, was white, their grandfathers were white, and their great-grandfathers were white. Jefferson went on to say that if such a person were to be emancipated, that person would become a 'citizen of the United States for all intents and purposes' " (Gordon-Reed 1997, 53).

21. Even before the period of Jefferson's alleged affair with Hemings, visitors to Monticello reported encountering white slaves at his estate. In 1796, the Duc de La Rochefoucauld-Liancourt described the sight of slaves with "neither in their color nor features a single trace of their origin, but they are sons of slave mothers and consequently slaves." During the same period, the Comte de Volney recorded seeing slaves at Monticello "as white as I am." Quoted in Stanton (1993, 152 [La

Rochefoucauld-Liancourt] and 173, n.18 [Volney]). Apparently, Jefferson at least tolerated and would have been aware of a practice that Phillip Morgan explains was common on plantations, in which "[y]oung white men were expected to sow their oats in the slave quarters" (1999, 63).

22. Similarities between Jefferson and Hemings's children have been established. All of Hemings's sons played the violin, an instrument that Jefferson played. They also served as apprentices to the best slave artisan at Monticello instead of working in the plantation's nail factory; some interpret this as proof that Jefferson wanted them to learn a trade prior to their emancipation. Others find significant the possibility that Beverly Hemings attended a balloon ascension on July 4, 1834, in Petersburg, Virginia; Jefferson attended balloon ascensions both at home and abroad. See Gordon-Reed (1997, 51; 151–52; 218).

23. Vidal (1973) also depicts Jefferson provocatively.

24. I retain this problematic term for the United States throughout this section in order to preserve the irony with which Erickson uses it. "America" in *Arc d'X* is less an actual place than a noble idea whose implementation has, in many ways, proved tragic. The novel refers, not so much to the United States as such, but to the laudable ideal that Jefferson regrettably labeled "America."

25. See also Genovese (1972).

26. Genovese also uses Hegel in his study of slave life (1972, 66–67; 86; 88; 89; 281; 465; 684, n5).

27. See also O'Brien (1996a).

28. See O'Brien (1996b); Onuf (1993); Schwarz (1997).

29. These thoughts on the nature of memory are inspired by Deleuze (1994).

CHAPTER 6. THE REST IS SILENCE

1. For more on the relationship between photography and colonial fantasy in French Algeria, see Clancy-Smith (1997); Graham-Brown (1988); Yegenoglu (1998). For other commentaries on *The Colonial Harem,* see Chow (1994); Mitchell (1994, 307–12).

2. For more on silence in either rhetorical or communication studies, see Brummett (1980); Bruneau (1973); Cloud (1999); Hedge (1996); Johannesen (1974); Olson (1997); Robert Scott (1972).

3. This paragraph is a gloss on Deleuze's interpretation of Foucault's historical methodology (1988, 47–69).

4. Foucault's notion of the "non-relation" between seeing and speaking is inspired by Blanchot; see, for example, Blanchot (1993, 25–32).

5. Mitchell, for one, pays too little attention to this caesura, claiming that in Alloula's study "[t]here is an equality of text and image" (1994, 308). His elaboration of the point undermines its very integrity, however, for "Alloula's text," in Mitchell's words, "presents itself as a substitute for a body of photographs that should have been taken, but never were" (1994, 308–309). Alloula's text, then, is a *substitute,* not a homology or a perfect equivalence; yet Mitchell's claim to an equality between text and image is doubly misleading here, for how can one offer up a positive equivalence for that which "should have been" but never was?

6. Derrida draws an analogy between Horatio and specifically those scholars who follow in the tradition of Marxist thought, even by breaking with it (1994, 175–76).

CONCLUSION

1. For further reflections on the practical entailments of such politics, see Adams and Minson (1978); Alcoff (1988); Butler (1990); Connolly (1991); Fuss (1989); Gates (1986); Giroux (1992); Goldstein and Rayner (1994).

2. Nealon's point is inspired by Emmanuel Levinas's philosophy; see Levinas (1969, 1981, 1985).

Bibliography

Abbott, Don P. 1996. *Rhetoric in the New World: Rhetorical Theory and Practice in Colonial Spanish America*. Columbia: University of South Carolina Press.

Adams, Parveen, and Jeff Minson. 1978. "The 'Subject' of Feminism." *m/f* 2: 43–61.

Aeschylus. 1979. *The Oresteia*. Translated by Robert Fagles. Rep. and rev. New York: Penguin Books.

Alcoff, Linda. 1988. "Cultural Feminism vs. Poststructuralism: The Identity Crisis in Feminist Theory." *Signs* 13: 405–36.

Alloula, Malek. 1986. *The Colonial Harem*. Translated by Myrna and Wlad Godzich. Minneapolis: University of Minnesota Press.

Anderson, Graham. 1993. *The Second Sophistic: A Cultural Phenomenon in the Early Roman Empire*. London: Routledge.

Andrews, Tina. 2001. *Sally Hemings: An American Scandal*. New York: Malibu Press.

Angus, Ian, and Lenore Langsdorf, eds. 1993. *The Critical Turn: Rhetoric and Philosophy in Postmodern Discourse*. Carbondale: Southern Illinois University Press.

Aristotle. 1954. *Rhetoric*. Translated by W. Rhys Roberts. Modern Library.

———. 1966. *Aristotle's Metaphysics*. Translated by Hippocrates G. Apostle. Bloomington: Indiana University Press.

———. 1991. *On Rhetoric: A Theory of Civic Discourse*. Translated by George A. Kennedy. New York: Oxford University Press.

Augustine. 1995. *De Doctrina Christiana: A Classic of Western Culture*. Edited by Duane W. H. Arnold and Pamela Bright. Notre Dame: University of Notre Dame Press.

Austin, J. L. 1962. *How to do Things With Words*. 2d ed. Cambridge: Harvard University Press.

Bacon, Francis. 2000. *The Advancement of Learning*. Edited by Michael Kiernan. Oxford: Clarendon Press, 2000.

Backman, Mark. 1991. *Sophistication: Rhetoric and the Rise of Self-consciousness*. Woodbridge, Conn.: Ox Bow.

Badir, Sémir. 2001. *Saussure: la langue et sa représentation*. Paris: L'Harmattan.

Baldwin, Charles S. 1928. *Medieval Rhetoric and Poetic (to 1400) Interpreted from Representative Works*. New York: Macmillan.

———. 1939. *Renaissance Literary Theory and Practice*, ed. Donald L. Clark. New York: Macmillan.

"

Barthes, Roland. 1972a. *Mythologies.* Translated by Annette Lavers. New York: The Noonday Press.

———. 1972b. "To Write: An Intransitive Verb?" In *The Languages of Criticism and the Sciences of Man: The Structuralist Controversy,* ed. Richard Macksey and Eugenio Donato, 134–56. Baltimore: Johns Hopkins University Press.

Bataille, Georges. 1988a. *Essential Writings.* Edited by Michael Richardson. London: Sage Publications.

———. 1988b. *Inner Experience.* Translated by Leslie Anne Boldt. Albany: State University of New York Press.

Baumlin, James S. 1994. "Introduction: Positioning *Ethos* in Historical and Contemporary Theory." In *Ethos: New Essays in Rhetorical and Critical Theory,* ed. James S. Baumlin and Tita French Baumlin, xi–xxxi. Dallas: Southern Methodist University Press.

———, and Tita French Baumlin, eds. 1994. *Ethos: New Essays in Rhetorical and Critical Theory.* Dallas: Southern Methodist University Press.

Behler, Ernst. 1995. "Nietzsche's Study of Greek Rhetoric." *Research in Phenomenology* 25: 3–26.

———. 1996. "Friedrich Nietzsche's Theory of Language and Its Reception in Contemporary Thought." In *Beyond the Symbol Model,* ed. John Stewart, 167–200. London: Sage.

Belenky, Mary Field, Blythe McVicker Clinchy, Nancy Rule Goldberger, and Jill Mattuck Tarule. 1986. *Women's Ways of Knowing: The Development of Self, Voice, and Mind.* New York: Basic Books.

Benardete, Seth. 1991. *The Rhetoric of Morality and Philosophy: Plato's Gorgias and Phaedrus.* Chicago: University of Chicago Press.

Benhabib, Seyla. 1986. *Critique, Norm, and Utopia: A Study of the Foundations of Critical Theory.* New York: Columbia University Press.

———, ed. 1996. *Democracy and Difference: Contesting the Boundaries of the Political.* Princeton: Princeton University Press.

Benjamin, Walter. 1968. "Theses on the Philosophy of History," In *Illuminations,* by Walter Benjamin. Translated by Harry Zohn, 253–64. New York: Schocken.

———. 1996. "On Language as Such and on the Language of Man." In *Walter Benjamin: Selected Writings, Volume I, 1913–1926,* ed. Marcus Bullock and Michael W. Jennings, 62–74. Cambridge: Harvard University Press.

Bennett, Larry J., and Wm. Blake Tyrrell. 1990. "Did Plato Coin *Rhētorikē*?" *American Journal of Philology* 111: 457–70.

Benson, Thomas W. 1989. "Rhetoric as a Way of Being." In *American Rhetoric: Context and Criticism,* ed. Thomas W. Benson, 293–322. Carbondale: Southern Illinois University Press.

Biesecker, Barbara. 1989. "Rethinking the Rhetorical Situation from Within the Thematic of *Differance.*" *Philosophy and Rhetoric* 22 (1989): 110–30.

———. 1992a. "Coming to Terms with Recent Attempts to Write Women into the History of Rhetoric." *Philosophy and Rhetoric* 25: 140–61.

———. 1992b. "Michel Foucault and the Question of Rhetoric." *Philosophy and Rhetoric* 25: 351–64.

———. 1997. *Addressing Postmodernity: Kenneth Burke, Rhetoric, and a Theory of Social Change.* Tuscaloosa: University of Alabama Press.

Bitzer, Lloyd. 1968. "The Rhetorical Situation." *Philosophy and Rhetoric* 1: 1–14.
————, and Edwin Black. 1971. *The Prospect of Rhetoric.* Englewood Cliffs, N.J.: Prentice-Hall.
Black, Edwin. 1970. "The Second Persona." *Quarterly Journal of Speech* 56: 109–19.
————. 2001. "Response to Being Honored." *Rhetoric and Public Affairs* 4: 540–41.
Blair, Carole. 1992. "Contested Histories of Rhetoric: The Politics of Preservation, Progress, and Change." *Quarterly Journal of Speech* 78: 403–28.
Blair, Hugh. [1819] 1993. *Lectures on Rhetoric and Belles Lettres.* Reprint. Delmar, N.Y.: Scholars' Facsimiles and Reprints.
Blanchot, Maurice. 1988. *The Unavowable Community.* Translated by Pierre Joris. Barrytown, N.Y.: Station Hill Press.
————. 1993. *The Infinite Conversation.* Translated by Susan Hanson. Minneapolis: University of Minnesota Press.
Blaug, Ricardo. 1996. "New Theories of Discursive Democracy: A User's Guide." *Philosophy and Social Criticism* 22.1: 49–80.
Bohman, James. 1996. *Public Deliberation: Pluralism, Complexity, and Democracy.* Cambridge: MIT Press.
Bonner, S. F. 1949. *Roman Declamation in the Late Republic and Early Empire.* Berkeley: University of California Press.
————. 1977. *Education in Ancient Rome.* Berkeley: University of California Press.
Brodie, Fawn M. 1974. *Thomas Jefferson: An Intimate History.* New York: W. W. Norton.
Brown, Peter. 1992. *Power and Persuasion in Later Antiquity: Towards a Christian Europe.* Madison: University of Wisconsin Press.
Browne, Stephen. 1995. "Reading, Rhetoric, and the Texture of Public Memory." *Quarterly Journal of Speech* 81: 237–50.
Brummett, Barry. 1980. "Towards a Theory of Silence as Political Strategy." *Quarterly Journal of Speech* 66: 289–303.
Bruneau, Thomas J. 1973. "Communicative Silences: Forms and Functions." *Journal of Communication* 23: 17–46.
Burke, Kenneth. 1966. *Language as Symbolic Action: Essays on Life, Literature, and Method.* Berkeley: University of California Press.
————. [1945] 1969a. *A Grammar of Motives.* London: Prentice Hall. Reprint, Berkeley: University of California Press.
————. [1945] 1969b. *A Rhetoric of Motives.* London: Prentice-Hall. Reprint, Berkeley: University of California Press.
Butler, Judith. 1990. *Gender Trouble.* New York: Routledge.
Cameron, Avril. 1991. *Christianity and the Rhetoric of Empire: The Development of Christian Discourse.* Berkeley: University of California Press.
Campbell, George. [1841] 1992. *The Philosophy of Rhetoric.* Reprint. Delmar, NY: Scholars' Facsimiles and Reprints.
Charland, Maurice. 1987. "Constitutive Rhetoric: The Case of the *Peuple Québécois.*" *Quarterly Journal of Speech* 73: 133–50.
Chase-Riboud, Barbara. 1979. *Sally Hemings: A Novel.* New York: Viking Press.
Cherwitz, Richard A., ed. 1990. *Rhetoric and Philosophy.* Hillsdale, N.J.: Lawrence Erlbaum.

Cheyfitz, Eric. 1997. *The Poetics of Imperialism: Translation and Colonization from "The Tempest" to "Tarzan."* Rev. ed. Philadelphia: University of Pennsylvania Press.

Chow, Rey. 1994. "Where Have All the Natives Gone?" In *Displacements: Cultural Identities in Question,* ed. Angelika Bammer, 125–51. Bloomington: Indiana University Press.

Cicero. 1942. *Brutus, Orator.* Translated by E. W. Sutton. Cambridge, Mass.: Loeb Classical Library.

———. 1949. *De Inventione, De Optimo Genere Oratorum, Topica.* Translated by H. M. Hubbell. Cambridge, Mass.: Loeb Classical Library.

———. [1939] 1988. *De Oratore.* In two volumes. Translated by H. M. Hubbell. Loeb Classical Library. Rev. and reprinted. Cambridge, Mass.: Harvard University Press.

Clair, Robin Patric. 1988. *Organizing Silence.* Albany: State University of New York Press.

Clancy-Smith, Julia. 1997. "The Colonial Gaze: Sex and Gender in the Discourses of French North Africa." In *Franco-Arab Encounters: Studies in Memory of David C. Gordon,* ed. Leon Carl Brown and Matthew S. Gordon, 201–28. Syracuse: Syracuse University Press.

Clark, Donald L. 1992. *Rhetoric and Poetry in the Renaissance.* New York: Columbia University Press.

Clarke, M. L. 1953. *Rhetoric at Rome: A Historical Survey.* London: Cohen and West.

Cloud, Dana L. 1999. "The Null Persona: Race and the Rhetoric of Silence in the Uprising of '34." *Rhetoric and Public Affairs* 2: 177–209.

Coates, Eyler Robert, Sr., ed. 2001. *The Jefferson-Hemings Myth: An American Travesty.* Charlottesville: Jefferson Editions.

Cole, Thomas. 1991. *The Origins of Rhetoric in Ancient Greece.* Baltimore: Johns Hopkins University Press.

Condillac, Etienne Bonnot de. 1974. *An Essay on the Origin of Human Knowledge.* New York: AMS Press.

Conley, Thomas M. [1990] 1993. *Rhetoric in the European Tradition.* New York: Longman. Reprint. Chicago: University of Chicago Press.

Connolly, William. 1991. *Identity/Difference.* Ithaca: Cornell University Press.

Copeland, Rita. 1991. *Rhetoric, Hermeneutics, and Translation in the Middles Ages.* New York: Cambridge University Press.

Corbett, Edward P. J. 1989. "Rhetoric, the Enabling Discipline." In *Selected Essays of Edward P. J. Corbett,* ed. Robert J. Connors, 194–208. Dallas: Southern Methodist University Press.

———. 1990. *The Rhetoric of Blair, Campbell, and Whately.* New York: Holt, Rinehart, and Winston.

Corbin, Carol, ed. 1998. *Rhetoric in Postmodern America: Conversations with Michael Calvin McGee.* New York: Guilford.

Corts, Thomas E. 1968. "The Derivation of Ethos." *Speech Monographs* 35: 201–202.

Crawford, Claudia. 1988. "The Beginnings of Nietzsche's Theory of Language." *Monographin und Texte sure Nietzsche-Forschung* 19. Berlin: de Gruyter.

Culler, Jonathan. 1974. "Introduction." In *Course in General Linguistics,* by Ferdinand de Saussure, xi–xv. Rev. ed. Translated by Wade Baskin. London: Fontana.

———. 1981. *The Pursuit of Signs: Semiotics, Literature, Deconstruction.* Ithaca: Cornell University Press.

———. 1986. *Ferdinand de Saussure.* Rev. ed. Ithaca: Cornell University Press.

Dabney, Virginius. 1981. *The Jefferson Scandals.* New York: Dodd, Mead and Co.

Darsey, James Francis. 1997. *The Prophetic Tradition and Radical Rhetoric in America.* New York: New York University Press.

Deleuze, Gilles. 1983. *Nietzsche and Philosophy.* Translated by Hugh Tomlinson. New York: Columbia University Press.

———. 1988. *Foucault.* Translated by Seán Hand. Minneapolis: University of Minnesota Press.

———. 1990. *The Logic of Sense.* Translated by Mark Lester with Charles Stivale. New York: Columbia University Press.

———. 1994. *Difference and Repetition.* Translated by Paul Patton. New York: Columbia University Press.

———, and Félix Guattari. 1987. *A Thousand Plateaus.* Translated by Brian Massumi. Minneapolis: University of Minnesota Press.

Derrida, Jacques. 1972. "Structure, Sign, and Play in the Discourse of the Human Sciences." In *The Structuralist Controversy: The Languages of Criticism and the Sciences of Man,* ed. Richard Macksey and Eugenio Donato, 247–72. Baltimore: Johns Hopkins University Press.

———. 1973. *Speech and Phenomena.* Translated by David B. Allison. Evanston: Northwestern University Press.

———. 1974. *Of Grammatology.* Translated by Gayatri Chakravorty Spivak. Baltimore: Johns Hopkins University Press.

———. 1978. "Cogito and the History of Madness." In *Writing and Difference.* Translated by Alan Bass, 31–63. Chicago: The University of Chicago Press.

———. 1981a. "Plato's Pharmacy." In *Dissemination.* Translated by Barbara Johnson, 61–172. Chicago: University of Chicago Press.

———. 1981b. *Positions.* Translated by Alan Bass. Chicago: University of Chicago Press.

———. 1982. *Margins of Philosophy.* Translated by Alan Bass. Chicago: University of Chicago Press.

———. 1984. "Deconstruction and the Other." In *Dialogues with Contemporary Continental Thinkers,* ed. Richard Kearney, 105–26. Manchester, UK: Manchester University Press.

———. 1998. *Limited Inc.* Translated by Samuel Weber. Evanston: Northwestern University Press.

———. 1994. *Specters of Marx.* Translated by Peggy Kamuf. New York: Routledge.

Dominik, William J., ed. 1997. *Roman Eloquence: Rhetoric in Society and Literature.* London: Routledge.

Doxtader, Erik W. 2000. "Characters in the Middle of Public Life: Consensus, Dissent, and *Ethos.*" *Philosophy and Rhetoric* 33: 336–69.

DuBois, Page. 1985. "Phallocentrism and Its Subversion in Plato's *Phaedrus.*" *Arethusa* 18: 91–103.

Eisenstein, Elizabeth L. 1979. *The Printing Press as an Agent of Change: Communications and Cultural Transformations in Early-Modern Europe*. 2 vols. Cambridge: Cambridge University Press.

Ellis, Joseph. 1997. *American Sphinx: The Character of Thomas Jefferson*. New York: Alfred A. Knopf.

Emerson, Ralph Waldo. 1964a. "Art." In *The Early Lectures of Ralph Waldo Emerson, Volume II, 1836–1838*, ed. Stephen E. Whicher, Robert E. Spiller, and Wallace E. Williams, 42–54. Cambridge: The Belknap Press of Harvard University Press.

———. 1964b. "Society." In *The Early Lectures of Ralph Waldo Emerson, Volume II, 1836–1838*, ed. Stephen E. Whicher, Robert E. Spiller, and Wallace E. Williams, 98–112. Cambridge: The Belknap Press of Harvard University Press.

Enos, Richard L. 1993. *Greek Rhetoric Before Aristotle*. Prospect Heights, Ill.: Waveland Press.

Erickson, Keith. 1975. *Aristotle's Rhetoric: Five Centuries of Philological Research*. Metuchen, N.J.: Scarecrow Press.

———, ed. 1974. *Aristotle: The Classical Heritage of Rhetoric*. Metuchen, N.J.: Scarecrow Press.

Erickson, Steve. 1993. *Arc d'X*. New York: Henry Holt.

Ewen, Stuart. 1988. *All Consuming Images: The Politics of Style in Contemporary Culture*. New York: Basic Books.

Farrell, Thomas B. 1993. *Norms of Rhetorical Culture*. New Haven: Yale University Press.

Ferrari, G. R. F. 1987. *Listening to the Cicadas: A Study of Plato's Phaedrus*. Cambridge: Cambridge University Press.

Ferraris, Maurizio. 1987. *Ermeneutica di Proust*. Milano: Ed. Guerini.

Finkelman, Paul. 1993. "Jefferson and Slavery: 'Treason Against the Hopes of the World.' " In *Jeffersonian Legacies*, ed. Peter S. Onuf, 181–221. Charlottesville: University of Virginia Press.

Fisher, Walter R., ed. 1975. *Rhetoric: A Tradition in Transition*. East Lansing: Michigan State University Press.

Fliegelman, Jay. 1993. *Declaring Independence: Jefferson, Natural Language, and the Culture of Performance*. Stanford: Stanford University Press.

Fogarty, Daniel John. 1959. *Roots for a New Rhetoric*. New York: Bureau of Publications, Teachers College, Columbia University.

Foster, Eugene A., et al. 1998. "Jefferson Fathered Slave's Last Child." *Nature* 196 (November): 27–28.

Foucault, Michel. 1972. *The Archaeology of Knowledge and the Discourse on Language*. Translated by A. M. Sheridan Smith. New York: Pantheon Books.

———. 1977. *Language, Counter-Memory, Practice*. Edited by Donald F. Bouchard. Ithaca: Cornell University Press.

———. 1979. *Discipline and Punish: The Birth of the Prison*. Translated by Alan Sheridan. New York: Vintage Books.

———. 1981. *This is not a pipe*. Translated by James Harkness. Berkeley: University of California Press.

———. 1988a. *Madness and Civilization: A History of Insanity in the Age of Reason.* Translated by Richard Howard. New York: Vintage Books.

———. 1988b. "The Minimalist Self." In *Politics, Philosophy, Culture: Interviews and Other Writings, 1977–1984,* ed. Lawrence D. Kritzman, 3–16. New York: Routledge.

———. 1990. *The History of Sexuality, Vol. I.* Translated by Robert Hurley. New York: Vintage Books.

———. 1994a. *The Birth of the Clinic: An Archaeology of Medical Perception.* Translated by A. M. Sheridan Smith. New York: Vintage Books.

———. 1994b. *The Order of Things: An Archaeology of the Human Sciences.* New York: Vintage Books.

———. 1998. "My Body, This Paper, This Fire." In *Aesthetics, Method, and Epistemology: Essential Works of Foucault 1954–1984,* ed. James D. Faubion, 393–417. New York: The New Press.

———. 2001. *Fearless Speech.* Edited by Joseph Pearson. Los Angeles: Semiotext(e).

Fox-Genovese, Elizabeth. 1988. *Within the Plantation Household: Black and White Women of the Old South.* Chapel Hill: The University of North Carolina Press.

Fraser, Nancy. 1985. "What's Critical About Critical Theory: The Case of Habermas and Gender." *New German Critique* 35: 97–132

———. 1989. *Unruly Practices: Power, Discourse, and Gender in Contemporary Social Theory.* Minneapolis: University of Minnesota Press.

———. 1992. "Rethinking the Public Sphere: A Contribution to the Critique of Actually Existing Democracy." In *Habermas and the Public Sphere,* ed. Craig Calhoun, 109–37. Cambridge: MIT Press.

Freeman, Charles. 1999. *The Greek Achievement: The Foundation of the Western World.* London: The Penguin Press.

French, Scot A., and Edward L. Ayers. 1993. "The Strange Career of Thomas Jefferson: Race and Slavery in American Memory, 1943–1993." In *Jeffersonian Legacies,* ed. Peter S. Onuf, 418–56. Charlottesville: University of Virginia Press.

Fumaroli, Marc. 1980. *L'Age de l'éloquence: Rhétorique et res litteraria de la Renaissance au seuil de l'époque classique.* Geneva: Droz.

Furley, David J., and Alexander Nehamas, eds. 1994. *Aristotle's Rhetoric: Philosophical Issues.* Princeton: Princeton University Press.

Fuss, Diana. 1989. *Essentially Speaking: Feminism, Nature, and Difference.* New York: Routledge.

Gadamer, Hans-Georg. 1976. *Philosophical Hermeneutics.* Translated by David E. Linge. Berkeley: University of California Press.

———. 1984. *Truth and Method.* New York: Crossroads.

Gaonkar, Dilip Parameshwar. 1997. "The Idea of Rhetoric in the Rhetoric of Science." In *Rhetorical Hermeneutics: Invention and Interpretation in the Age of Science,* ed. Alan G. Gross and William M. Keith, 25–85. Albany: State University of New York Press.

Garin, Eugenio. 1965. *Italian Humanism: Philosophy and Civic Life in the Renaissance.* Translated by Peter Munz. New York: Harper and Row.

Garver, Newton. 1973. Preface. *Speech and Phenomena,* by Jacques Derrida. Translated by David B. Allison, ix–xxix. Evanston: Northwestern University Press.

———. 1994. *Aristotle's Rhetoric: An Art of Character.* Chicago: University of Chicago Press.

Gates, Henry Louis, ed. 1986. *"Race," Writing, and Difference.* Chicago: University of Chicago Press.

Genovese, Eugene D. 1972. *Roll, Jordan, Roll: The World the Slaves Made.* New York: Vintage Books.

Gilman, Sander, Carole Blair, and David J. Parent, eds. 1989. *Friedrich Nietzsche on Rhetoric and Language.* New York: Oxford University Press.

Giroux, Henry. 1992. "Post-Colonial Ruptures and Democratic Possibilities." *Cultural Critique* 21: 4–39.

Golden, James L., and Edward P. J. Corbett. 1990. *The Rhetoric of Blair, Campbell, and Whatley.* Carbondale: Southern Illinois University Press.

Goldman, Richard P. 1980. *Devavanitravesika, an Introduction to the Sanskrit Language.* Berkeley: University of California Press.

Goldstein, Jonah, and Jeremy Rayner. 1994. "The Politics of Identity in Late Modern Society." *Theory and Society* 23: 367–84.

Goody, Jack. 1986. *The Logic of Writing and Organization of Society.* Cambridge: Cambridge University Press.

———. 1987. *The Interface between the Written and the Oral.* Cambridge: Cambridge University Press.

Gordon-Reed, Annette. 1997. *Thomas Jefferson and Sally Hemings: An American Controversy.* Charlottesville: University of Virginia Press.

———. 1999. "The Memories of a Few Negroes." In *Sally Hemings and Thomas Jefferson: History, Memory and Civic Culture,* ed. Jan Ellen Lewis and Peter S. Onuf, Charlottesville: University of Virigina Press, 236–52.

Gorgias. 1972. "Encomium of Helen." In *The Older Sophists,* ed. Rosamond Kent Sprague, 50–54. Columbia: University of South Carolina Press.

Graham-Brown, Sarah. 1988. *Images of Women: The Portrayal of Women in Photography of the Middle East 1860–1950.* New York: Columbia University Press.

Grassi, Ernesto. 1980. *Rhetoric as Philosophy: The Humanist Tradition.* University Park: Pennsylvania State University Press.

Gray, Hanna H. 1963. "Renaissance Humanism: The Pursuit of Eloquence." *Journal of the History of Ideas* XXIV (Oct.–Dec.): 497–514.

Gray-Rosendale, Laura, and Sibylle Gruber, eds. 2001. *Alternative Rhetorics: Challenges to the Rhetorical Tradition.* Albany: State University of New York Press.

Greenblatt, Stephen. 1991. *Marvelous Possessions: The Wonder of the New World.* Chicago: University of Chicago Press.

Griswold, Charles L. 1986. *Self-Knowledge in Plato's Phaedrus.* New Haven: Yale University Press.

Gross, Alan G., and Arthur E. Walzer, eds. 2000. *Rereading Aristotle's Rhetoric.* Carbondale: Southern Illinois University Press.

Grossberg, Lawrence. 1979. "Marxist Dialectics and Rhetorical Criticism." *Quarterly Journal of Speech* 65: 235–49.

Guazzo, Stefano. 1856. *La civile conversazione.* Venice.

Gustafson, Sandra M. 2000. *Eloquence Is Power: Oratory and Performance in Early America*. Chapel Hill: University of North Carolina Press.

Guthrie, W. K. C. [1971] 1998. *The Sophists*. Reprint. Cambridge: Cambridge University Press.

———. 1975. *The Greek Philosophers from Thales to Aristotle*. New York: Harper and Row.

Halliday, E. M. 2001. *Understanding Thomas Jefferson*. New York: HarperCollins.

Hariman, Robert. 1995. *Political Style*. Chicago: University of Chicago Press.

Havelock, Eric A., and Jackson Hershbell. 1978. *Communication Arts in the Ancient World*. Mamaroneck, N.Y.: Hastings House.

Hawkes, Terence. 1977. *Structuralism and Semiotics*. Berkeley: University of California Press.

Heath, Malcolm. 1987. "The Unity of Plato's *Phaedrus*." *Oxford Studies in Ancient Philosophy* 7: 150–73.

Hedge, Radha S. 1996. "Narratives of Silence: Rethinking Gender, Agency, and Power from the Communication Experiences of Battered Women in South India." *Communication Studies* 47: 303–17.

Hedges, Elaine, and Shelly Fisher Fishkin, eds. 1994. *Listening to Silences*. New York: Oxford University Press.

Hegel, G. W. F. 1971. *Hegel's Philosophy of Mind*. Translated by A. V. Miller. Oxford: Clarendon Press.

———. 1977. *Phenomenology of Spirit*. Translated by A. V. Miller. Oxford: Clarendon Press.

———. 1995. *Lectures on the History of Philosophy*. 3 vols. Translated by E. S. Haldane. Lincoln: University of Nebraska Press.

Heidegger, Martin. 1958. *The Question of Being*. Bilingual ed. Translated by William Kluback and Jean T. Wilde. New Haven: College and University Press.

———. 1973. *The End of Philosophy*. Translated by Joan Stambaugh. New York: Harper and Row.

———. 1993. "The End of Philosophy and the Task of Thinking." In *Basic Writings*. Ed. David Farrell Krell, 369–92. San Francisco: Harper San Francisco.

———. 1996. *Being and Time*. Translated by Joan Stambaugh. Albany: State University of New York Press.

———. 1997. *Plato's Sophist*. Translated by Richard Rojcewicz and André Schuwer. Bloomington: Indiana University Press.

———. 1999. *Contributions to Philosophy* (From Enowning). Translated by Parvis Emad and Kenneth Maly. Bloomington: Indiana University Press.

Heidlebaugh, Nolah J. 2001. *Judgment, Rhetoric, and the Problem of Incommensurability: Recalling Practical Wisdom*. Columbia: South Carolina University Press.

Holdcroft, David. 1991. *Saussure: Signs, System, and Arbitrariness*. Cambridge: Cambridge University Press.

Horner, Winifrid B. 1993. *Nineteenth-Century Scottish Rhetoric: The American Connection*. Carbondale: Southern Illinois University Press.

———, ed. 1990. *The Present State of Scholarship in Historical and Contemporary Rhetoric*. Rev. ed. Columbia: University of Missouri Press.

Howell, Wilbur S. 1971. *Eighteenth-Century British Logic and Rhetoric.* Princeton: Princeton University Press.

Hubbell, Harry M. 1913. *The Influence of Isocrates on Cicero, Dionysius, and Aristides.* New Haven: Yale University Press.

Hume, David. 1975. *Enquiries Concerning Human Understanding.* 3d ed. Oxford: Clarendon Press.

———. 2000. *A Treatise of Human Nature.* Edited by David Fate Norton and Mary J. Norton. Oxford: Oxford University Press.

Hyde, Michael J. 2001. *The Call of Conscience: Heidegger and Levinas, Rhetoric and the Euthanasia Debate.* Columbia: University of South Carolina Press.

Ingraham, Laura. 2000. *The Hillary Trap: Looking for Power in All the Wrong Places.* New York: Hyperion Press.

Isaac, Rhys. 1999. "Monticello Stories Old and New." In *Sally Hemings and Thomas Jefferson: History, Memory and Civic Culture,* ed. Jan Ellen Lewis and Peter S. Onuf, 114–26. Charlottesville: University of Virginia Press.

Isocrates. [1928] 2000. "Panegyricus." In *Isocrates.* Vol. 1. Translated by George Norlin, 117–241. Loeb Classical Library. Reprint. Cambridge: Harvard University Press.

———. [1929] 2000. "Antidosis." In *Isocrates.* Vol. 2. Translated by George Norlin, 179–365. Loeb Classical Library. Reprint. Cambridge: Harvard University Press.

Jaeger, Werner. 1961. *Early Christianity and Greek Paideia.* Cambridge: Harvard University Press.

James, William. 1985. *The Varieties of Religious Experience: A Study in Human Nature.* New York: Penguin Books.

Jarratt, Susan C. 1987. "Toward a Sophistic Historiography." *Pre/Text* 8: 9–26.

———. 1991. *Rereading the Sophists: Classical Rhetoric Refigured.* Carbondale: Southern Illinois University Press.

Jaworski, Adam, ed. 1997. *Silence: Interdisciplinary Perspectives.* Berlin: Mouton de Gruyter.

Jay, Martin. 1993. "Experience Without a Subject: Walter Benjamin and the Novel." *New Formations* 20: 145–55.

Jefferson in Paris. 1995. Produced by Donald Rosenfield, Humbert Balsan, Ismail Merchant, Paul Bradley. Directed by James Ivory. 2 hr. 24 min. Merchant-Ivory, Videocassette.

Jefferson, Thomas. 1982. *Notes on the State of Virginia.* Edited by William Peden. Chapel Hill: University of North Carolina Press.

Johannesen, Richard L. 1974. "The Functions of Silence: A Plea for Communication Research." *Western Speech* 38: 25–35.

Johnson, Barbara. 1981. Translator's Introduction. *Dissemination,* by Jacques Derrida. Translated by Barbara Johnson, vii–xxxiii. Chicago: The University of Chicago Press.

Johnstone, Christopher L. 1996. *Theory, Text, Context: Issues in Greek Rhetoric and Oratory.* Albany: State University of New York Press.

Jordan, Winthrop D. 1968. *White over Black: American Attitudes toward the Negro, 1550–1812.* Chapel Hill: University of North Carolina Press.

Kastley, James L. 1997. *Rethinking the Rhetorical Tradition: From Plato to Postmodernism.* New Haven: Yale University Press.

———. 2002. "Respecting the Rupture: Not Solving the Problem of Unity in Plato's *Phaedrus.*" *Philosophy and Rhetoric* 35: 138–52.

Kennedy, George A. 1963. *The Art of Persuasion in Greece.* Princeton: Princeton University Press.

———. 1972. *The Art of Rhetoric in the Roman World.* Princeton: Princeton University Press.

———. 1994. *A New History of Classical Rhetoric.* Princeton: Princeton University Press.

———. 1999. *Classical Rhetoric and its Christian and Secular Tradition from Ancient to Modern Times.* 2d ed. Rev. and enl. Chapel Hill: University of North Carolina Press.

Kerferd, G. B., 1981a. "The Future Direction of Sophistic Studies." In *The Sophists and Their Legacy,* ed. G. B. Kerferd, 1–6. Wiesbaden: Franz Steiner.

———. 1981b. *The Sophistic Movement.* Cambridge: Cambridge University Press.

Kimball, Bruce A. 1986. *Orators and Philosophers: A History of the Idea of a Liberal Education.* New York: Teachers College Press.

Kinneavy, James I. 1987. *Greek Rhetorical Origins of Christian Faith.* New York: Oxford University Press.

Kostman, James. 1989. "Ambiguity of Partaking in Plato's *Sophist.*" *Journal of the History of Philosophy* 27: 343–63.

Kurzon, Dennis. 1998. *Discourse of Silence.* Philadelphia: J. Benjamins. Lander, Eric, and Joseph Ellis. 1998. "Founding Father." *Nature* 196 (November): 13–14.

Landes, Joan, ed. 1998. *Feminism: The Public and the Private.* Oxford: Oxford University Press.

Lanham, Richard A. 1976. *The Motives of Eloquence: Literary Rhetoric in the Renaissance.* New Haven: Yale University Press.

Ledgin, Norm. 2000. *Diagnosing Jefferson.* Arlington, Tex.: Future Horizons.

Leff, Michael. 1993. "The Uses of Aristotle's Rhetoric in Contemporary American Scholarship." *Argumentation* 7: 291–96.

Lemen, Donald. 1957. *Rhetoric in Greco-Roman Education.* New York: Columbia University Press.

Lesko, Barbara S. 1997. "The Rhetoric of Women in Pharaonic Egypt." In *Listening to Their Voices: The Rhetorical Activities of Historical Women,* ed. Molly Meijer Wertheimer, 89–111. Columbia: University of South Carolina Press.

Lévi-Strauss, Claude. 1994. *Tristes Tropiques.* Translated by John and Doreen Weightman. New York: Penguin Books.

Levinas, Emmanuel. 1969. *Totality and Infinity.* Translated by Alphonso Lingis. Pittsburgh: Duquesne University Press.

———. 1981. *Otherwise than Being, or Beyond Essence.* Translated by Alphonso Lingis. The Hague: Martinus Nijhoff.

———. 1985. *Ethics and Infinity.* Translated by Richard A. Cohen. Pittsburgh: Duquesne University Press.

Lewis, Jan Ellis. 1999. "The White Jeffersons." In *Sally Hemings and Thomas Jefferson: History, Memory, and Civic Culture,* ed. Jan Ellen Lewis and Peter S. Onuf, 127–60. Charlottesville: University Press of Virginia.

Lewis, Jan Ellen, and Peter S. Onuf. 1998. "American Synecdoche: Thomas Jefferson as Image, Icon, Character, and Self." *American Historical Review* 103: 125–36.

———. 1999a. "Introduction." In *Sally Hemings and Thomas Jefferson: History, Memory, and Civic Culture,* ed. Jan Ellen Lewis and Peter S. Onuf, 1–16. Charlottesville: University of Virginia Press.

———, eds. 1999b. *Sally Hemings and Thomas Jefferson: History, Memory, and Civic Culture.* Charlottesville: University Press of Virginia.

Lingis, Alphonso. 1994. *The Community of Those Who Have Nothing in Common.* Bloomington: Indiana University Press.

———. 1998. *The Imperative.* Bloomington: Indiana University Press.

Locke, John. 1979. *An Essay Concerning Human Understanding.* Edited by Peter H. Nidditch. Oxford: Oxford University Press.

McCarthy, Thomas. 1994. "Legitimacy and Diversity: Dialectical Reflections on Analytical Distinctions." *Protosoziologie* 6: 199–228.

McDermott, Hubert. 1989. *Novel and Romance: The Odyssey to Tom Jones.* Basingstoke: MacMillan.

McGee, Michael Calvin. 1975. "In Search of 'The People': A Rhetorical Alternative." *Quarterly Journal of Speech* 61: 235–49.

———. 1980. "The Ideograph: A Link Between Rhetoric and Ideology." *Quarterly Journal of Speech* 66: 1–16.

McKeon, Richard. 1942. "Rhetoric in the Middle Ages." *Speculum* 17: 1–32.

———. 1987. *Rhetoric: Essays in Invention and Discovery.* Edited by Mark Backman. Woodbridge, Conn.: Ox Bow.

———. 1998. *Selected Writings of Richard McKeon.* Edited by Zahava K. McKeon and William G. Swenson. Chicago: Chicago University Press.

McKerrow, Raymie E. 1989. "Critical Rhetoric: Theory and Praxis." *Communication Monographs* 56: 91–111.

McLuhan, Marshall. 1962. *The Gutenburg Galaxy: The Making of Typographic Man.* Toronto: University of Toronto Press.

McMurray, Rebecca L., and James F. McMurray, Jr. 2002. *Anatomy of a Scandal: Thomas Jefferson and the Sally Story.* Shippensburg, Pa.: White Mane Books.

Mack, Peter. 1993. *Renaissance Argument: Valla and Agricola in the Traditions of Rhetoric and Dialectic.* Leiden: Brill.

———, ed. 1994. *Renaissance Rhetoric.* New York: St. Martin's Press.

Mackenzie, Mary Margaret. 1982. "Paradox in Plato's *Phaedrus.*" *Proceedings of the Cambridge Philological Society* 28: 64–76.

Maffesoli, Michel. 1993. *The Shadow of Dionysus: A Contribution to the Sociology of the Orgy.* Translated by Cindy Linse and Mary Kristina Palmquist. Albany: State University of New York Press.

———. 1996a. *The Contemplation of the World: Figures of Community Style.* Translated by Susan Emanuel. Minneapolis: University of Minnesota Press.

———. 1996b. *The Time of the Tribes: The Decline of Individualism in Mass Society.* Translated by Don Smith. London: Sage.

Mailloux, Steven, ed. 1981. *Rhetoric, Sophistry, Pragmatism.* New York: Cambridge University Press.

Malone, Dumas. 1948–1981. *Jefferson and His Time.* Boston: Little, Brown.

Marback, Richard. 1999. *Plato's Dream of Sophistry*. Columbia: University of South Carolina Press.

Mauss, Marcel. 1985. "A Category of the Human Mind: The Notion of Person, the Notion of Self." In *The Category of the Person: Anthropology, Philosophy, History*, ed. Michael Carrithers, Steven Collins, and Steven Lukes, 1–25. Cambridge: Cambridge University Press.

May, James M. 1988. *Trials of Character: The Eloquence of Ciceronian Ethos*. Chapel Hill: University of North Carolina Press.

Meyer, Michael. 1994. *Rhetoric, Language, and Reason*. University Park: Pennsylvania State University Press.

Mill, Thomas P. 1997. *The Formation of College English: Rhetoric and Belles Lettres in the British Cultural Provinces*. Pittsburgh: University of Pittsburgh Press.

Miller, John Chester. 1977. *The Wolf by the Ears: Thomas Jefferson and Slavery*. New York: The Free Press.

Miller, Joseph M., Michael H. Prosser, and Thomas W. Benson, eds. 1973. *Readings in Medieval Rhetoric*. Bloomington: Indiana University Press.

Mitchell, W. J. T. 1994. *Picture Theory*. Chicago: University of Chicago Press.

Morgan, Edmund S. 1975. *American Slavery—American Freedom*. New York: Norton.

Morgan, Phillip D. 1999. "Interracial Sex in the Chesapeake and the British Atlantic World, c. 1700–1820." In *Sally Hemings and Thomas Jefferson: History, Memory, and Civic Culture*, ed. Jan Ellen Lewis and Peter S. Onuf, 52–84. Charlottesville: University of Virginia Press.

Muckelbauer, John. 2001. "Sophistic Travel: Inheriting the Simulacrum Through Plato's 'The Sophist.' " *Philosophy and Rhetoric* 34: 225–44.

Murphy, James J. 1971a. *Medieval Rhetoric: A Select Bibliography*. Toronto: Center for Medieval Studies.

———. 1974. *Rhetoric in the Middle Ages: A History of Rhetorical Theory from Saint Augustine to the Renaissance*. Berkeley: University of California Press.

———, 1981. *Renaissance Rhetoric: A Short-Title Catalogue of Works on Rhetorical Theory from the Beginning of Printing to A. D. 1700*. New York: Garland.

———, ed. 1971b. *Three Medieval Rhetorical Arts*. Berkeley: University of California Press.

———, ed. 1978. *Medieval Eloquence: Studies in the Theory and Practice of Medieval Rhetoric*. Berkeley: University of California Press.

———, ed. 1983. *Renaissance Eloquence: Studies in the Theory and Practice of Renaissance Rhetoric*. Berkeley: University of California Press.

Naas, Michael. 1995. *Turning: From Persuasion to Philosophy*. Atlantic Highlands, N.J.: Humanities Press.

Nealon, Jeffrey. 1998. *Alterity Politics*. Durham: Duke University Press.

Nietzsche, Friedrich. 1968. *The Will to Power*. Translated by Walter Kaufmann and R. J. Hollingdale. New York: Vintage Books.

———. 1974. *The Gay Science*. Translated by Walter Kaufmann. New York: Vintage Books.

———. 1982. "Thus Spoke Zarathustra." In *The Portable Nietzsche*. Edited and translated by Walter Kaufmann, 103–439. New York: Penguin Books.

———. 1989a. *On the Genealogy of Morals and Ecce Homo*. Translated by Walter Kaufmann and R. J. Hollingdale. New York: Vintage Books.

———. 1989b. "On Truth and Lying in an Extra-Moral Sense." In *Friedrich Nietzsche on Rhetoric and Language,* ed. and trans. Sander L. Gilman, Carole Blair, and David J. Parent, 246–57. New York: Oxford University Press.

———. 1990. *Twilight of the Idols/The Anti-Christ.* Translated by R. J. Hollingdale. New York: Penguin Books.

O' Brien, Conor Cruise. 1996a. *The Long Affair: Thomas Jefferson and the French Revolution, 1785–1800.* Chicago: University of Chicago Press.

———. 1996b. "Thomas Jefferson: Radical and Racist." *Atlantic Monthly* (October): 53–74.

Olson, Lester C. 1997. "On the Margins of Rhetoric: Audre Lorde Transforming Silence into Language and Action." *Quarterly Journal of Speech* 83: 49–70.

Ong, Walter J. 1967. *The Presence of the Word: Some Prolegomena For Cultural and Religious History.* New Haven: Yale University Press.

———. 1982. *Orality and Literacy: The Technologizing of the Word.* London: Methuen.

Onuf, Peter S. 1988. " 'To Declare Them a Free and Independent People': Race, Slavery, and National Identity in Jefferson's Thought." *Journal of the Early American Republic* 18: 1–46.

———, ed. 1993. *Jeffersonian Legacies.* Charlottesville: University Press of Virginia.

Parton, James. 1874. *Life of Thomas Jefferson.* Boston: James R. Osgood and Company.

Perelman, Chaïm. 1979. *The New Rhetoric and the Humanities: Essays on Rhetoric and Its Applications.* Boston: D. Reidel.

———. 1982. *The Realm of Rhetoric.* Translated by William Kluback. Notre Dame: University of Notre Dame Press.

———, and L. Olbrechts-Tyteca. 1969. *The New Rhetoric: A Treatise on Argumentation.* Translated by John Wilkinson and Purcell Weaver. Notre Dame: Notre Dame University Press.

Perry, Ben Edwin. 1967. *The Ancient Romances: A Literary-Historical Account of their Origins.* Berkeley: University of California Press.

Peters, John Durham. 1999. *Speaking into the Air: A History of the Idea of Communication.* Chicago: University of Chicago Press.

Peterson, Merrill D. 1960. *The Jefferson Image in the American Mind.* New York: Oxford University Press.

———. 1970. *Thomas Jefferson and the New Nation: A Biography.* New York: Oxford University Press.

Phillips, Kendall R. 1996. "The Spaces of Public Dissension." *Communication Monographs* 63: 231–48.

Plato. 1969. "Sophist." In *The Collected Dialogues of Plato,* ed. Edith Hamilton and Huntington Cairns, 957–1017. Princeton: Princeton University Press.

———. 1999. "Gorgias." In *The Collected Dialogues of Plato,* ed. Edith Hamilton and Huntington Cairns, 229–307. Princeton: Princeton University Press.

———. 1999. "Meno." In *The Collected Dialogues of Plato,* ed. Edith Hamilton and Huntington Cairns, 353–84. Princeton: Princeton University Press.

———. 1999. "Phaedo." In *The Collected Dialogues of Plato,* ed. Edith Hamilton and Huntington Cairns, 40–98. Princeton: Princeton University Press.

———. 1999. "Phaedrus." In *The Collected Dialogues of Plato,* ed. Edith Hamilton and Huntington Cairns, 475–525. Princeton: Princeton University Press.

————. 1999. "Socrates' Defense (Apology)." In *The Collected Dialogues of Plato*, ed. Edith Hamilton and Huntington Cairns, 3–26. Princeton: Princeton University Press.

Poulakos, John. 1983. "Towards a Sophistic Definition of Rhetoric." *Philosophy and Rhetoric* 16: 35–48.

————. 1984. "Rhetoric, the Sophists, and the Possible." *Communication Monographs* 51: 215–26.

————. 1987. "Sophistical Rhetoric as a Critique of Culture." In *Argument and Critical Practices: Proceedings of the Fifth SCA/AFA Conference on Argumentation*, ed. J. W. Wenzel, 97–101. Annandale, Va.: Speech Communication Association.

————. 1990. "Interpreting Sophistical Rhetoric: A Response to Schiappa." *Philosophy and Rhetoric* 23: 218–28.

————. 1994. *Sophistical Rhetoric in Classical Greece*. Columbia: University of South Carolina Press.

Poulakos, Takis. 1997. *Speaking for the Polis: Isocrates' Rhetorical Education*. Columbia: University of South Carolina Press.

————, ed. 1993. *Rethinking the History of Rhetoric: Multidisciplinary Essays on the Rhetorical Tradition*. Boulder: Westview Press.

Quintilian. [1920–1922] 1996–1998. *Institutio Oratoria*. Translated by H. E. Butler. 4 vols. Loeb Classical Library. Cambridge: Harvard University Press.

Reid, Ronald F., ed. 1995. *American Rhetorical Discourse*. 2d. ed. Prospect Heights, Ill.: Waveland Press.

Reynolds, Suzanne. 1996. *Medieval Reading: Grammar, Rhetoric, and the Classical Text*. Cambridge: Cambridge University Press.

Ricoeur, Paul. 1976. *Interpretation Theory*. Fort Worth: Texas Christian University Press.

Robbins, Bruce. 1990. "Interdisciplinarity in Public: A Rhetoric of Rhetoric." *Social Text* 25/26: 103–18.

Romilly, Jacqueline de. 1998. *Les Grands sophistes dans l'Athènes de Périclès*. Paris: De Fallois.

Rorty, Amélie O., ed. 1996. *Essays on Aristotle's Rhetoric*. Berkeley: University of California Press.

Rosen, Stanley. 1983. *Plato's Sophist: The Drama of Original and Image*. South Bend: St. Augustine's Press.

Rosteck, Thomas, ed. 1999. *At the Intersection: Cultural Studies and Rhetorical Studies*. New York: Guilford Press.

Rothman, Joshua. 1999. "James Callender and Social Knowledge of Interracial Sex in Antebellum Virginia." In *Sally Hemings and Thomas Jefferson: History, Memory, and Civic Culture*, ed. Jan Ellen Lewis and Peter S. Onuf, 87–113. Charlottesville: University of Virginia Press.

Rousseau, Jean-Jacques. 1999. *Essay on the Origin of Languages*. Translated by John T. Scott. Hanover: University Press of New England.

Rowe, C. J. 1986. "The Argument and Structure of Plato's *Phaedrus*." *Proceedings of the Cambridge Philological Society* 32: 106–25.

Sallis, John. 1995. *Delimitations: Phenomenology and the End of Metaphysics*. 2d ed. Bloomington: Indiana University Press.

Sally Hemings: An American Scandal. 2000. Produced by Gerrit van der Meer. Directed by Charles Haid. Written by Tina Andrews. 4 hrs. CBS, 13, 16 February.

Salutati, Lino Coluccio. 1951. *De laboribus Herculis.* Edited by B. L. Ullman. 2 vols. Zurich.

Saussure, Ferdinand de. 1972. *Course in General Linguistics.* Translated by Roy Harris. La Salle: Open Court.

———. 1974. *Course in General Linguistics.* Rev. ed. Translated by Wade Baskin. London: Fontana.

Schiappa, Edward. 1990a. "Neo-Sophistic Rhetorical Criticism or the Historical Reconstruction of Sophistic Doctrines?" *Philosophy and Rhetoric* 23: 192–217.

———. 1990b. "History and Neo-Sophistic Criticism: A Reply to Poulakos." *Philosophy and Rhetoric* 23: 307–15.

———. 1992. "*Rhêtorikê:* What's in a Name? Toward a Revised History of Early Greek Rhetorical Theory." *Quarterly Journal of Speech* 78: 1–15.

———. 1999. *The Beginnings of Rhetorical Theory in Ancient Greece.* New Haven: Yale University Press.

Schildgen, Brenda Deen, ed. 1997. *The Rhetoric Canon.* Detroit: Wayne State University Press.

Schrag, Calvin O. 1985. "Rhetoric Resituated at the End of Philosophy." *Quarterly Journal of Speech* 71: 164–74.

Schwarz, Benjamin. 1997. "What Jefferson Helps to Explain." *Atlantic Monthly* (March): 60–72.

Scott, Charles E. 1987. *The Language of Difference.* Atlantic Highlands, N.J.: Humanities Press.

———. 1990. *The Question of Ethics: Nietzsche, Foucault, Heidegger.* Bloomington: Indiana University Press.

———. 1996. *On the Advantages and Disadvantages of Ethics and Politics.* Bloomington: Indiana University Press.

———. 1999. *The Time of Memory.* Albany: State University of New York Press.

Scott, James C. 1990. *Domination and the Arts of Resistance: Hidden Transcripts.* New Haven: Yale University Press.

Scott, Robert L. 1967. "On Viewing Rhetoric as Epistemic." *Central States Speech Journal* 18: 9–7.

———. 1972. "Rhetoric and Silence." *Western Speech* 36: 146–58.

———. 1976. "On Viewing Rhetoric as Epistemic: Ten Years Later." *Central States Speech Journal* 27: 258–66.

———. 2000. "Between Silence and Certainty: A Codicil to 'Dialectical Tensions of Speaking and Silence.'" *Quarterly Journal of Speech* 86: 108–10.

Searle, John R. 1969. *Speech Acts: An Essay in the Philosophy of Language.* London: Cambridge University Press.

———. 1979. *Expression and Meaning: Studies in the Theory of Speech.* Cambridge: Cambridge University Press.

Sebeok, Thomas Albert. 2001. *Signs: An Introduction to Semiotics.* Toronto: University of Toronto Press.

Seigel, Jerold E. 1968. *Rhetoric and Philosophy in Renaissance Humanism: The Union of Eloquence and Wisdom, Petrarch to Valla.* Princeton: Princeton University Press.

Shakespeare, William. 1969. "Hamlet Prince of Denmark." In *William Shakespeare: The Complete Works,* ed. Alfred Harbage, 930–74. New York: Penguin Books.

Sheridan, Thomas. [1796] 1991. *A Course of Lectures on Elocution 1762.* Reprint. Delmar, N.Y.: Scholars' and Facsimiles Reprints.

Silverman, Kaja. 1983. *The Subject of Semiotics.* New York: Oxford University Press.

Simons, Herbert W. 1989. *Rhetoric in the Human Sciences.* London: Sage.

Simpson, David. 2002. *Situatedness, or, Why We Keep Saying Where We're Coming From.* Durham: Duke University Press.

Smith, Craig R. 1998. *Rhetoric and Human Consciousness: A History.* Prospect Heights, Ill.: Waveland.

Smith, Leef. 2000. "Jefferson Paternity Called Likely." *Washington Post* 27 (January): B01.

Sonnino, Lee A. 1968. *A Handbook to Sixteenth-Century Rhetoric.* London: Routledge and Kegan Paul.

Spivak, Gayatri. 1974. Translator's Preface. *Of Grammatology,* by Jacques Derrida, ix–lxxxvii. Baltimore: Johns Hopkins University Press.

Sprague, Rosamond K., ed. 1972. *The Older Sophists.* Columbia: University of South Carolina Press.

Stanton, Lucia C. 1993. " 'Those Who Labor For My Happiness': Thomas Jefferson and His Slaves." In *Jeffersonian Legacies,* ed. Peter S. Onuf, 147–80. Charlottesville: University of Virginia Press.

———, and Dianne Swann-Wright. 1999. "Bonds of Memory: Identity and the Hemings Family." In *Sally Hemings and Thomas Jefferson: History, Memory, and Civic Culture,* ed. Jan Ellen Lewis and Peter S. Onuf, 161–83. Charlottesville: University of Virginia Press.

Strozier, Robert M. 1988. *Saussure, Derrida, and the Metaphysics of Subjectivity.* Berlin: Mouton de Gruyter.

Struever, Nancy S. 1970. *The Language of History in the Renaissance: Rhetoric and Historical Consciousness in Florentine Humanism.* Princeton: Princeton University Press.

Sullivan, Andrew. 1995. *Virtually Normal: An Argument About Homosexuality.* New York: Alfred A. Knopf.

Svenbro, Jesper. 1988. *Phrasikleia: Anthropologie de la lecture en Grèce ancienne.* Paris: Éditions la Découverte.

Swartz, Omar. 1998. *The Rise of Rhetoric and Its Intersections with Contemporary Critical Thought.* Boulder: Westview Press.

Tannen, Deborah, and Muriel Saville-Troike, eds. 1985. *Perspectives on Silence.* Norwood, N.J.: Ablex.

Thomas, Douglas. 1999. *Reading Nietzsche Rhetorically.* New York: Guilford.

Too, Yun Lee. 1995. *The Rhetoric of Identity in Isocrates: Text, Power, Pedagogy.* Cambridge: Cambridge University Press.

Toulmin, Stephen. 1964. *The Uses of Argument.* Cambridge: Cambridge University Press, 1964.

Untersteiner, Mario. 1953. *The Sophists*. Translated by Kathleen Freeman. Oxford: Basil Blackwell.

Valesio, Paolo. 1980. *Novantiqua: Rhetoric as a Contemporary Theory*. Bloomington: Indiana University Press.

Vickers, Brian. 1988. *In Defence of Rhetoric*. Oxford: Clarendon Press.

———, ed. 1982. *Rhetoric Revalued: Papers from the International Society for the History of Rhetoric*. Binghamton, N.Y.: Center for Medieval and Early Renaissance Studies.

Vico, Giambattista. 1965. *On the Study Methods of Our Time*. Translated by Elio Gianturco. Indianapolis: Bobbs-Merrill.

Vidal, Gore. 1973. *Burr*. New York: Random House.

Vitanza, Victor J. 1997. *Negation, Subjectivity, and the History of Rhetoric*. Albany: State University of New York Press.

———, ed. 1994. *Writing Histories of Rhetoric*. Carbondale: Southern Illinois University Press.

Vries, Gerrit Jacob de. 1969. *A Commentary on the Phaedrus of Plato*. Amsterdam: Hakket.

Wander, Phillip C. 1984. "The Third Persona: An Ideological Turn in Rhetorical Theory." *Central States Speech Journal* 35: 197–216.

Warnick, Barbara. 1993. *The Sixth Canon: Belletristic Rhetorical Theory and Its French Antecedent*. Columbia: University of South Carolina Press.

Weaver, Richard M. 1953. *The Ethics of Rhetoric*. Chicago: H. Regnery.

———. 1970. *Language is Sermonic: Richard M. Weaver on the Nature of Rhetoric*. Edited by Richard I. Johannesen, Rennard Strickland, and Ralph T. Eubanks. Baton Rouge: Louisiana State University Press.

Webster's Ninth New Collegiate Dictionary. 1990. Springfield, Mass.: Merriam-Webster.

Weinberg, Bernard. 1961. *A History of Literary Criticism in the Italian Renaissance*. 3 vols. Chicago: University of Chicago Press.

White, Deborah Gray. 1985. *Ar'n't I a Woman?: Female Slaves in the Plantation South*. New York: W. W. Norton.

White, Eugene E., ed. 1980. *Rhetoric in Transition: Studies in the Nature and Uses of Rhetoric*. University Park: Pennsylvania State University Press.

White, Hayden. 1992. "Writing in the Middle Voice." *Stanford Literature Review* 9: 179–87.

Whitson, Steve, and John Poulakos. 1993. "Nietzsche and the Aesthetics of Rhetoric." *Quarterly Journal of Speech* 79: 131–45.

Wichelns, Herbert A. 1993. "The Literary Criticism of Oratory." In *Landmark Essays on American Public Address*, ed. Martin J. Medhurst, 1–32. Davis, Cal.: Hermagoras Press.

Williams, Wendy J. 2000. "Miniseries Tackles Jefferson 'Scandal.' " *Boston Herald* 13 (February): 66.

Wilson, Elizabeth A. 1998. *Neural Geographies: Feminism and the Microstructure of Cognition*. New York: Routledge.

Wittgenstein, Ludwig. 1990. *Tractatus Logico-Philosophicus*. Translated by C. K. Ogden. London: Routledge.

Wood, Gordon S. 1999. "The Ghosts of Monticello." In *Sally Hemings and Thomas Jefferson: History, Memory, and Civic Culture*, ed. Jan Ellen Lewis and Peter S. Onuf, 19–34. Charlottesville: University of Virginia Press.

Woodson, Byron W., Sr. 2001. *A President in the Family: Thomas Jefferson, Sally Hemings, and Thomas Woodson.* Westport: Praeger.

Yarborough, Stephen R. 1999. *After Rhetoric: The Study of Discourse Beyond Language and Culture.* Carbondale: Southern Illinois University Press.

Yegenoglu, Meyda. 1998. *Colonial Fantasies: Towards a Feminist Reading of Orientalism.* Cambridge: Cambridge University Press.

Yoos, George E. 1979. "A Revision of the Concept of Ethical Appeal." *Philosophy and Rhetoric* 12: 41–58.

Young, Iris Marion. 1987. "Impartiality and the Civic Public." In *Feminism as Critique,* ed. Seyla Benhabib, 56–76. Minneapolis: University of Minnesota Press, 1987.

———. 1990. *Justice and the Politics of Difference.* Princeton: Princeton University Press.

Young, James E. 1993. *The Texture of Memory: Holocaust Memorials and Meaning.* New Haven: Yale University Press.

Index